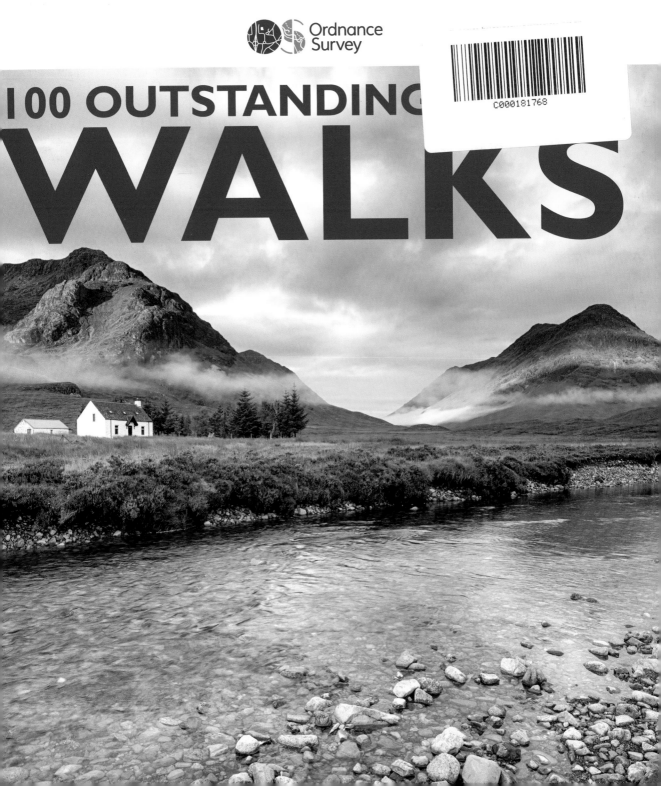

Ordnance Survey

100 OUTSTANDING
WALKS

Contents

Introduction

Britain's National Parks, Areas of Outstanding Natural Beauty, National Scenic Areas, Heritage Coastline, National Trails and UNESCO World Heritage Sites provide the most scenically splendid countryside across England, Wales and Scotland, and by far the best way of exploring these very special places is on foot. This magnificent compendium of outstanding British walks brings together the finest selection of Pathfinder Walks in Britain's officially designated places of scenic beauty and historic interest.

There are 100 walking gems in this collection: inspirational outings for a wide range of walking experience and abilities, whether new to country walking or seasoned ramblers. There are easy-paced short walks, half-day rambles, and more energetic and challenging full-day excursions in a combined total of 625 miles (over 1,000km) of richly rewarding routes.

Great natural wonders include the awesome chasm of Cheddar Gorge in Somerset, the mighty curtain-wall of water at Sgŵd yr Eira in the Brecon Beacons, and the majestic mountain grandeur of Lochnagar in the Cairngorms. The iconic Seven Sisters where the South Downs meet the sea, the rugged Northumbrian coastline between Craster and Dunstanburgh, and Porthgain to Abereiddi on the Pembrokeshire Coast are but three of the splendid seascape adventures. There's natural quietude at Leighton Moss in Lancashire, Dunwich Heath in Suffolk and at Camasunary on the Isle of Skye. Britain's history-packed industrial past is encountered at Cornish tin mines and at Ironbridge in the Midlands. Legacies of international importance visited from centuries past include prehistoric Stonehenge, Iron Age Cissbury Ring, Roman Hadrian's Wall, Norman Durham Cathedral and Castle, and Georgian Bath and Edinburgh.

While these pages will whet the appetite for the best country walking Britain has to offer, the accompanying subscription to OS Maps enables all 100 walks to be accessed online. OS Maps is available in both a web version and an app for Android and Apple devices. Before setting off on one of our walks we recommend you use the app to download the map of your route to your phone for offline use and, if you wish, print off a large-scale map with a route card featuring detailed directions.

> '...I'll walk, to still my beating mind.'
> **William Shakespeare (1564–1616),**
> *The Tempest* 4.1

> 'Adopt the pace of nature: her secret is patience.'
> **Ralph Waldo Emerson (1803–1882)**

At-a-glance

Walk	Page	Start	Distance	Height Gain	Time	Difficulty
South-West of England						
① Wistman's Wood	18	Two Briges Hotel	4½ M (7.2km)	345 Ft (105m)	2½ hrs	●●
② Rippon Tor, Pil Tor and Buckland Beacon	20	Cold East Cross	6½ M (10.3km)	1,035 Ft (315m)	3½ hrs	●●●
③ Lynton and Valley of Rocks	24	Lynton	5½ M (8.8km)	1,130 Ft (315m)	3 hrs	●●
④ Simonsbath and the River Barle	26	Simonsbath	7½ M (12.1km)	1,000 Ft (305m)	4 hrs	●●
⑤ Hurlstone and Selworthy Beacon	28	Bossington	6¼ M (10.1km)	1,150 Ft (350m)	3½ hrs	●●
⑥ Helford, Little Dennis and Manaccan	32	Helford	5 M (8km)	670 Ft (205m)	2½ hrs	●
⑦ Tollard Royal and Win Green	34	Tollard Royal	7 M (11.3km)	670 Ft (205m)	3½ hrs	●●
⑧ Corfe Castle and the Purbeck Ridge	36	Corfe Castle	6 M (9.7km)	1,035 Ft (315m)	3 hrs	●●
⑨ Beer and Branscombe	38	Beer	6¼ M (9.9km)	1,180 Ft (360m)	3½ hrs	●●
⑩ Cheddar Gorge and Velvet Bottom	40	Cheddar	6½ M (10.5km)	1,215 Ft (370m)	3½ hrs	●●
⑪ Baggy Point and Saunton Down	42	Croyde	7¼ M (11.4km)	1,065 Ft (325m)	3½ hrs	●●
⑫ Wills Neck and Triscombe Combe	44	Lydeard Hill	6½ M (10.5km)	1,150 Ft (350m)	3½ hrs	●●
⑬ Kingston and the River Erme	46	Kingston	5¾ M (9.1km)	1,035 Ft (315m)	3 hrs	●●
⑭ Cotehele	48	Calstock	3½ M (5.6km)	525 Ft (160m)	1½ hrs	●
⑮ Around St Agnes	52	Trevaunance Cove	6¼ M (10km)	1,080 Ft (330m)	3½ hrs	●●
⑯ Golden Cap	54	Seatown	6½ M (10.5km)	1,675 Ft (510m)	4 hrs	●●●
⑰ Bath and Claverton Down	56	Bath Abbey	8½ M (13.5km)	625 Ft (190m)	4 hrs	●●●
⑱ Avebury, West Kennett and Silbury Hill	58	Avebury	6½ M (10.5km)	310 Ft (95m)	3 hrs	●●
⑲ Stonehenge	60	Amesbury	8 M (12.9km)	445 Ft (135m)	4 hrs	●●●
South-East of England						
⑳ New Forest Snapshot	68	Millyford Bridge	2¾ M (4.5km)	130 Ft (40m)	1½ hrs	●
㉑ Around Burley	70	Burbush Hill	4¼ M (6.8km)	245 Ft (75m)	2½ hrs	●
㉒ Firle Beacon and Charleston Farmhouse	74	Firle	5 M (8km)	740 Ft (225m)	2½ hrs	●
㉓ Friston Forest, the Seven Sisters and Cuckmere Haven	76	Exceat	6½ M (10.5km)	1,150 Ft (350m)	3½ hrs	●●

Walk	Page	Start	Distance	Height Gain	Time	Difficulty
㉔ Cissbury and Chanctonbury Rings	78	Findon Valley	11 M (17.6km)	1,360 Ft (415m)	5½ hrs	●●●
㉕ The Chidham Peninsula	82	Chidham	5 M (8km)	Negligible	2½ hrs	●
㉖ Ibstone, Turville and Fingest	84	Ibstone Common	7¾M (12.3km)	855 Ft (260m)	4 hrs	●●●
㉗ Aldbury, Ivinghoe Beacon and Ashridge	86	Aldbury	7½M (11.8km)	805 Ft (245m)	4 hrs	●●●
㉘ Cranbrook and Sissinghurst	88	Cranbrook church	7¼M (11.6km)	410 Ft (125m)	3½ hrs	●●
㉙ Freshwater and Tennyson Down	90	Highdown Lane	3¾M (6km)	475 Ft (145m)	2 hrs	●
㉚ Wye and Crundale Downs	92	Wye	8½M (13.5km)	1,050 Ft (320m)	4 hrs	●●●
㉛ Albury Downs and St Martha's Hill	94	Newlands Corner	7M (11.2km)	985 Ft (300m)	3½ hrs	●●
㉜ Whitehall St James's	98 100	Charing Cross Westminster	¾M (1.4km) 2M (3.2km)	Negligible Negligible	1 hr 1½ hrs	● ●

Heart of England						
㉝ Shugborough Park and Sherbrook Valley	108	Milford Common	7½M (12km)	670 Ft (205m)	3½ hrs	●●
㉞ Wotton-under-Edge and the Tyndale Monument	110	Wotton-under-Edge	4 M (6.5km)	460 Ft (140m)	2¼ hrs	●
㉟ Bourton-on-the-Water, the Slaughters and Naunton	112	Bourton-on-the-Water	10M (16km)	705 Ft (215m)	5 hrs	●●●
㊱ Great Malvern and the Worcestershire Beacon	114	Great Malvern	5½M (8.9km)	1,360 Ft (415m)	3 hrs	●●
㊲ Corvedale and Wenlock Edge	116	Aston Munslow	6¾M (10.9km)	1,000 Ft (305m)	3½ hrs	●●
㊳ Caer Caradoc and Cardington	118	Hazler	7¼M (11.6km)	1,720 Ft (525m)	4½ hrs	●●●
㊴ Goodrich Castle	120	Goodrich	8¼M (13.3km)	310 Ft (95m)	3½ hrs	●●
㊵ Blenheim Park	124	Woodstock	6½M (10.5km)	360 Ft (110m)	3½ hrs	●
㊶ Ironbridge World Heritage Site	126	Ironbridge	7¼M (11.6km)	525 Ft (160m)	3½ hrs	●●
㊷ Cromford and Matlock Bath	128	Cromford Wharf	7M (11.3km)	1,390 Ft (425m)	3½ hrs	●●

East of England						
㊸ Horsey	136	Horsey	3¾M (6km)	Negligible	1½ hrs	●
㊹ River Bure and Upton Marshes	138	S Walsham Broad	6M (9.7km)	Negligible	2½ hrs	●
㊺ The Weavers' Way to the Berney Arms	140	Halvergate	9M (14.5km)	Negligible	4 hrs	●●
㊻ Constable Country – Flatford and East Bergholt	144	East Bergholt	5½M (8.9km)	230 Ft (70m)	2½ hrs	●
㊼ Walesby, Claxby and Normanby le Wold	146	Walesby	5¼M (8.4km)	690 Ft (210m)	3 hrs	●●
㊽ Castle Rising	148	Castle Rising	2¼M (3.6km)	130 Ft (40m)	1 hr	●
㊾ West Runton and Beacon Hill	150	East Runton	7¼ (11.7km)	575 Ft (175m)	3½ hrs	●●
㊿ Dunwich Heath and Minsmere Marsh	152	Dunwich Heath	5M (8km)	215 Ft (65m)	2 hrs	●

Walk	Page	Start	Distance	Height Gain	Time	Difficulty
North of England						
51 **Elterwater**	160	Elterwater village	5½ M (8.9km)	310 Ft (95m)	3 hrs	●
52 **Wray Castle and Blelham Tarn**	162	Red Nab, High Wray	6 M (9.7km)	785 Ft (240m)	3 hrs	●●
53 **Crummock Water**	164	Scalehill Bridge	8½ M (13.8km)	1,050 Ft (320m)	4 hrs	●●●
54 **Kielder Water and the Bull Crag Peninsula**	168	Leaplish	6¼ M (10.1km)	650 Ft (200m)	2½ hrs	●
55 **Hartside, Salter's Road and High Cantle**	170	Hartside	8½ M (13.7km)	1,590 Ft (485m)	4½ hrs	●●●
56 **Farndale**	174	Low Mill	3½ M (5.6km)	245 Ft (75m)	2 hrs	●
57 **The Cook Monument and Roseberry Topping**	176	Gribdale Gate	6½ M (10.5km)	1,315 Ft (400m)	3½ hrs	●●
58 **Robin Hood's Bay and Ravenscar**	178	Robin Hood's Bay	9 M (14.5km)	605 Ft (185m)	4½ hrs	●●●
59 **Stanage Edge and Higger Tor**	182	Upper Burbage	3½ M (5.6km)	375 Ft (115m)	1½ hrs	●
60 **Lose Hill**	184	Edale	6 M (9.7km)	1,650 Ft (505m)	3½ hrs	●●
61 **The Manifold Valley**	186	Wetton	6½ M (10.5km)	1,420 Ft (435m)	3½ hrs	●●
62 **Malham Cove, Gordale Scar and Janet's Foss**	190	Malham	5 M (8km)	640 Ft (195m)	2½ hrs	●●
63 **Pen-y-ghent**	192	Horton-in-Ribblesdale	6 M (9.5km)	1,610 Ft (490m)	3½ hrs	●●
64 **Gunnerside, Kisdon and Muker**	194	Gunnerside	11¼ M (18km)	1,790 Ft (545m)	6 hrs	●●●
65 **Leighton Moss**	198	Yealand Storrs	4½ M (7.3km)	345 Ft (105m)	2½ hrs	●●
66 **Kirkham Priory and the River Derwent**	200	Kirkham	4¾ M (7.6km)	280 Ft (85m)	2½ hrs	●
67 **High Cup Nick**	202	Dufton	8 M (12.9km)	1,445 Ft (440m)	4 hrs	●●●
68 **How Stean Gorge and Upper Nidderdale**	204	Lofthouse	4¼ M (7km)	670 Ft (205m)	2½ hrs	●
69 **Craster and Dunstanburgh Castle**	206	Craster	4¾ M (7.6km)	380 Ft (115m)	2 hrs	●
70 **Fountains Abbey**	210	Fountains Abbey	5¾ M (9.3km)	550 Ft (165m)	3 hrs	●
71 **Durham – Riverside and Woods**	212	Durham	5 M (8km)	215 Ft (65m)	2½ hrs	●
72 **Hadrian's Wall at Walltown and Thirlwall Castle**	214	Walltown Quarry	7¾ M (12.5km)	1,020 Ft (310m)	3½ hrs	●●

Walk		Page	Start	Distance	Height Gain	Time	Difficulty
Wales							
73	Llyn y Fan Fach and the Carmarthen Fans	222	Near Llanddeusant	6 M (9.7km)	2,130 (650m)	4 hrs	●●●
74	Waterfalls Walk	224	Cwm Porth	9 M (14.5km)	2,100 Ft (640m)	5 hrs	●●●
75	Brecon Beacons Horseshoe	226	Cwm Gwdi	8½ M (13.7km)	2,890 Ft (880m)	5 hrs	●●●
76	Porthgain and Abereiddi	230	Porthgain	3½ M (5.6km)	260 Ft (80m)	2 hrs	●
77	St David's, Porth Clais and Ramsey Sound	232	St David's	9 M (14.5km)	770 Ft (235m)	4½ hrs	●●●
78	Precipice Walk	236	Near Dolgellau	3½ M (5.5km)	705 Ft (215m)	2 hrs	●
79	Conwy Mountain and Sychnant Pass	238	Conwy	6 M (9.5km)	1,215 Ft (370m)	3 hrs	●●
80	Cnicht	240	Croesor	6¾ M (10.7km)	1,950 Ft (595m)	4½ hrs	●●●
81	Moel Famau	244	Moel Famau	5¼ M (8.25km)	1,265 Ft (385m)	3 hrs	●●
82	Llanmadoc Hill	246	Llanmadoc	6½ M (10.5km)	1,000 Ft (305m)	3½ hrs	●●
83	Aberdaron and Land's End	248	Aberdaron	7½ M (12km)	1,280 Ft (390m)	4½ hrs	●●●
84	Wynford Vaughan Thomas' Viewpoint	252	Aberhosan	6 M (9.7km)	1,605 Ft (490m)	3½ hrs	●●
85	Ty Mawr and the Pontcysyllte Aqueduct	254	Ty Mawr	5½ M (9km)	500 Ft (150m)	3 hrs	●
86	Saundersfoot and Tenby	256	Saundersfoot	4 M (6.5km)	1,085 Ft (330m)	2½ hrs	●

Walk		Page	Start	Distance	Height Gain	Time	Difficulty
Scotland							
87	Glen Feshie	264	Near Achlean	3½ M (5.5km)	415 Ft (125m)	2 hrs	●
88	The Lily Loch and Loch an Eilein from Inverdruie	266	Inverdruie	6 M (9.7km)	445 Ft (135m)	3 hrs	●
89	Morrone	268	Braemar	7 M (11.3km)	2,015 Ft (615m)	4 hrs	●●●
90	Lochnagar and Loch Muick	270	Spittal of Glenmuick	14 M (22.4km)	2,790 Ft (850m)	8 hrs	●●●
91	Lochgoilhead and Donich Water	274	Lochgoilhead	2½ M (4km)	625 Ft (190m)	1½ hrs	●
92	Ben Lomond	276	Rowardennan	7¼ M (11.7km)	3,135 Ft (955m)	5 hrs	●●●
93	Ben Venue	278	Loch Achray	8¼ M (13.3km)	2,670 Ft (815m)	5½ hrs	●●●
94	Pap of Glencoe	282	Glencoe village	5 M (8km)	2,490 Ft (760m)	3½ hrs	●●
95	Isle of Iona	284	Iona	8½ M (13.7km)	690 Ft (210m)	4½ hrs	●●
96	Dunkeld, The Hermitage and Birnam	286	Dunkeld	7¾ M (12.4km)	655 Ft (200m)	4 hrs	●●
97	Camasunary – Elgol – Glasnakille	288	Kilmarie	11¼ M (18km)	2,280 Ft (695m)	6½ hrs	●●●
98	The Quiraing and Meall na Suiramach	290	Bealach Ollasgairte	4 M (6.5km)	1,360 Ft (415m)	3 hrs	●●
99	Rascarrel Bay and Balcary Point	292	Balcary Bay	5 M (8km)	310 Ft (95m)	2½ hrs	●●
100	Grassmarket and Greyfriars Georgian New Town	296 298	Princes Street Princes Street	1½ M (2.3km) 2¾ M (4.7km)	Negligible Negligible	2 hrs 2 hrs	● ●

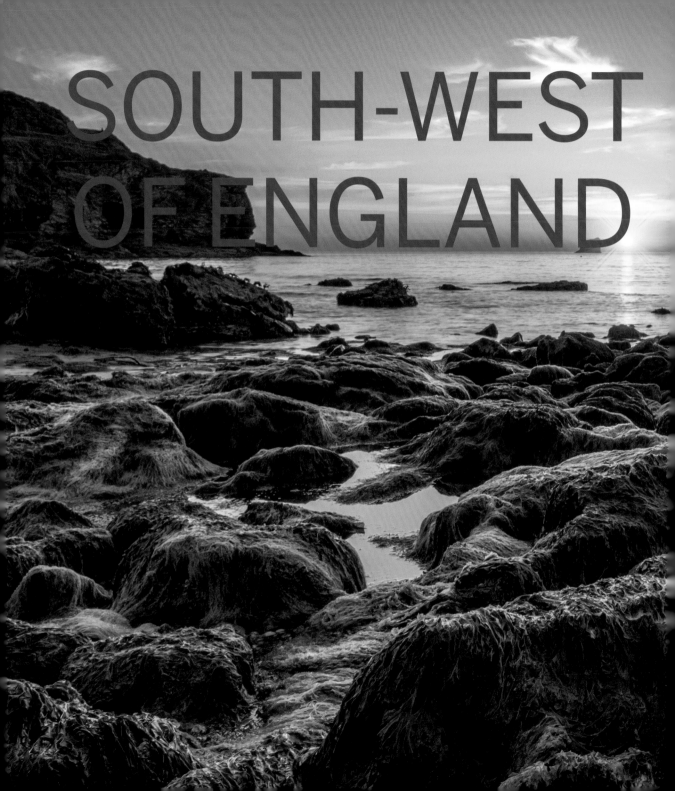

SOUTH-WEST OF ENGLAND

The Walks

Top: Swanage railway runs from Corfe Castle to Swanage.
Bottom: Rippon Tor.
Previous page: Trevaunance Cove, Cornwall.

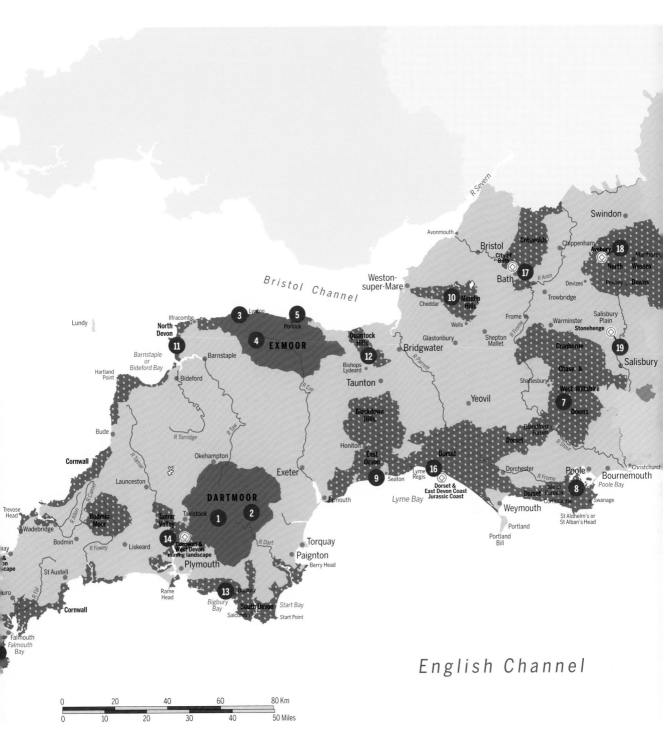

Lundy

Bristol Channel

Weston-super-Mare

Avonmouth

R Severn

Swindon

Bristol

City of Bath

Cotswolds

Chippenham

Avebury

Marlborough

18 North

Wessex

Downs

17

Bath

R Avon

Devizes

Pewsey

Trowbridge

Ilfracombe

3 Lynton

5 Porlock

North Devon

11

4 EXMOOR

Quantock Hills

10 Mendip Hills

Cheddar

Wells

Frome

Shepton Mallet

Warminster

Salisbury Plain

Stonehenge

19 Salisbury

Cranborne

Hartland Point

Barnstaple or Bideford Bay

Barnstaple

Bideford

12

Bishops Lydeard

Glastonbury

Bridgwater

R Parrett

Shaftesbury

Chase &

West Wiltshire

Downs

7

Trevose Head

Bude

R Torridge

R Taw

R Exe

Taunton

Yeovil

R Stour

Cornwall

Okehampton

Exeter

Blackdown Hills

Blandford Forum

Dorset

Launceston

R Tamar

R Camel

DARTMOOR

Honiton

East Devon

9 Seaton

Dorchester

R Frome

Dorset

Poole

8

Bournemouth

Christchurch

Bodmin Moor

R Allen

Tavistock

1

2

Exmouth

Lyme Regis

16 Dorset & East Devon Coast Jurassic Coast

Isle of Purbeck

Corfe Castle

Swanage

Wadebridge

Bodmin

R Fowey

Liskeard

14 Cornwall & West Devon mining landscape

R Dart

Torquay

Lyme Bay

Poole Bay

St Aldhelm's or St Alban's Head

St Austell

R Fal

Plymouth

Paignton

Berry Head

Weymouth

Portland

Falmouth

Falmouth Bay

Rame Head

13 Bigbury

Bigbury Bay

South Devon

Salcombe

Start Bay

Start Point

Portland Bill

English Channel

0   20   40   60   80 Km
0 10 20 30 40 50 Miles

Dartmoor National Park

To anyone, like myself, who found their walking legs on the crags of Snowdonia or the Lake District, Dartmoor comes as a shock. The contrast between the crag-girt heights of north Wales and north-west England, hemmed in by neighbouring summits, and Dartmoor's open panorama of granite tors, wooded river valleys and heather-covered moorland could not be more marked. Yet, to look on yourself as an all-round walker, you need to experience not only soaring crags, but soft, undulating landscapes, too. And there is no better place than Dartmoor to embark on that transition.

Naturally, on my first visit to the National Park, my instinct was to find the highest point, and go for it; the 'big is best' mentality is a common malaise among walkers! So, I launched myself onto Yes Tor and High Willhays (known in combination as the 'Roof of Devon'), as much beguiled by the strange names as by the prospect of a challenging ascent. I knew these were the only summits in southern England to rise above 2,000 feet (610m), which, in those days, was the minimum height for qualification as a mountain.

In the event, while High Willhays may have been somewhat undistinguished, my first skirmish with Dartmoor did much to awaken the realisation that, although it was a different kind of magnificence from that to which I'd been accustomed, there was immense beauty among the heather, tors and tumbling streams. Moreover, it had also become clear that this ancient landscape held a wealth of Neolithic tombs, Bronze Age stone circles and long-abandoned medieval farmhouses.

Dartmoor encompasses the largest area of granite in Britain, 240 square miles (622sqkm) at the surface, yet most of it is buried beneath superficial peat deposits. That peat, incidentally, releases its water slowly, so the moors are rarely dry, forming into bogs and mires, which will quickly teach the walker much about landscape observation ... and navigation.

Sir Arthur Conan Doyle was inspired to write the Sherlock Holmes novel *Hound of the Baskervilles* by the tales of Dartmoor he heard while staying at the Duchy Hotel in Princetown. Fox Tor Mire is said to be the inspiration for Great Grimpen Mire in the book.

AMAZING BUT TRUE ...

Pursued by millions of people worldwide, the modern hobby of geocaching has its foundations in a long-established Dartmoor pursuit called 'letterboxing'. It was started in 1854 by James Perrott of Chagford, who left what today would be called a cache on a small crag at Cranmere Pool.

WALK 1 Wistman's Wood

DARTMOOR NATIONAL PARK

DIFFICULTY ●●

START Two Bridges Hotel

DISTANCE 4½ miles (7.2km)

HEIGHT GAIN 345 feet (105m)

APPROXIMATE TIME 2½ hours

ROUTE TERRAIN Rough, open moorland beyond Wistman's Wood; river crossing at weir or on granite boulders

PARKING Parking area opposite the Two Bridges Hotel, just west of the B3212/3357 junction

OS EXPLORER OL28

OS PATHFINDER Short Walks Dartmoor

 DETAILED ROUTE DOWNLOAD
os.uk/obw

An absolute must-do for any woodland lover looking to get away from it all, this walk provides an escape from any signs of civilisation within minutes of leaving the start. Crockern Tor, passed early in the route, is the ancient site of the Great Court, the stannary parliament where tin-mining representatives met to regulate the industry. A rough track leads to Wistman's Wood National Nature Reserve (NNR), an ancient upland oak woodland of stunted, contorted and thickly moss-laden trees, which on misty days create ghostly forms. On leaving the wood, the way is across open moorland to cross the West Dart on stepping stones, before an easy final section accompanying the Devonport Leat. *Do not attempt this walk after a prolonged wet spell or after very heavy rainfall, as the river crossing at the weir and via the nearby stepping stones is only advisable when river levels are average or lower.*

Right: Wistman's Wood.
Opposite page top: Two Bridges.
Opposite page bottom: Devonport Leat.

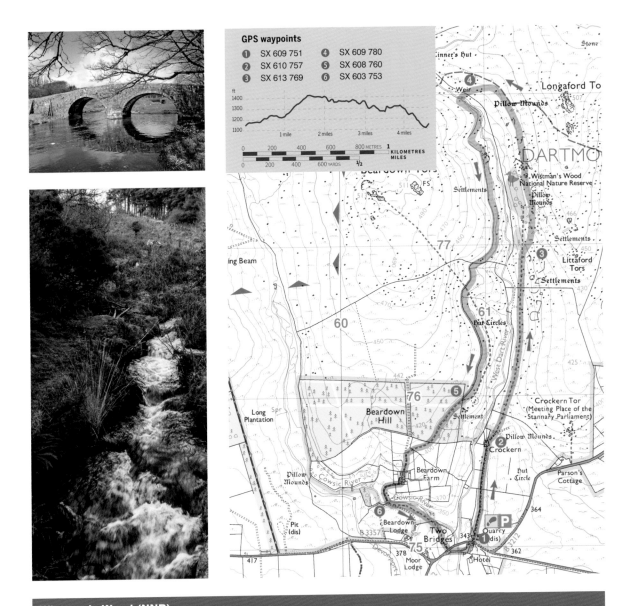

GPS waypoints

①	SX 609 751	④	SX 609 780
②	SX 610 757	⑤	SX 608 760
③	SX 613 769	⑥	SX 603 753

Wistman's Wood (NNR)

Wistman's Wood is one of only three remaining areas of ancient upland oak woodland on the moor, the others being Piles Copse, on the Erme, and Blackator Copse, on the West Okement River. It is an enchanting place: the twisted, stunted oaks grow from a bed of moss-covered boulders and are festooned with tree ferns and lichens, many of which survive here because of the clean air.

Rippon Tor, Pil Tor and Buckland Beacon

DARTMOOR NATIONAL PARK

DIFFICULTY ●●●

START Cold East Cross, a crossroads 2¾ miles (4.4km) north-east of Buckland in the Moor

DISTANCE 6½ miles (10.3km)

HEIGHT GAIN 1,035 feet (315m)

APPROXIMATE TIME 3½ hours

ROUTE TERRAIN Moorland paths and woodland tracks, sometimes boggy and rough; there's a steady descent/ascent to/from Buckland in the Moor

PARKING Cold East Cross

OS EXPLORER OL28

OS PATHFINDER South Devon and Dartmoor

⬇ **DETAILED ROUTE DOWNLOAD** os.uk/obw

The views on this walk across open moorland, especially over west Devon, are amazing. Apart from the initial climb to Rippon Tor, this route offers dramatic and ever-changing views over Dartmoor for relatively little effort. This is very much a 'tor-bagging' walk that takes in Rippon Tor (the highest point on the walk at just over 1,551 feet (473m), Top Tor, Pil Tor, Tunhill Rocks and last, but not least, Buckland Beacon, which is a particularly outstanding viewpoint. There's also a very worthwhile detour to the attractive hamlet of Buckland in the Moor – a small group of thatched cottages nestling below the steep, wooded slopes of Buckland Beacon. *This would be a difficult walk to follow in misty weather, without the tors to act as guides, unless you are competent in navigating in such conditions, so save it for a fine weather day to make the most of the amazing views and to safeguard route-finding.*

Right: Dartmoor ponies near Rippon Tor.
Opposite page: Looking north from Rippon Tor.

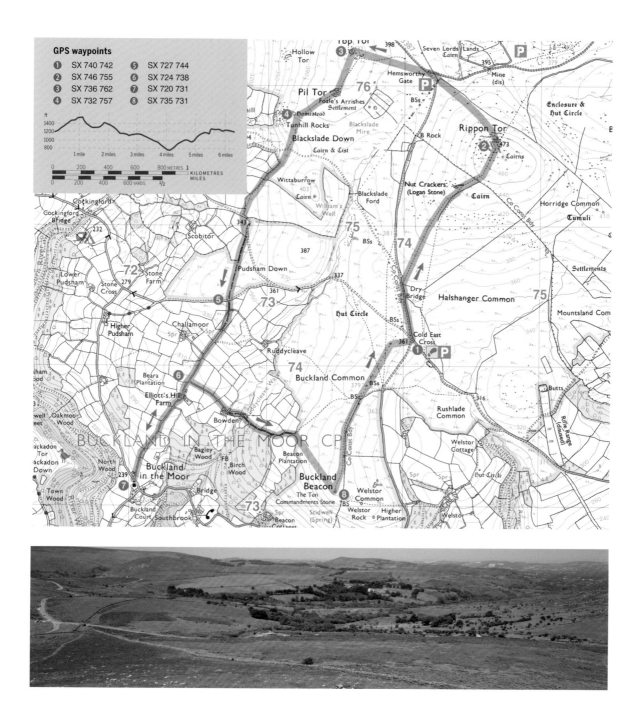

GPS waypoints

①	SX 740 742	⑤	SX 727 744
②	SX 746 755	⑥	SX 724 738
③	SX 736 762	⑦	SX 720 731
④	SX 732 757	⑧	SX 735 731

Exmoor National Park

The appeal of Exmoor for the walker lies in its diversity. Designated a National Park in 1954, the hills of Exmoor offer a warm embrace in their steep-sided valleys and something a little more bracing on the open tops. This is a region of austere moorland and atmospheric, sometimes eerie, wooded combes that inspired the Romantic poets Shelley and Coleridge, and, later, R. D. Blackmore, whose novel *Lorna Doone* did much to raise the profile of the region.

Exmoor also has a dramatic and spectacular coastline, stretching from Minehead to Combe Martin, that boasts the highest sea cliffs in England. There is particular appeal in strolling down from the South West Coast Path to find a glorious beach, a welcoming village (and pub, of course) or just an isolated cliff-enclosed cove that may once have been used by smugglers.

It was amid the folds of Exmoor, somewhere along the Tarka Trail, that I first spent a wild night under canvas, with heather for comfort, the remains of a sheepfold for shelter, a roof of stellar magnificence, a coffee in hand, and liver and onions warming on the Trangia. Years later, Exmoor National Park was to be designated an International Dark Sky Reserve, the first in Europe. With appropriate experience, walking here need not be solely a daytime activity; this is a great place to discover that night-time brings its own rewards.

To the perceptive walker, the Exmoor landscape is a chronicle of how people from as long ago as Mesolithic times have exploited the region and left behind outstanding archaeological wealth; they traded, travelled, worshipped and interred their dead here, and, little by little, helped to fashion the landscape we see today. Moreover, the heather and grass moorland and the natural woodland are internationally important for their scenic beauty and wildlife, including red deer and wild Exmoor ponies.

The Exmoor pony is native to the British Isles and is among the most ancient of horse breeds in Britain, having been recorded as long ago as the Domesday Book in 1086. It is said that they almost became extinct during World War Two because soldiers used them for target practice, and thieves stole them for meat, but today some herds still roam the National Park in a semi-feral state.

> **AMAZING BUT TRUE ...**
> The 'Beast of Exmoor' is a crypto-zoological cat reported to roam the National Park. If it does exist, it is possibly a black leopard released after it became illegal to keep big cats in captivity outside zoos.

Lynton and Valley of Rocks

EXMOOR NATIONAL PARK

DIFFICULTY ●●

START Lynton

DISTANCE 5½ miles (8.8km)

HEIGHT GAIN 1,130 feet (315m)

APPROXIMATE TIME 3 hours

ROUTE TERRAIN Well-surfaced coast path, woodland tracks and quiet lanes

PARKING Lynton

OS EXPLORER OL9

OS PATHFINDER Exmoor and the Quantocks

 DETAILED ROUTE DOWNLOAD os.uk/obw

The Valley of Rocks is probably the most dramatic geological feature on Exmoor. Its jagged and weirdly shaped tors rise craggily above the valley floor, and its hillsides are covered in scree, adding to the rugged appearance. This is an exceptionally varied and attractive but, at the same time, easy-going route. Starting from the once isolated but now bustling community of Lynton, the walk rises along a splendid path that leads through the spectacular valley. The second half of the walk is through pleasant woodland, by a quiet combe and along a narrow winding lane. Views inland are over the wonderfully wooded East Lyn River, and there are fine prospects over Lynton's near neighbour Lynmouth – don't miss the chance to ride on the cliff railway linking these close coastal neighbours. Both towns became fashionable resorts in the 19th century, when their outstanding setting and mild climate made them popular with affluent Victorian visitors.

Right: Castle Rock, Valley of Rocks.
Opposite page top: Looking down on Lynmouth from Lynton.
Opposite page bottom: Valley of Rocks.

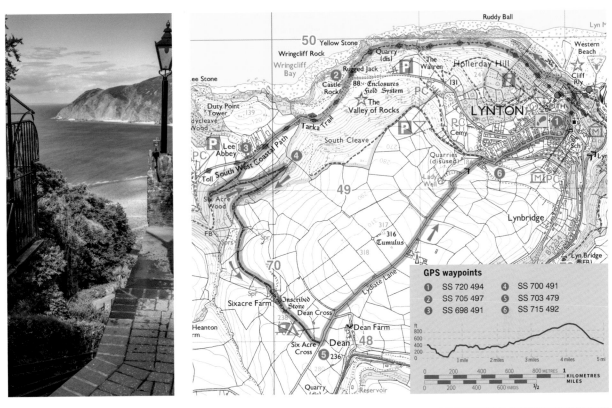

GPS waypoints

❶	SS 720 494	❹	SS 700 491
❷	SS 705 497	❺	SS 703 479
❸	SS 698 491	❻	SS 715 492

Simonsbath and the River Barle

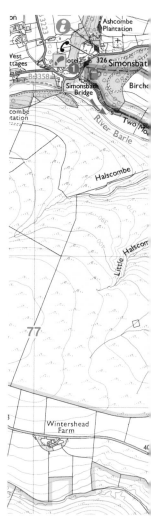

EXMOOR NATIONAL PARK

DIFFICULTY ●●

START Simonsbath

DISTANCE 7½ miles (12.1km)

HEIGHT GAIN 1,000 feet (305m)

APPROXIMATE TIME 4 hours

ROUTE TERRAIN Woodland tracks, field and riverside paths, muddy and uneven in places

PARKING Simonsbath

OS EXPLORER OL9

OS PATHFINDER Exmoor and the Quantocks

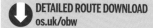 **DETAILED ROUTE DOWNLOAD** os.uk/obw

Simonsbath is the centre of the former Royal Forest of Exmoor. The whole length of the River Barle is delightful, but no stretch can compare with the river downstream from Simonsbath, where glorious woodland soon gives way to a peaceful and remote steep-sided and bracken-covered valley. The first part of the walk follows the riverbank, passing the ruins of a 19th-century copper mine, Wheal Eliza, and Cow Castle, a prehistoric earthwork; the second part returns high above the valley, giving superb views all the way back to Simonsbath.

The Exmoor Forest Hotel was the only building in Simonsbath until the 19th century. Originally the residence of the Warden of the Forest, it was purchased by John Knight, a Worcestershire industrialist, when the forest was sold off in 1818. The Knight family built the village church and Wheal Eliza mine, which was not a successful venture. Today, the Two Moors Way threads its way alongside the Barle en route from Lynmouth to Ivybridge.

Right: The River Barle.

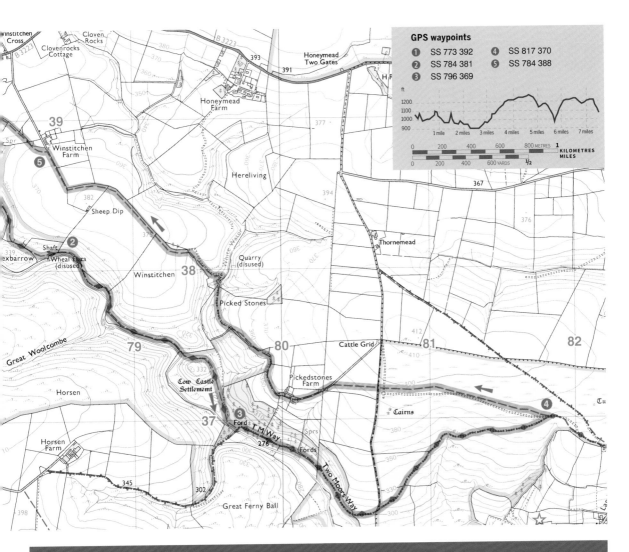

❶	SS 773 392	❹	SS 817 370
❷	SS 784 381	❺	SS 784 388
❸	SS 796 369		

The Two Moors Way

The Two Moors Way is followed for the first half of this delightful walk through the Barle Valley. This long-distance path links Ivybridge, on the southern edge of Dartmoor National Park, to Lynmouth in Exmoor National Park on the Bristol Channel coast, passing through both of South-west England's national parks, and extending through 90 miles (145km) of glorious Devon countryside across wild moorland and along river valleys. By using the Erme-Plym Trail, running between Wembury and Ivybridge, a trans-Devon coast-to-coast walk is possible of 102 miles (164km).

SOUTH-WEST OF ENGLAND | Simonsbath and the River Barle ● 27

Hurlstone and Selworthy Beacon

EXMOOR NATIONAL PARK

DIFFICULTY ●●

START Bossington

DISTANCE 6¼ miles (10.1km)

HEIGHT GAIN 1,150 feet (350m)

APPROXIMATE TIME 3½ hours

ROUTE TERRAIN Woodland tracks, coast path and quiet lanes, with a very steep climb through Hurlstone Combe to attain Bossington Hill

PARKING Bossington

OS EXPLORER OL9

OS PATHFINDER Exmoor and the Quantocks

 **DETAILED ROUTE DOWNLOAD** os.uk/obw

The countryside between the three picturesque villages of Selworthy, Allerford and Bossington is Exmoor at its finest, combining a steep combe, open moorland and wonderful woodland, with excellent views over the coast, the Vale of Porlock and inland to high Exmoor – the latter dominated by Dunkery Beacon, the highest point on the moor. The only climbing comes soon after the start: a lengthy, steady and, eventually, very steep ascent along the side of Bossington Hill and up through Hurlstone Combe, later passing on to Selworthy Beacon, which is the finest of many great viewpoints on a splendid and outstandingly attractive walk.

Much of this walk is on land that was part of the extensive Holnicote estate, formerly owned by the Acland family and given to the National Trust in 1944. Selworthy is almost unreal in its picturesque perfection and was purpose-built by the Aclands in the 19th century to house their retired tenants and estate workers.

Right: Packhorse bridge, Allerford.
Opposite page top: The church at Selworthy.
Opposite page middle: Bossington village.
Opposite page bottom: Path leading to Dunkery Beacon.

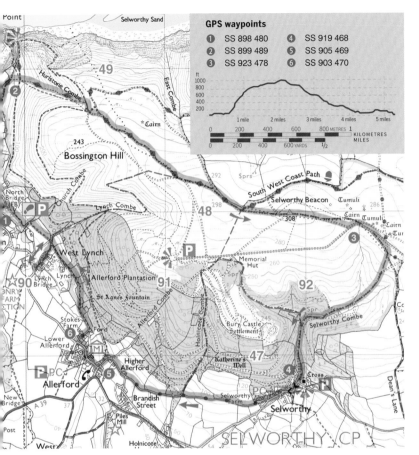

Areas of Outstanding Natural Beauty

The south-west of England is blessed with numerous Areas of Outstanding Natural Beauty; in fact, many would argue that the whole region is one huge AONB. Moreover, the varied landscapes are best appreciated by touring leisurely on foot, rather than driving around in haste.

The Mendip Hills offer a splendid diversity of limestone landscapes: steep slopes, undulating plateaux, gorges and rocky tors. And, there is a vast assortment of ancient monuments, too, all adding interest to any walk across the flower-rich grasslands and wooded hollows. Here, it is Cheddar Gorge that holds sway; England's largest gorge is a 400-foot (122m) deep, three-mile (4.8km) long chasm formed during the last ice age. This is one of the few places where I've spent the night out under the stars, with just a bivvy bag as shelter, surrounded by pinnacles and weather-fractured crags. It was a memorable experience, because, for a short while, I had a curious fox for company. I am curious by nature, too, and so, the next day, I extended the walk into the intriguingly named Velvet Bottom, mainly to get some idea of what such a place might look like.

Some years later, while working as a volunteer warden in the Lake District, trying to figure out how I felt about Wordsworth, I discovered that he had visited Somerset with his sister, Dorothy, and had stayed with Samuel Taylor Coleridge at his cottage in Nether Stowey. Throw that lovely gaggle of hills known as the Quantocks into the equation, and it was only a matter of time before I, too, found my way into Somerset. I never did take to poetry, but the hillwalking was sublime compensation. I later discovered that these undulating uplands of gorse, heather, bracken and conifer had been designated England's first AONB; I could see why.

Dorset, for me, is a long way from home, but the intricate ways of the so-called Isle of Purbeck were quite a pull in the days when I hoped to have my photographs on the cover of Ordnance Survey maps. Corfe Castle (*left*) was an evocative sight, but, if I'm being honest, the long thin line of the Purbeck Hills was an even greater draw.

> **AMAZING BUT TRUE ...**
> Burgh Island, off the South Devon coast, was the setting for Agatha Christie's novel, *Three Little Indians*. Today, Agatha Christie mystery weekends are held at the art deco Burgh Island Hotel (www.burghisland.com).

Helford, Little Dennis and Manaccan

CORNWALL AONB

DIFFICULTY ●

START Helford

DISTANCE 5 miles (8km)

HEIGHT GAIN 670 feet (205m)

APPROXIMATE TIME 2½ hours

ROUTE TERRAIN Moderate coast path, lanes and woodland paths

PARKING Helford

OS EXPLORER 103

OS PATHFINDER Cornwall

DETAILED ROUTE DOWNLOAD
os.uk/obw

South Cornish perfection is all wrapped up in this short walk that follows the South West Coast Path and field paths in a clockwise circuit from Helford. The Helford River itself is a fine example of a ria – the lower reaches of a river valley that were inundated by the sea following sea level rise after the last ice age. There are views across the river to the stunning gardens at Trebah and Glendurgan, both of which are open to the public and renowned for their collections of camellias, rhododendrons and azaleas. Dennis Head is a lovely headland offering a grand panorama of Falmouth Bay, while Gillan Creek is a narrow and secretive arm of the sea whose estuary is a paradise for wading birds. Stroll through ancient coastal woodland and explore the charming village of St Anthony-in-Meneage with its beautiful church, before rounding off a memorable walk with a cream tea, Cornish pasty or fish and chips in Helford.

Right: Helford.
Opposite page left: Hydrangea Valley, Trebah Garden.
Opposite page right: Cornish cream tea.

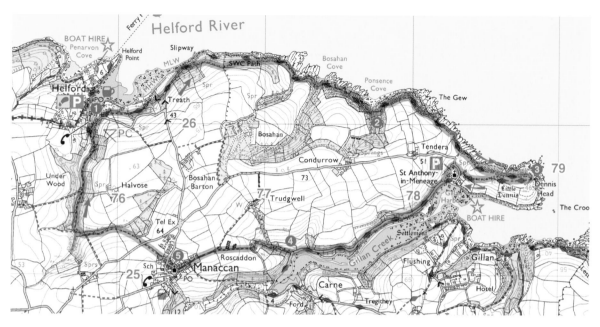

GPS waypoints

① SW 759 261 ④ SW 771 251
② SW 777 260 ⑤ SW 764 250
③ SW 788 256

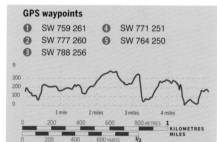

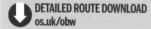

Tollard Royal and Win Green

WALK 7

CRANBORNE DOWNS AND WEST WILTSHIRE DOWNS AONB

DIFFICULTY ●●

START Tollard Royal

DISTANCE 7 miles (11.3km)

HEIGHT GAIN 670 feet (205m)

APPROXIMATE TIME 3½ hours

ROUTE TERRAIN Undulating downland tracks and woodland paths with one section of lane

PARKING Limited space by the village pond at Tollard Royal; alternative parking is available at the National Trust's Win Green car park, approximately half way round the route; pick up the route directions from waypoint 4

OS EXPLORER 118

OS PATHFINDER Somerset, the Mendips and Wiltshire

⬇ **DETAILED ROUTE DOWNLOAD** os.uk/obw

Located amid the dry wooded valleys and the curvaceous chalk uplands of the north Dorset-south Wiltshire border, Tollard Royal has a medieval church and a former 13th-century hunting lodge known as King John's House. It lies at the heart of Cranborne Chase, a favourite hunting ground of King John and other medieval monarchs. This fit-for-a-king walk leaves Tollard Royal to climb up to Win Hill; at 911 feet (277m), it's the highest point on Cranborne Chase and a tremendous vantage point, with a toposcope to aid orientation. Views extend across the wooded slopes of the Chase to the Mendips, Marlborough Downs, New Forest, Dorset coast and, on a clear day, the Isle of Wight. A splendid ridge walk follows thereafter, with more outstanding views and a descent via a parallel valley to return to the village. Towards the end, the route passes through an exemplar dry valley with the splendid name of Tinkley Bottom.

Right: Cranborne Chase.

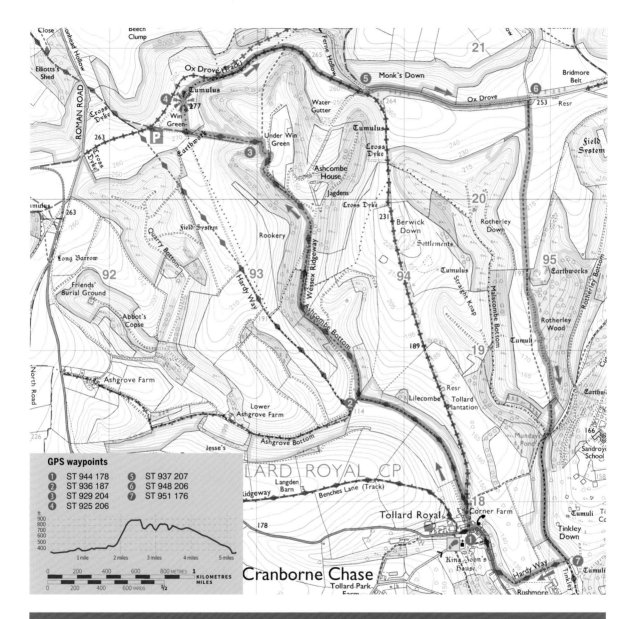

GPS waypoints

❶	ST 944 178	❺	ST 937 207
❷	ST 936 187	❻	ST 948 206
❸	ST 929 204	❼	ST 951 176
❹	ST 925 206		

Cranborne Chase

Cranborne Chase is an area of wooded valleys and rolling chalk uplands on the borders of Wiltshire and Dorset. In the Middle Ages it was a royal forest – a favourite hunting ground of King John. It became a private chase in the early 17th century when James I bestowed it upon Robert Cecil, Earl of Salisbury.

Corfe Castle and the Purbeck Ridge

DORSET AONB

DIFFICULTY ●●

START Corfe Castle

DISTANCE 6 miles (9.7km)

HEIGHT GAIN 1,035 feet (315m)

APPROXIMATE TIME 3 hours

ROUTE TERRAIN Rolling downland tracks, woodland paths with boardwalk and field paths

PARKING Castle View car park, Corfe Castle

OS EXPLORER OL15

OS PATHFINDER Dorset

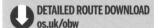
DETAILED ROUTE DOWNLOAD
os.uk/obw

No visit to Dorset would be complete without seeing Corfe Castle, which occupies a break in the long ridge of the Purbeck Hills; its hilltop ruin is one of Dorset's most evocative and much-photographed sights. This walk follows the ridge to the west, from which there are wonderful views across the Dorset heathlands to the coast. The return is through the village of East Creech and very pleasant woodland nestling in the lee of the down. The route's finale has vantage points affording magnificently photogenic views of Corfe Castle.

The route passes old clay workings. Purbeck blue clay was first excavated here in Roman times; during the 18th century, Josiah Wedgwood considered it the best clay in the world and used it to create his 'Queen's Ware'. Additionally, the walk passes through two nature reserves – Stonehill Down and Kilwood Coppice and Meadows – and there's an opportunity to ride on the Swanage Railway from Corfe's station.

Right: Corfe Castle railway station.
Opposite page: Corfe Castle.

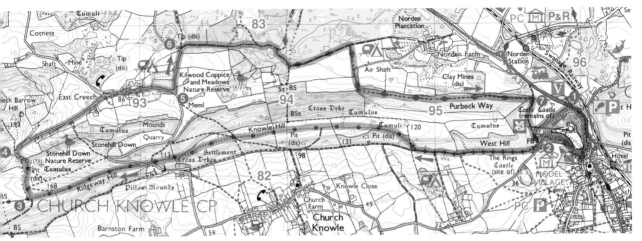

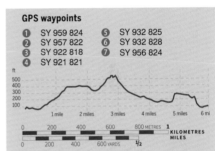

GPS waypoints

❶	SY 959 824	❺	SY 932 825
❷	SY 957 822	❻	SY 932 828
❸	SY 922 818	❼	SY 956 824
❹	SY 921 821		

Edward the Martyr

Edward II, the Saxon boy king of England, was murdered in Corfe in 978. One theory puts the guilt on his stepmother, wanting her own son Æthelred on the throne, but the lack of contemporary chronicles leaves the event shrouded in mystery. Partly fuelled by his body being found incorrupt when removed from Wareham for reburial at Shaftesbury Abbey in 980, a cult grew around Edward and he became venerated as a saint.

Beer and Branscombe

EAST DEVON AONB

DIFFICULTY ●●

START Beer

DISTANCE 6¼ miles (9.9km)

HEIGHT GAIN 1,180 feet (360m)

APPROXIMATE TIME 3½ hours

ROUTE TERRAIN Field paths, woodland tracks and coast path, uneven in places; a couple of steady ascents

PARKING Beer Cliff Top car park

OS EXPLORER 115

OS PATHFINDER South Devon and Dartmoor

 DETAILED ROUTE DOWNLOAD os.uk/obw

This exceptionally attractive walk takes in the two idyllic villages of Beer and Branscombe, a picturesque Norman church, beautiful woodland, impressive cliffs and superlative views over Lyme Bay from Portland Bill near Weymouth to Berry Head on the far side of Torbay. Setting out from Beer the route heads inland along tracks and field paths to Branscombe, continuing through coastal woodland before descending steeply to the beach at Branscombe Mouth. The final leg of the walk takes the Undercliff path, a narrow and winding way beneath the sheer chalk face of Beer Head, then climbs to the top of the cliff and follows the South West Coast Path back to Beer.

As well as being a fishing village, Beer was also known for its local freestone, worked since Roman times and used in buildings all over the country. The underground caverns of Beer Quarry caves – once a hiding place for smuggled goods – are well worth a visit.

Right: Branscombe church and war memorial.
Opposite page left: The beach at Beer.
Opposite page right: Beer Quarry Caves.

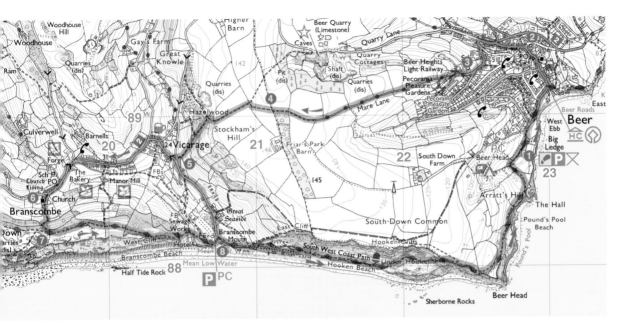

GPS waypoints

1 SY 228 888
2 SY 228 894
3 SY 224 892
4 SY 211 890
5 SY 204 886
6 SY 195 884
7 SY 196 882
8 SY 207 881

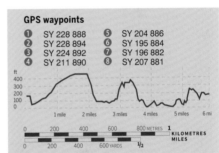

Cheddar Gorge and Velvet Bottom

MENDIP HILLS AONB

DIFFICULTY ●●

START Cheddar

DISTANCE 6½ miles (10.5km)

HEIGHT GAIN 1,215 feet (370m)

APPROXIMATE TIME 3½ hours

ROUTE TERRAIN Woodland and field paths with some steep climbs, often rocky and uneven and slippery in places; there are unguarded cliff edges above Cheddar Gorge

PARKING Cliff Street car park, Cheddar

OS EXPLORER 141

OS PATHFINDER Short Walks Somerset: Bath to the Quantocks

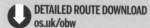 **DETAILED ROUTE DOWNLOAD** os.uk/obw

With a depth of 450-feet (137m) and a length of one-mile (1.6km), Cheddar Gorge is one of the great natural wonders of Britain, its amazing caves drawing visitors from across the world to this chasm in the Mendip Hills. However, few have discovered its continuation to the east, Velvet Bottom. Beyond a disused quarry lies a now quiet and beautiful valley that was once the location of lead ore mining. Cheddar Gorge is a relic of past glacial periods when torrents of meltwater, unabsorbed by the permafrosted limestone, cascaded off the Mendip plateau, exploiting a line of weakness in the geology to gouge out a canyon-like valley. This route goes out along the north rim of Cheddar Gorge, descending at Black Rock for the exploration eastwards to Velvet Bottom, and climbing to return along the south rim of the gorge, with dramatic views down into it – *be careful, there are some sheer drops*. There are also extensive views over the Mendips and across the Somerset Levels.

Right: Wild mountain goat.
Opposite page: Cheddar Gorge.

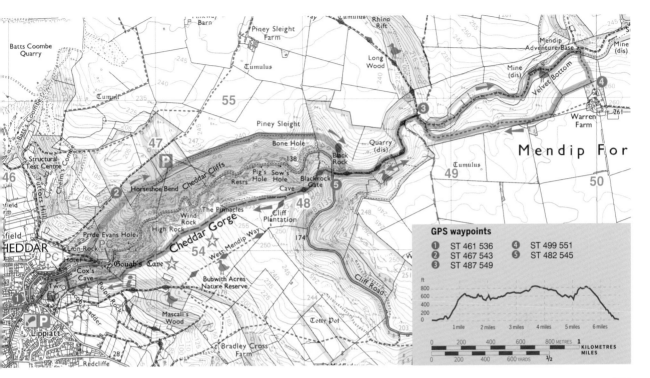

GPS waypoints

① ST 461 536		④ ST 499 551
② ST 467 543		⑤ ST 482 545
③ ST 487 549		

Velvet Bottom

Although Velvet Bottom was a lead-mining area before the Romans arrived, the most intensive periods of mining took place during the Roman occupation and then later in the Middle Ages. The mines were finally abandoned in the 1880s, and nature has since begun to reclaim the land. It is a long and slow process, for few plants can tolerate the high lead levels in the soil of the valley floor. Now it is a 43-acre (17.4-ha) nature reserve managed by Somerset Wildlife Trust; wildflowers noted at the site include spring sandwort, common spotted orchid and rock stonecrop.

Baggy Point and Saunton Down

NORTH DEVON AONB

DIFFICULTY ●●

START Croyde

DISTANCE 7¼ miles (11.4km)

HEIGHT GAIN 1,065 feet (325m)

APPROXIMATE TIME 3½ hours

ROUTE TERRAIN Lanes, farm tracks, coast path (level-going), and a steep ascent of Saunton Down

PARKING Croyde village hall car park

OS EXPLORER 139

OS PATHFINDER North and Mid Devon

 **DETAILED ROUTE DOWNLOAD** os.uk/obw

The surfing hotspot of Croyde Bay is flanked by the craggy headland of Baggy Point to the north and lofty Saunton Down to the south. Much of Baggy Point is a Site of Special Scientific Interest (SSSI), designated for its geological features, which include raised beaches, wave-cut platforms and erratic boulders; the Promontory here is popular with climbers. In the custodianship of the National Trust, the Sandleigh Tearoom offers a mid-walk refreshment stop. The South West Coast Path is not too strenuous here, with a section across the beach at the foot of the dunes of Croyde Burrows. However, at low tide, it may be easier to walk on the harder sand close to the sea and then to wade across the stream emptying into Croyde Bay. There's one short, steep pull up on to Saunton Down, for which the sea views over Croyde Bay are ample compensation. Henry Williamson, author of *Tarka the Otter*, published in 1927, lived locally.

Right: Baggy Point.

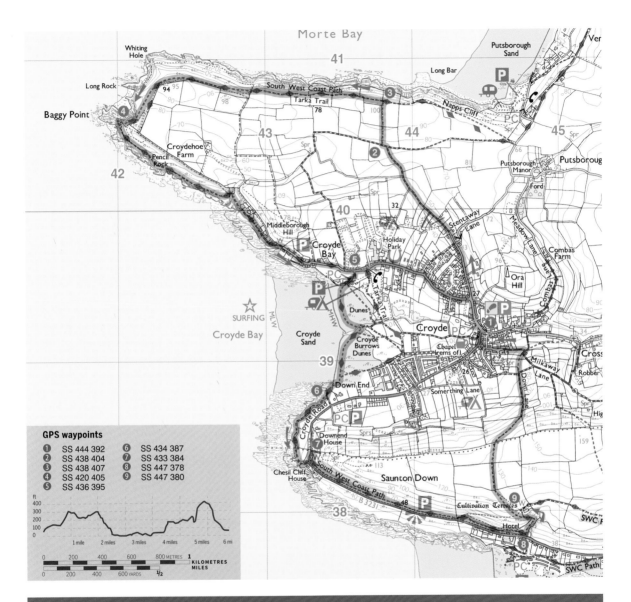

GPS waypoints

1	SS 444 392	6	SS 434 387
2	SS 438 404	7	SS 433 384
3	SS 438 407	8	SS 447 378
4	SS 420 405	9	SS 447 380
5	SS 436 395		

Croyde Beach

The beach at Croyde is beautiful and sandy and set in a wide bay between Baggy Point and Saunton Down. A very pretty spot on the Barnstaple Bay coastline, its fine golden sands make it a popular destination in summer and it has some of the best surfing conditions in Britain. Behind the beach is a hummocky sand dune system called Croyde Burrows.

Wills Neck and Triscombe Combe

QUANTOCK HILLS AONB

DIFFICULTY ●●

START Lydeard Hill

DISTANCE 6½ miles (10.6km)

HEIGHT GAIN 1,150 feet (350m)

APPROXIMATE TIME 3½ hours

ROUTE TERRAIN Moorland and woodland tracks, and field paths; the return to Lydeard Hill is a long, steady ascent

PARKING Lydeard Hill

OS EXPLORER 140

OS PATHFINDER Exmoor and the Quantocks

 **DETAILED ROUTE DOWNLOAD** os.uk/obw

'Upon smooth Quantock's airy ridge we roved unchecked, or loitered mid her sylvan combes …' wrote William Wordsworth, describing walks in the countryside hereabouts, where he and his sister Dorothy lived in 1797-8. This walk follows the Quantock ridge north-west from Lydeard Hill, from where there are superb all-round views, and over its highest point at Wills Neck, 1,260 feet (386m) above sea level. To the east lie the Somerset Levels with the Mendips on the horizon; to the north, the Quantock ridge continues to Great Hill; to the west are the Brendon Hills and Exmoor, and to the south, there's a lovely vista over the Vale of Taunton Deane to the Blackdown Hills. The patchwork of fields, hedges and woods viewed from the ridge reveal the English countryside at its finest and most archetypal. The route descends through Triscombe Combe, continuing to West Bagborough, sheltering beneath wooded slopes, before regaining the ridge to provide an energetic conclusion to the walk.

Right: Wild pony upon the Quantocks.
Opposite page top: William Wordsworth.
Opposite page middle: Purple heather on Lydeard Hill.
Opposite page bottom: On top of the Quantock Hills.

GPS waypoints

❶	ST 180 338	❻	ST 155 355
❷	ST 174 344	❼	ST 160 344
❸	ST 165 351	❽	ST 168 335
❹	ST 163 359	❾	ST 170 334
❺	ST 161 362		

Map labels: at Hill, Cairn, 337, 323, Cairn, Quarry (disused), Marrow Hill, Triscombe Stone, 323, Cairn, Triscombe Quarry, Cairn, Boxenwood Cottage, 386, Cairns, Wills Neck, 384, Fire Signal Pit, 357, Tumuli, Macmillan Way West, Bagborough Hill, Smokeham Farm, 194, Rock Farm, Bagborough Plantation, Middle Hill, Black Knap, Gate, Aisholt Common, WEST BAGBOROUGH CP, Wood Barn, West Bagborough, Heathfield, 124, Reservoir, 135, 130, 120, Bagborough House, War Memorial, Bashford Stables, Milton Farm, 172, Lydeard Hill, 364, Cairn, Tumulus, Cattle Grid, Tilbury Farm, Birches Corner, Quarry (disused), Tilbury Park, 296, 280, ckham Cross, WDW, 185

Elevation profile: ft 1200 1000 800 600 — 1 mile, 2 miles, 3 miles, 4 miles, 5 miles

Scale: 0 200 400 600 800 METRES / 1 KILOMETRES MILES / 0 200 400 600 YARDS / ½

Kingston and the River Erme

SOUTH DEVON AONB

DIFFICULTY ●●

START Kingston

DISTANCE 5¾ miles (9.1km)

HEIGHT GAIN 1,035 feet (315m)

APPROXIMATE TIME 3 hours

ROUTE TERRAIN Field paths and undulating coast path; there are steep and taxing descents to the River Erme and Westcombe Beach, and the track near Okenbury is often muddy

PARKING By the church in Kingston

OS EXPLORER OL20

OS PATHFINDER South Devon and Dartmoor

 DETAILED ROUTE DOWNLOAD os.uk/obw

Exploring probably South Devon's least visited corner, this walk is a little off the beaten track, but the drive along narrow, high-hedged lanes is well worth it. The pretty village of Kingston dates back to King Aethulwulf, who acquired land here in AD876. This is a walk that starts gently and builds up, both in terms of energy expenditure and grandeur. Heading first to the loveliest and most peaceful of Devon's estuaries, the Erme, the walk then joins the South West Coast Path for an equally lovely but rugged stretch of coast to Westcombe Beach. At Hoist Point the cliffs are at their most stunning and dramatic, with seascape views eastwards to Burgh Island and its art deco hotel. The return leg is along a path ascending through the secluded Wiscombe valley. On reaching Kingston, the 16th-century Dolphin Inn, which sits in the heart of the village, is the perfect place to reflect upon the day's outing.

Right: Westcombe's prehistoric rock formations.
Opposite page: Wonwell Beach.

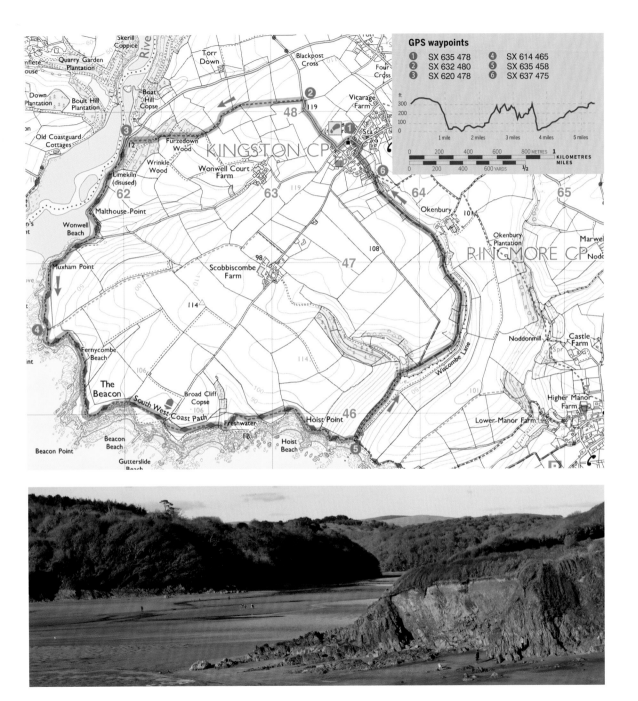

GPS waypoints

1	SX 635 478	**4**	SX 614 465
2	SX 632 480	**5**	SX 635 458
3	SX 620 478	**6**	SX 637 475

Cotehele

WALK 14

TAMAR VALLEY AONB

DIFFICULTY ●

START Calstock

DISTANCE 3½ miles (5.6km)

HEIGHT GAIN 525 feet (160m)

APPROXIMATE TIME 1½ hours

ROUTE TERRAIN Riverside lane and woodland tracks and paths, with a fairly steep climb up through the woods from Cotehele Quay

PARKING Calstock

OS EXPLORER 108

OS PATHFINDER Short Walks Cornwall

 DETAILED ROUTE DOWNLOAD os.uk/obw

The historic village of Calstock, tucked away in a meandering fold of the Tamar, provides a fitting start for a gentle riverside stroll that leads through woodland to beautiful Cotehele House and its sympathetically restored quay, once a bustling port and lifeline for the Tamar Valley. The 12-arched Tamar viaduct, which the route passes beneath, is an impressive sight.

Cotehele is a most beautifully preserved and atmospheric Tudor house, built largely between 1485 and 1539 by the Edgcumbe family. Owned by the National Trust since 1947, Cotehele is still a working estate, as it has been for more than 600 years, focussing on market gardening, flower growing and small-scale farming. The gardens are varied, and there is plenty to see all year round. The last working sailing barge on the Tamar, *Shamrock*, has been restored and can be seen at Lime Quay; is now owned by the National Trust and National Maritime Museum.

Right: Cotehele Quay.
Opposite page top: Entrance to Cotehele House.
Opposite page bottom: Cotehele House and Gardens.

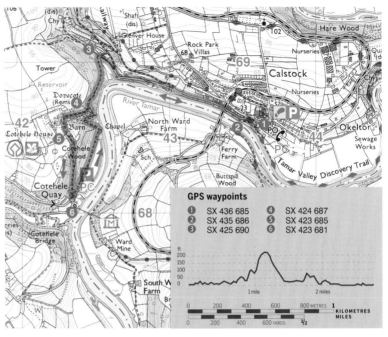

GPS waypoints

1	SX 436 685	**4**	SX 424 687
2	SX 435 686	**5**	SX 423 685
3	SX 425 690	**6**	SX 423 681

UNESCO World Heritage Sites

The four World Heritage Sites in the south-west of England serve to highlight what a richly diverse corner of the country this is. At one extreme is the Cornwall and West Devon Mining Landscape, a testament to past industry; at the other is the world-renowned City of Bath, a synergy of human achievements over almost 2,000 years. Between the two, the naturally occurring cliff exposures along the Dorset and East Devon Coast, of which Durdle Door (the limestone arch near Lulworth) is arguably the best known, provide a counterpoint to the man-made prehistoric sites at Stonehenge and Avebury.

When it comes to inscribing new entries into the World Heritage list, you can be certain that those that make the grade have a weight of validating evidence behind them. The Dorset and East Devon Coasts, commonly known together as the Jurassic Coast, for example, display a formidable sequence of Triassic, Jurassic and Cretaceous rock that documents over 185 million years of the Earth's history. When I first started my outdoor walking life, a rock was a rock, but, over time, I have become more aware of geology, and my interest has been piqued, leading to a whole litany of absorbing questions and discoveries.

No-one, for example, could admire the standing stones of Stonehenge (*left*) and learn that they originated in south Wales, without wondering how they were transported and what purpose they served. The geology of Cornwall and West Devon is also key to an understanding of that region's mining heritage. It takes a while to feel comfortable exploring this industrial landscape, compared with the more evident beauty of a sylvan dale, but it instils a healthy respect for the hardened breed of men that worked here in often hazardous conditions.

That heritage comes in all shapes and sizes is well illustrated in the City of Bath, renowned for its neoclassical public buildings and Roman remains that reflect two great eras in British history. Moreover, Bath represents an attempt to unify nature and the urban setting through careful planning and design; the resultant townscape incorporates picturesque vistas and gives this ancient city on the edge of the Cotswolds such a distinctive appearance.

AMAZING BUT TRUE ...
Dozmary Pool on Bodmin Moor is where King Arthur received his sword, Excalibur from the Lady of the Lake. On the king's death, the sword was returned to the lake, seized by a woman's white-clad arm, which rose from the pool to grasp it.

Around St Agnes

CORNWALL AND WEST DEVON MINING LANDSCAPE (UNESCO)

DIFFICULTY ●●

START Trevaunance Cove, St Agnes

DISTANCE 6¼ miles (10km)

HEIGHT GAIN 1,080 feet (330m)

APPROXIMATE TIME 3½ hours

ROUTE TERRAIN Field paths and tracks, exposed coast path with a steep ascent from Trevallas Porth, and some lane and road walking

PARKING Trevaunance Cove

OS EXPLORER 104

OS PATHFINDER Cornwall

 DETAILED ROUTE DOWNLOAD os.uk/obw

Like many Cornish coast walks, there is more to this route than the distance implies. Although of modest length, this walk has some energy-sapping gradients, and it is a sobering thought that miners who worked here in the 19th century had to climb these paths after a gruelling 16 or so hours underground. Just offshore at Newdowns Head are the jagged Bawden Rocks, more memorably known as 'Man and his Man'. The National Trust is the guardian of Newdowns Head from where there are lovely panoramas of Perran Bay, with Newquay in the distance. On a clear day you can see Trevose Head on the far side of Newquay Bay. Views from St Agnes Beacon are stupendous, as well, and well worth the climb. The Blue Hills Tin Streams, passed near the end of the walk, is a working tin museum. The cove at Trevallas Porth is a refreshing place to paddle.

Right: Coastal path at Trevellas Coombe.
Opposite page: The beach at Trevaunance Cove.

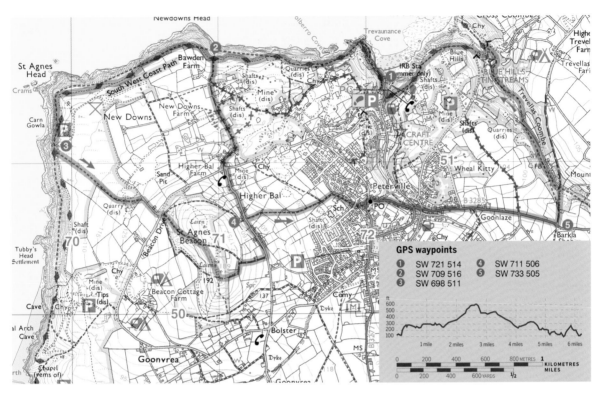

GPS waypoints

①	SW 721 514	④	SW 711 506
②	SW 709 516	⑤	SW 733 505
③	SW 698 511		

The Blue Hills Tin Streams

A working tin museum – Blue Hills Tin Streams – can be found on the coast just upstream of Trevellas Porth. Here the process of alluvial tin mining is explained and you can watch craftsmen working the tin in a tour of the site. Overlooked by the dramatically perched ruins of engine-houses, the nearby cove is a refreshing place to paddle, *but bathing is dangerous at any time*.

Golden Cap

DORSET AND EAST DEVON COAST (UNESCO)

DIFFICULTY ●●●

START Seatown

DISTANCE 6½ miles (10.5km)

HEIGHT GAIN 1,675 feet (510m)

APPROXIMATE TIME 4 hours

ROUTE TERRAIN Coast path, coastal downland tracks and field paths

PARKING Next to the beach at Seatown

OS EXPLORER 116

OS PATHFINDER Dorset and the Jurassic Coast

 DETAILED ROUTE DOWNLOAD os.uk/obw

Rising to 626 feet (191m), Golden Cap is the highest point along the English Channel coast and boasts spectacular views in all directions. On the summit is a memorial to the Earl of Antrim, who was chairman of the National Trust from 1966 until his death in 1977. One of his great concerns was the ongoing loss of coastline to development; in response, he helped launch Enterprise Neptune, a project aimed at protecting coastal heritage and habitats, which now safeguards 700 miles (1127km) of Britain's finest coastline.

This classic walk from Seatown skirts Langdon Hill and St Gabriel's Wood before rising on to Stonebarrow Hill; the return follows the South West Coast Path. Much of the coast between Seatown and Charmouth is owned by the National Trust, and there is a wealth of paths linking coastal cliffs with the sylvan downs behind. Inevitably, this is an energetic walk, but the superb scenery more than repays the effort involved. Allow time to enjoy Seatown's splendid beach, or to hunt for fossils beneath the cliffs.

Right: Seatown.
Opposite page left: Coastal path above Seatown, looking down on Chesil Beach.
Opposite page right: Fishermen at Seatown.

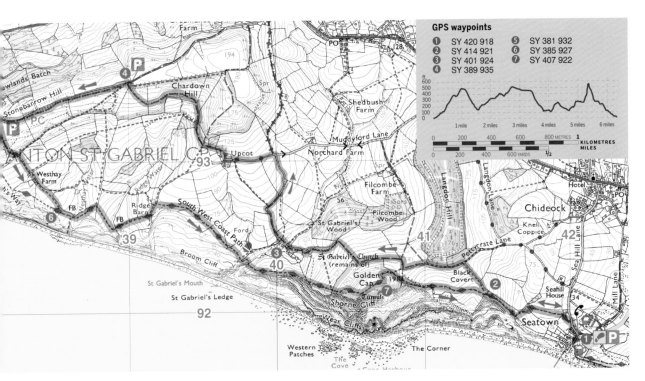

WALK 17

Bath and Claverton Down

CITY OF BATH (UNESCO)

DIFFICULTY ●●●

START Bath Abbey

DISTANCE 8½ miles (13.5km)

HEIGHT GAIN 625 feet (190m)

APPROXIMATE TIME 4 hours

ROUTE TERRAIN City streets and suburban roads, canal towpath, lanes, field and woodland paths

PARKING Bath

OS EXPLORER 155

OS PATHFINDER Cotswolds

DETAILED ROUTE DOWNLOAD os.uk/obw

Bath is located at the southern edge of the Cotswolds, where the hills descend abruptly to the Avon valley; its Georgian buildings rising up the valley sides give the city its distinctive appearance. Bath's spa heritage dates to about AD60, when the Romans exploited the naturally occurring hot water to create a bathing complex at the centre of their settlement, known then as Aquae Sulis. Bath Abbey dates from the 12th century and was built on the site of a Benedictine monastery, originally founded in the 7th century. The popularity of Bath as a spa tourism destination really took off in the Georgian period, as can be seen by the grandeur of the Pump Room and Assembly Rooms; the city's wealth and status generated a proliferation of splendid Georgian architecture, such as the Royal Crescent and the Circus.

Commencing and ending at Bath Abbey, the route crosses Pulteney Bridge to head for Bathwick, where it follows the Kennet and Avon Canal around Bathampton to Claverton. The return leg crosses Claverton Down to Sham Castle before dropping back into the city.

Right: Bath Abbey.

GPS waypoints

1	ST 752 648	6	ST 788 639
2	ST 758 654	7	ST 779 640
3	ST 776 665	8	ST 778 651
4	ST 790 642	9	ST 766 648
5	ST 787 642	10	ST 758 652

Claverton Pumping Station

Claverton Pumping Station opened in 1813 and was built to utilise the power of the River Avon to raise water from the river to feed into the Kennet and Avon Canal. Restored between 1967 and 1975, the pumping machinery is maintained and operated by the Claverton Group, all volunteers, and can be viewed on open days over scheduled weekends throughout the summer.

Avebury, West Kennett and Silbury Hill

STONEHENGE AND AVEBURY AND ASSOCIATED SITES (UNESCO)

DIFFICULTY ●●

START Avebury

DISTANCE 6½ miles (10.5km)

HEIGHT GAIN 310 feet (95m)

APPROXIMATE TIME 3 hours

ROUTE TERRAIN Downland tracks and gently undulating field paths

PARKING National Trust car park, Avebury

OS EXPLORER 157

OS PATHFINDER Somerset, the Mendips and Wiltshire

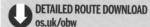

DETAILED ROUTE DOWNLOAD
os.uk/obw

A fascinating walk on the Marlborough Downs links the most outstanding collection of prehistoric remains in the country. It starts at Avebury, whose great stone circle is more complex than it seems, with two smaller circles within the main outer ring of standing stones, protected by a ditch and embankment. The size of the outer circle and the proximity of other monuments suggest it was a highly significant place in Neolithic Britain. It's also worth visiting Elizabethan Avebury Manor, now a National Trust property, and the village's fine medieval church. Beyond Avebury, the walk follows part of the Ridgeway, a prehistoric trackway that is probably the oldest long-distance track still in use in Britain. The route also passes West Kennett Long Barrow, the largest burial chamber in Britain, and Silbury Hill, the tallest prehistoric man-made mound in Europe.

Right: Prehistoric Silbury Hill.
Opposite page top: Avebury's Norman church.
Opposite page bottom: Avebury stone circle.

GPS waypoints
① SU 099 696
② SU 099 698
③ SU 125 708
④ SU 118 680
⑤ SU 119 674
⑥ SU 114 678
⑦ SU 104 681

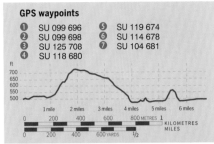

st Kennett Long Barrow

st Kennett Long Barrow is a stone-chambered tomb dating n around 3700BC, and is the largest burial chamber ngland at nearly 350 feet (106m) long. It is one of the most impressive Neolithic chambered tombs in Britain and 50 people were interred here. The three huge stones at the entrance probably date from when the tomb was sealed up.

Stonehenge

STONEHENGE AND AVEBURY AND ASSOCIATED SITES (UNESCO)

DIFFICULTY ●●●

START Amesbury

DISTANCE 8 miles (12.9km)

HEIGHT GAIN 445 feet (135m)

APPROXIMATE TIME 4 hours

ROUTE TERRAIN Downland tracks and gently undulating field paths, roadsides and lanes

PARKING Recreation Ground car park at Amesbury

OS EXPLORER 130

OS PATHFINDER Somerset, the Mendips and Wiltshire

 DETAILED ROUTE DOWNLOAD os.uk/obw

The highlight of this thoroughly absorbing walk is the sudden view of Stonehenge ahead, dominating the skyline, and the approach to the site across the wide expanses of Salisbury Plain, from where its location can be fully appreciated. The walk begins and finishes in nearby Amesbury, an attractively situated town enfolded within a great loop of the River Avon.

Stonehenge is one of the best-known prehistoric monuments in the world. Mysteries abound and controversies persist about its purpose and construction, in particular why and how the smaller bluestones were brought from the Preseli Hills in Pembrokeshire to be erected here. Stonehenge appears to have been built in three main phases over 1,500 years, beginning with the construction of a large circular bank and ditch around 3000BC. About 2000BC the circles of bluestones were erected and subsequently rearranged, and, lastly, the circle of giant sarsen blocks with lintels – the most striking feature of the monument – was completed around 1400BC.

Right: Stonehenge.

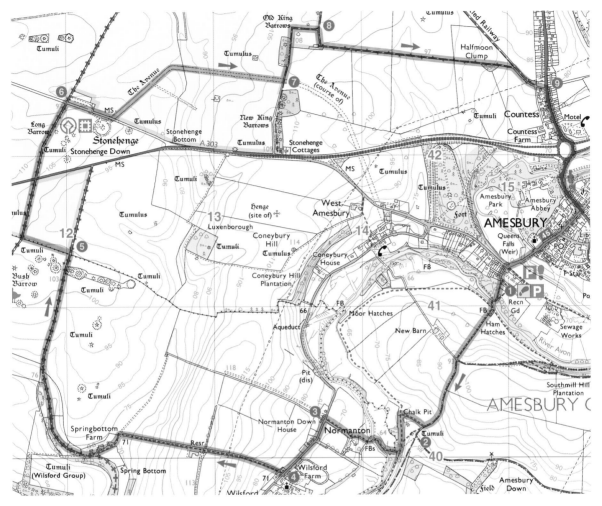

Amesbury

Amesbury is situated on the River Avon which does a great loop to the south-west of the town. The church, with its Norman nave and 13th-century central tower is strikingly imposing and was believed to have been the church of a medieval nunnery that stood nearby. After the dissolution of the monasteries in the 1530s, a house, Amesbury Abbey, was built on the site, and rebuilt in the 19th century. The house is privately owned and not open to the public.

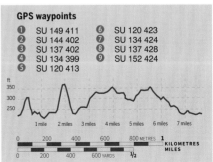

GPS waypoints

❶	SU 149 411	❻	SU 120 423
❷	SU 144 402	❼	SU 134 424
❸	SU 137 402	❽	SU 137 428
❹	SU 134 399	❾	SU 152 424
❺	SU 120 413		

SOUTH-EAST
OF ENGLAND

The Walks

Top: Footpath through Friston Forest in the South Downs National Park.
Bottom: St Martha's Church.
Previous page: Sussex Weald and the South Downs.

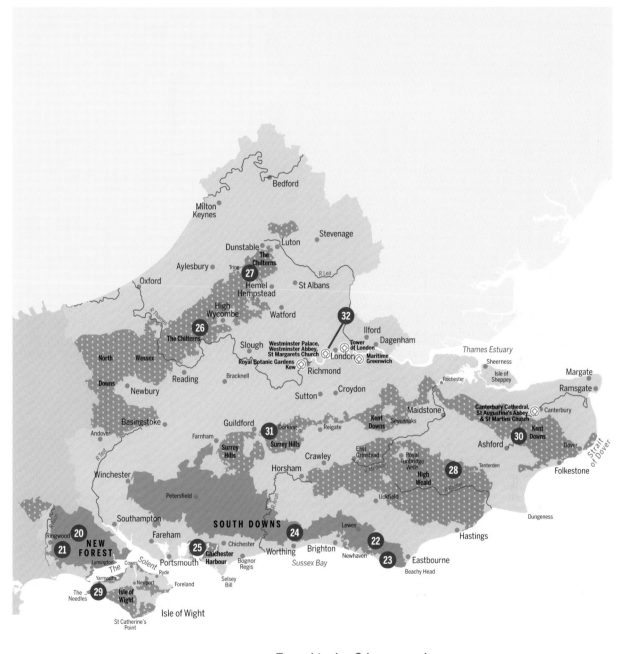

Bedford

Milton
Keynes

Dunstable

Luton

Stevenage

Aylesbury

The
Chilterns

Tring

27

R Lea

Oxford

Hemel
Hempstead

St Albans

High
Wycombe

Watford

26

R Thames

The Chilterns

Slough

32

Ilford

Dagenham

North

Wessex

Westminster Palace,
Westminster Abbey,
St Margarets Church

Tower
of London

Royal Botanic Gardens
Kew

London

Maritime
Greenwich

Sheerness

Margate

Downs

Reading

Bracknell

Richmond

Rochester

Isle of
Sheppey

Ramsgate

Newbury

Sutton

Croydon

Basingstoke

Andover

Guildford

31

Farnham

Dorking

Reigate

Kent
Downs

Sevenoaks

Maidstone

Canterbury Cathedral,
St Augustine's Abbey
& St Martins Church

Canterbury

R Test

Surrey
Hills

Surrey Hills

Crawley

East
Grinstead

Ashford

30

Kent
Downs

Dover

Strait of Dover

Winchester

Horsham

R Medway

Royal
Tunbridge
Wells

Folkestone

Petersfield

R Arun

High
Weald

28

Tenterden

Southampton

Fareham

SOUTH DOWNS

24

Uckfield

Lewes

R Rother

Dungeness

20

**NEW
FOREST**

R Avon

25

Chichester
Harbour

Chichester

Worthing

Brighton

Hastings

Ringwood

21

Lymington

Cowes

Portsmouth

Bognor
Regis

Sussex Bay

Newhaven

22

23

Eastbourne

Beachy Head

The
Solent

Ryde

Selsey
Bill

Yarmouth

Newport

Foreland

The
Needles

29

Isle of
Wight

St Catherine's
Point

Isle of Wight

English Channel

Thames Estuary

0	20	40	60	80 Km
0	10	20	30	40	50 Miles

New Forest National Park

The great attraction of the New Forest National Park is its diverse landscape. This alluring blend of ancient and ornamental woodland, open heaths swathed in heather, coastal mudflats, salt marshes and rivers, not to mention a profusion of appealing historic villages, was granted National Park status as recently as 2005. As with many large tracts of land in England, the New Forest is an ancient designation. It was first defined as a 'Royal Forest' in 1079 by William the Conqueror and was used for hunting deer. It appears in the Domesday Book in 1086 as 'Nova Foresta'.

I first visited the New Forest long before the area became a National Park, in the days when I was researching in the nearby Ordnance Survey archive. I was struck by the acute sense of place that can be felt in forests and heaths of antiquity, almost as though I was walking back through time.

Like all the National Parks, this is a landscape fashioned by man's endeavour and by the animals that live there to this day. Commoners' cattle, ponies and donkeys roam the open heath and woodland, and it is largely their grazing that maintains the open character of the forest. The New Forest pony is one of the indigenous horse breeds of Britain and one of the National Park's most famous attractions, although Shetland ponies can be found here, too.

Large areas within the National Park are woodland enclosures that owe their existence to the demand for timber; Knightwood Inclosure, near Lyndhurst, and Amberwood Inclosure near Fritham are classic examples of this practice of producing timber, both deciduous and coniferous. But the National Park also encompasses a splendid and varied medley of other habitats that are host to bats, beetles and butterflies, as well as all three British native species of snake: the adder, the grass snake and the rarer smooth snake. In fact, more than half the National Park comprises Sites of Special Scientific Interest.

Walking is by far the best way to explore the New Forest, bringing you close encounters with the thousands of free-roaming ponies and donkeys. There are countless potential routes here, because there are very few restrictions on walking, but if free-range rambling isn't your thing, then you can make the most of more than 140 miles (225km) of maintained tracks.

AMAZING BUT TRUE ...
The Beaulieu country estate in the heart of the New Forest was used to train spies before they were deployed into occupied Europe, yet none of the villagers knew what was happening under their noses.

WALK 20

New Forest Snapshot

NEW FOREST NATIONAL PARK

DIFFICULTY ●

START Millyford Bridge

DISTANCE 2¾ miles (4.5km)

HEIGHT GAIN 130 feet (40m)

APPROXIMATE TIME 1½ hours

ROUTE TERRAIN Woodland and heathland tracks and paths

PARKING Millyford Bridge car park, one mile (1.6km) west of Emery Down on the back road to Linwood

OS EXPLORER OL22

OS PATHFINDER New Forest, Hampshire and South Downs

⬇ **DETAILED ROUTE DOWNLOAD** os.uk/obw

This magical little walk packs in three of the New Forest's best-known sites: the Portuguese Fireplace, the Reptile Centre, where all native reptiles and amphibians found in the New Forest can be seen, and the Knightwood Oak, at least 400 years of age and one of the Forest's noblest and oldest trees. In between, the route passes through typical New Forest scenery of wooded pasture, heath and broadleaved woodland. It's the perfect introduction to the New Forest and its various habitats.

Starting out along a New Forest lane, bordered by old and ornamental trees, the route soon reaches the Portuguese Fireplace. During World War One, Portuguese troops were stationed in the New Forest to help provide vitally important timber and to meet the shortfall in local manpower at a time when most forest workers were doing military service. Troops constructed the fireplace to ensure meals were cooked in the traditional Portuguese way, and it now stands as a memorial to their wartime assistance.

Right: New Forest wild pony.
Opposite page left: The Knightwood Oak at 500 years old is the largest oak in the New Forest.
Opposite page right: The Portuguese Fireplace.

GPS waypoints

1. SU 267 079
2. SU 264 078
3. SU 270 070
4. SU 269 064
5. SU 263 064
6. SU 264 070

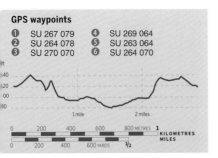

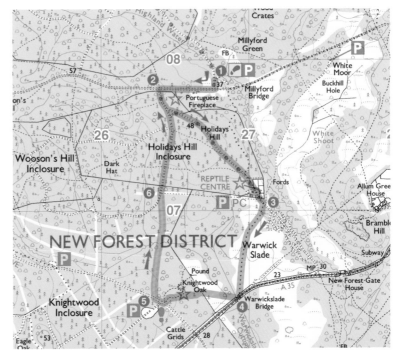

Around Burley

NEW FOREST NATIONAL PARK

DIFFICULTY ●

START Burbush Hill

DISTANCE 4¼ miles (6.8km)

HEIGHT GAIN 245 feet (75m)

APPROXIMATE TIME 2½ hours

ROUTE TERRAIN Old railway track bed, heathland tracks and village lane

PARKING Forestry Commission car park at Burbush Hill

OS EXPLORER OL22

OS PATHFINDER Short Walks New Forest National Park

 DETAILED ROUTE DOWNLOAD os.uk/obw

Burley is a bustling village in the heart of the New Forest, reached here via a path from Burbush Hill, along an old railway line and then across the heather-clad slopes of Turf Hill. The railway ran between Southampton and Dorchester and was promoted by Dorset solicitor Charles Castleman, but it took such a slow, roundabout route that it earned the nickname, 'Castleman's Corkscrew'; it closed in the mid-1960s. Over Turf Hill, the walk winds through the village of Burley, where the old-fashioned craft of cider-making has been revived, and visitors can watch traditional cider apples being pressed (in season). The walk concludes with a peaceful stroll across the sandy heath of Kingston Great Common National Nature Reserve. Managed by Natural England this 138-acre (56ha) reserve comprises lowland heath and waterlogged (particularly in winter) valley mire. Look out here for rare birds, such as woodlark, nightjar and Dartford warbler, as well as colourful dragonfly species.

Right: Castleman's Corkscrew.
Opposite page top: Banded demoiselle.
Opposite page bottom: Turf Hill.

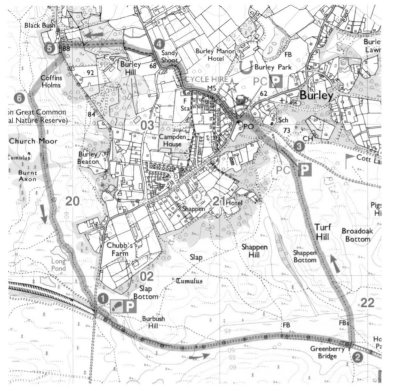

GPS waypoints

① SU 202 017   ④ SU 205 034
② SU 218 015   ⑤ SU 199 035
③ SU 214 028   ⑥ SU 197 031

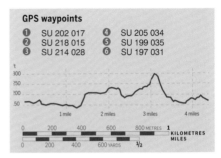

South Downs National Park

An extravagant and rich tapestry of rolling hills and busy market towns characterises England's newest National Park, the South Downs, created in 2011. This glorious blend of farmland, ancient woodland and lowland heath extends from Winchester in the west to Eastbourne; they even produce wine here.

Much of the geography we see today is the result of man's efforts to clear and manage the landscape for thousands of years. It is a setting that has inspired writers, artists and musicians, including JMW Turner, Jane Austen and Edward Elgar.

Today, the South Downs continue to inspire and invigorate walkers to explore, for example, the rides of Friston Forest and the open downland that leads to the chalk cliffs of the Seven Sisters. Central to the whole National Park is the 100-mile (160-km) South Downs Way, an imaginative linking of ancient paths and tracks that have been in use for more than 8,000 years. But the notion of a long walk through the South Downs is nothing new. In 1911, author Hilaire Belloc wrote a novel, *The Four Men: A Farrago*, in which he describes a 90-mile (140km) walk across Sussex and into the area today encompassed by the National Park. People still follow in Belloc's footsteps; *The Four Men* has even been made into a play and performed at the Brighton Fringe.

In recent years, my regular visits to France via Portsmouth have been supplemented by additional days spent dipping into the South Downs. That glorious broad stretch of the South Downs Way up to the hilltop fort on Chanctonbury Hill was one of my first jaunts. I was drawn to this by the often-repeated comment of philosopher Bertrand Russell: 'It can be regarded as an axiom that any view which includes Chanctonbury Ring is a good view'. I wanted to see the view for myself; the presence of an increasingly rare dew pond near the summit made the visit even more agreeable.

But, before you gain the impression that the chalky undulations of the South Downs are a walk in the park, bear in mind that stretches have been used for Oxfam's Trailwalker, probably the UK's toughest team charity challenge.

> **AMAZING BUT TRUE ...**
> The Long Man of Wilmington on Windover Hill – 230 feet (70m) high and 235 feet (72m) wide – is one of only two extant human hill figures in England; the other is the Cerne Abbas Giant.

Firle Beacon and Charleston Farmhouse

SOUTH DOWNS NATIONAL PARK

DIFFICULTY ●

START Firle

DISTANCE 5 miles (8km)

HEIGHT GAIN 740 feet (225m)

APPROXIMATE TIME 2½ hours

ROUTE TERRAIN Downland and field tracks and paths

PARKING Firle

OS EXPLORER OL25

OS PATHFINDER South Downs National Park and East Sussex

 DETAILED ROUTE DOWNLOAD os.uk/obw

From Firle, a seemingly timeless feudal estate village, this short ramble on to the Downs climbs to Firle Beacon to take in far-reaching Wealden and sea views, descending to Charleston Farmhouse, home of the Bloomsbury set, and returning past the mansion of Firle Place.

Firle is a rare example of an estate village, tucked away below the South Downs escarpment amid a patchwork of fields and hedgerows. Nearby Charleston Farmhouse was the bohemian country retreat of the Bloomsbury group of post-Victorian artists, writers and intellectuals, including Vanessa Bell and Duncan Grant, who set up home here in 1916. It has been restored and preserved by the Charleston Trust, and a rewarding visit will reveal some fine examples of colourful murals and painted furniture. In the churchyard of St Peter's in Firle are the graves of Vanessa Bell and her son, Quentin Bell, both Bloomsbury artists. This route also passes the Palladian mansion and parkland of Firle Place.

Right: The studio of Bloomsbury set member Duncan Grant at Charleston. **Opposite page**: View from Firle Beacon.

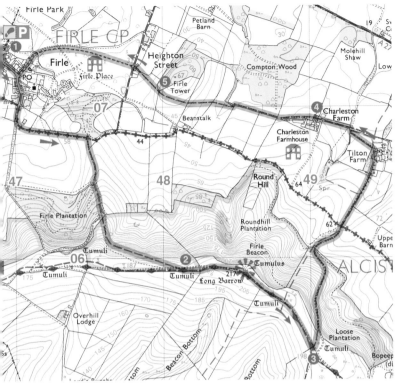

GPS waypoints

① TQ 469 074   ④ TQ 490 069
② TQ 481 059   ⑤ TQ 479 070
③ TQ 490 054

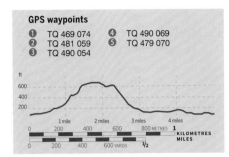

Firle Place

Home to the Gage family for over 500 years, Firle Place is a fine Palladian mansion. Throughout the year it hosts various events, exhibitions and concerts and the house and tearoom is open to the public four days each week in summer. Firle Tower, passed earlier in the walk, was built in 1822 by Viscount Gage to house his head gamekeeper.

Friston Forest, the Seven Sisters and Cuckmere Haven

SOUTH DOWNS NATIONAL PARK

DIFFICULTY ●●

START Exceat, Seven Sisters Country Park

DISTANCE 6½ miles (10.5km)

HEIGHT GAIN 1,150 feet (350m)

APPROXIMATE TIME 3½ hours

ROUTE TERRAIN Forest and downland tracks, clifftop and riverside field paths; the route rollercoasters up and down on the South Downs Way across the Seven Sisters

PARKING Riverside car park at Exceat

OS EXPLORER OL25

OS PATHFINDER South Downs National Park and East Sussex

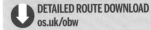

DETAILED ROUTE DOWNLOAD
os.uk/obw

A hugely satisfying and superbly varied walk takes you along the wide rides of Friston Forest, over open downland to the spectacular Seven Sisters and along a clifftop rollercoaster stretch of the South Downs Way, before descending to Cuckmere Haven for a stroll across the floodplain at the foot of the Downs, adjacent to the looping coils of the Cuckmere.

Now little more than a name on a map, Exceat, at the start of the walk, was a village abandoned after the Black Death in the mid-14th century. The delightful mixed woodland of Friston Forest is managed by the Forestry Commission. Upon reaching the coast, the route crosses a succession of hanging dry valleys of the iconic chalk cliffs of the Seven Sisters, over which the South Downs Way rises and falls, offering one of the most memorable walking experiences in England. Gazing down upon the extravagant meanders of the Cuckmere River and the shingle beach, marsh and lagoons of Cuckmere Haven is also thrilling.

Right: Seven Sisters.

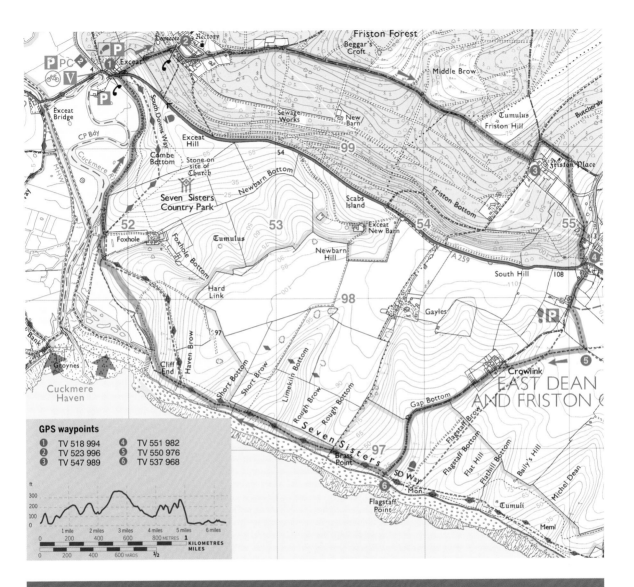

GPS waypoints

1. TV 518 994
2. TV 523 996
3. TV 547 989
4. TV 551 982
5. TV 550 976
6. TV 537 968

The River Cuckmere

Noted for its extravagant meanders and ox-bow lakes, the River Cuckmere rises on the High Weald near Heathfield. Over its comparatively short 18-mile (29-km) course, the Cuckmere initially descends at quite a gradient – its name probably derived from Old English meaning 'fast-flowing' – to cross the farmland of the Low Weald, passing Hailsham to flow through a gap in the South Downs at Alfriston, before looping over its floodplain to issue into the English Channel between the Seven Sisters and Seaford.

Cissbury and Chanctonbury Rings

SOUTH DOWNS NATIONAL PARK

DIFFICULTY ●●●

START Combe Rise car park, Findon Valley

DISTANCE 11 miles (17.6km)

HEIGHT GAIN 1,360 feet (415m)

APPROXIMATE TIME 5½ hours

ROUTE TERRAIN Undulating downland tracks and field paths

PARKING Combe Rise car park

OS EXPLORER OL10

OS PATHFINDER West Sussex and the South Downs

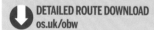

DETAILED ROUTE DOWNLOAD
os.uk/obw

A highlight for anyone walking the Downs, this lengthy ramble has broad sweeping vistas embracing some of the finest scenery in the South Downs National Park. In passing through Cissbury Ring and Chanctonbury Ring, the route links two of the finest Iron Age hill forts in the country. Reaching more than 600 feet (184m) above sea level, Cissbury Ring is the largest hill fort in Sussex, its massive earthwork ramparts enclose an area of 65 acres, and the inner bank has a circumference of over one mile. Cissbury Ring was constructed around 400BC, developed on a site that had been mined for flint since Neolithic times. The remains of the mining activity can be seen after passing through the ramparts.

Famously, Chanctonbury Ring is capped by beech trees, and some replanting has taken place since the 1987 hurricane to preserve this landmark feature. Infamously, Chanctonbury has long been associated with mysterious forces, and folklore has it that if you run backwards round the ring six times you can summon the Devil from the underworld.

Right: Cissbury Ring.

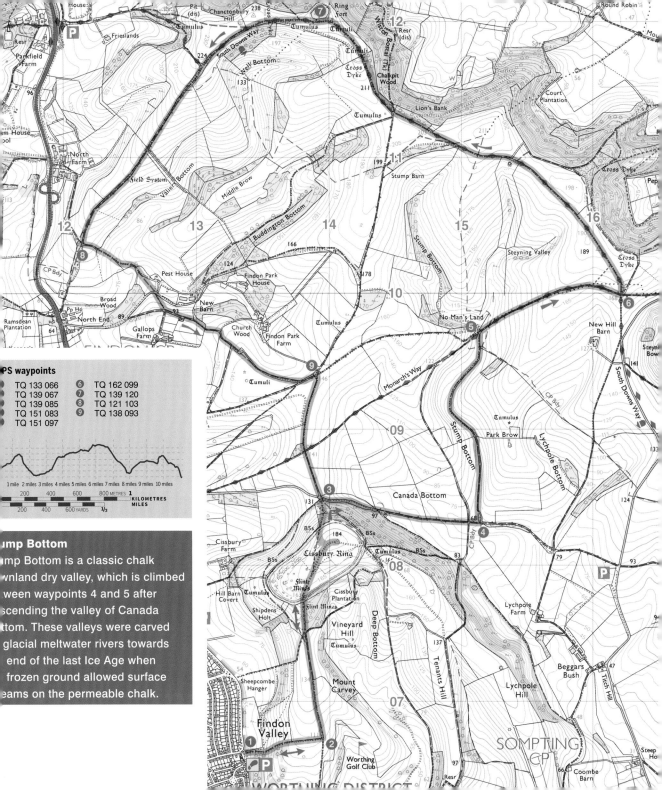

Stump Bottom

Stump Bottom is a classic chalk downland dry valley, which is climbed between waypoints 4 and 5 after descending the valley of Canada Bottom. These valleys were carved by glacial meltwater rivers towards the end of the last Ice Age when frozen ground allowed surface streams on the permeable chalk.

Areas of Outstanding Natural Beauty

About half of the Isle of Wight – England's largest offshore island – is designated as an AONB. This is a comparatively small, intimate landscape, but the scene can change in an instant, from fecund and lush, to rugged and wild. This is especially evident in the climb over Tennyson Down, which ascends gradually to a tremendous viewpoint, looking one way to The Needles and Alum Bay, and the other towards the north-west of the island.

Along the coast of the Isle of Wight, the landscape is reminiscent of the South Downs and the Kent Downs: gently undulating chalk cliffs that provide airy walks that are easy on the legs. Like much of this southern part of Britain, the Kent Downs are a farmed landscape, their character evolving from human endeavour that is manifested in tiny lanes, isolated farmsteads, churches, castles, coast houses and orchards. Moreover, the ancient woodland and chalk grassland are rich in wildlife, while the renowned White Cliffs of Dover are as iconic a symbol of England as Big Ben.

The High Weald promises more of the same – gently rolling countryside and beautiful villages; the wonder is that the whole of southern England, from Dover to Southampton, hasn't been designated as one huge National Park. There is, perhaps, a little more woodland in the High Weald and more sandstone outcrops, but, overall, the picture is one of isolated farmsteads and ancient sunken lanes created by Saxon drovers and Tudor ironworkers – very much a medieval landscape.

The almost legendary Ashdown Forest (*left*) was a deer-hunting forest in Norman times and is now south-east England's largest expanse of heathland, where richly purpled heather and bright-yellow gorse enrich the countryside and bring joy to the soul. Ashdown is the best surviving example of four medieval forests along the Weald Forest Ridge and a reminder of a vital landscape that is fast disappearing.

Although they are far from my home in north-west England, the Chilterns have consumed much of my time, mostly while updating Pathfinder guides. I still remember with affection the walk up onto Ivinghoe Beacon; it's not the highest point, but it stands apart and so has a splendid view. Near the Elstree Studios, I even discovered Hagrid's Cottage from the early Harry Potter films, before they moved it to Glen Coe.

AMAZING BUT TRUE …

A network of tunnels cut into the Kent chalk cliffs date from the Napoleonic Wars. Famous for their use as a military command post during World War Two, the tunnels remained in use through the Cold War, until 1984.

The Chidham Peninsula

CHICHESTER HARBOUR AONB

DIFFICULTY ●

START Chidham

DISTANCE 5 miles (8km)

HEIGHT GAIN Negligible

APPROXIMATE TIME 2½ hours

ROUTE TERRAIN Field and shore paths

PARKING Cobnor Farm amenity car park

OS EXPLORER OL8

OS PATHFINDER West Sussex and the South Downs

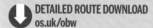 **DETAILED ROUTE DOWNLOAD** os.uk/obw

Chidham faces picturesque Bosham across one of the many narrow, finger-like inlets of Chichester Harbour. A peaceful walk, ideal for birdwatchers, this route follows the shore path beside the Bosham Channel, around Cobnor Point and fringing Nutbourne Marsh Nature Reserve to Chidham Point. The shallow tidal waters and mudflats are home to curlew, dunlin, redshank and oystercatcher. *At exceptionally high tides the section between Cobnor and Chudham points may be inundated.*

From the start of the walk there are lovely views of photogenic Bosham, framed by the South Downs behind. Herons frequent the lagoons on the landward side of Cobnor Point. To seaward, the spit of estuarine mud and silt has the remains of old piling dating from the 19th century, when an attempt was made to reclaim a wide tract of land from the sea. Before that there was a tidal mill here. Nowadays, it is an important nesting site for three species of tern.

Right: Bosham harbour.
Opposite page: Curlew.

GPS waypoints
1. SU 793 034
2. SU 796 034
3. SU 788 020
4. SU 780 046
5. SU 787 044

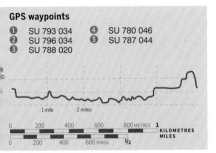

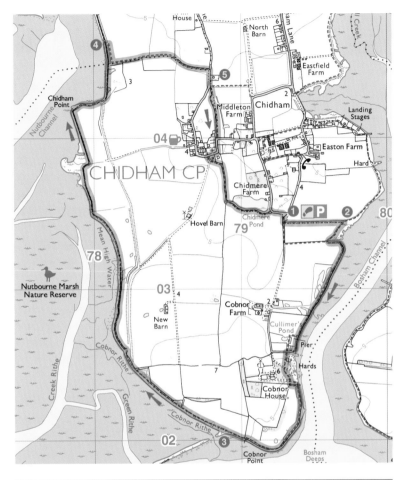

The Chidham Peninsula

The Chidham Peninsula lies within the relatively unspoilt natural estuary of Chichester Harbour, which is a haven of tranquillity, natural beauty and internationally recognised wetland wildlife habitat. Chidham lies between the Bosham and Nutbourne channels, 'fingers' of tidal water amid the mudflats, salt marsh and low-lying land of Chichester Harbour. Nutbourne Marsh, passed on the western side of the peninsula, is a Site of Special Scientific Interest, its inter-tidal mud providing feeding grounds and over-wintering quarters for migratory waterfowl.

Ibstone, Turville and Fingest

CHILTERNS AONB

DIFFICULTY ●●●

START Ibstone Common

DISTANCE 7¾ miles (12.3km)

HEIGHT GAIN 855 feet (260m)

APPROXIMATE TIME 4 hours

ROUTE TERRAIN Rolling downland and woodland paths and tracks

PARKING Roadside parking beside Ibstone Common

OS EXPLORER 171

OS PATHFINDER Thames Valley and Chilterns

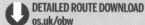 **DETAILED ROUTE DOWNLOAD**
os.uk/obw

Set in the characteristic Chilterns countryside of beech woodland and sweeping dry chalk valleys, there is a tranquillity and away-from-it-all feel about this walk which belies its location in home-counties Buckinghamshire. The sense of remoteness is further reinforced by the two small, apparently timeless villages of Turville and Fingest, which are encountered en route. Turville is an idyllic village of old brick and half-timbered cottages grouped around a green, with a pub and a restored late-medieval church; it is set amid beech woods and chalk downs that are unmistakeably Chiltern in character. Fingest is similarly picturesque but even smaller. Its church is notable for its plainbut massive, twin-gabled Norman tower, which looks out of proportion to the rest of the building. This walk passes three pubs: the Fox Country Inn at Ibstone, the Bull and Butcher at Turville and the Chequers Inn at Fingest.

Right: Cobstone Mill on Turville Hill.

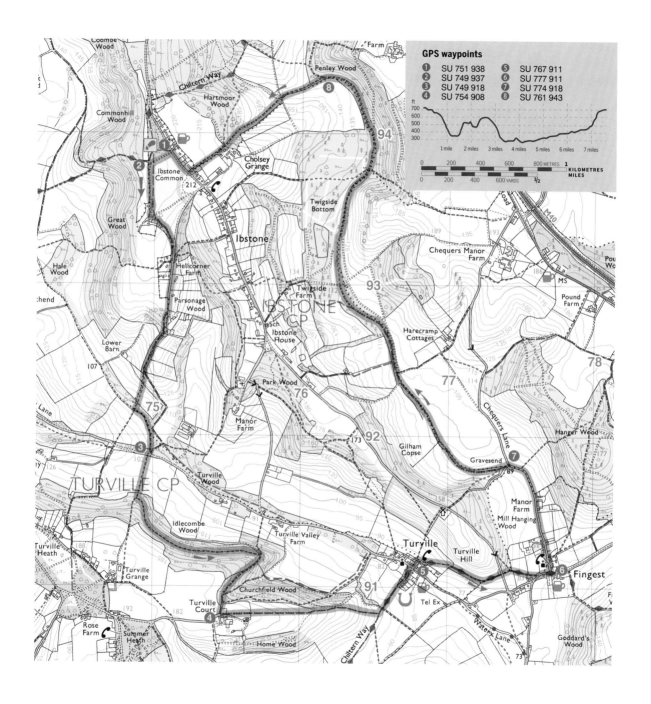

GPS waypoints

①	SU 751 938	⑤	SU 767 911
②	SU 749 937	⑥	SU 777 911
③	SU 749 918	⑦	SU 774 918
④	SU 754 908	⑧	SU 761 943

Aldbury, Ivinghoe Beacon and Ashridge

CHILTERNS AONB

DIFFICULTY ●●●

START Aldbury

DISTANCE 7½ miles (11.8km)

HEIGHT GAIN 805 feet (245m)

APPROXIMATE TIME 4 hours

ROUTE TERRAIN Good field and woodland paths and tracks

PARKING Laneside (with consideration) in Aldbury; alternative parking at Pitstone Hill (waypoint 3) and the Bridgewater Monument (waypoint 7)

OS EXPLORER 181

OS PATHFINDER Thames Valley and Chilterns

 DETAILED ROUTE DOWNLOAD os.uk/obw

Combining superb views from the Chilterns escarpment on the outward leg with some immensely pleasurable walking through the National Trust's Ashridge Estate on the return, this outstanding circuit sets out from the picturesque village of Aldbury to Ivinghoe Beacon, which, at 764 feet (233m), is one of the highest viewpoints in the Chilterns. There are magnificent panoramas over the Vale of Aylesbury, along the Chiltern escarpment from Dunstable Downs to Coombe Hill and across to the slopes of Ashridge Park.

It is unsurprising, given its classic English village composition of charming cottages and triangular green – complete with stocks, whipping-post and duck pond – backed by the beech-clad Chiltern Hills, that Aldbury has frequently been used as a film set. The Bridgewater Monument, passed near the end of the walk, was erected in 1832 in memory of the great canal builder and owner of the Ashridge Estate, the third Duke of Bridgewater. The beautiful and extensive woodlands of the estate are at their phenomenal best in autumn.

Right: Ashridge Estate.
Opposite page: Chiltern Hills' Ridgeway path.

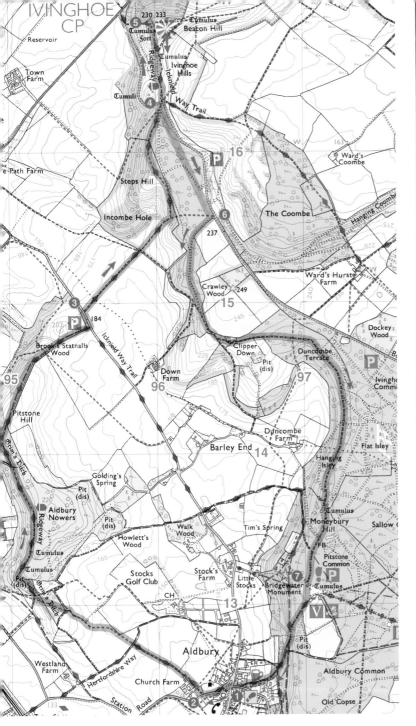

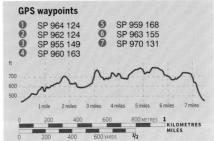

WALK 28

Cranbrook and Sissinghurst

HIGH WEALD AONB

DIFFICULTY ●●

START Cranbrook church

DISTANCE 7¼ miles (11.6km)

HEIGHT GAIN 410 feet (125m)

APPROXIMATE TIME 3½ hours

ROUTE TERRAIN Field paths and woodland tracks

PARKING Jockey Lane car park, on the north side of Cranbrook church

OS EXPLORER 136, 137

OS PATHFINDER Kent

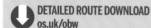 **DETAILED ROUTE DOWNLOAD** os.uk/obw

Cranbrook church is known in Kent as the 'cathedral of the Weald', and the hilltop town in which it is located may well be justified in claiming to be the capital of the High Weald. Certainly in medieval times Cranbrook was the most prosperous wool town of the Weald, and this wealth is reflected in the airy, spaciousness of St Dunstan's Church with its rich workmanship in both stone masonry and stained glass. The walk sets out on the footpath leading north-eastwards from St Dunstan's, striking across pastures and fields and through woodland to the village of Sissinghurst, famous across the globe for the gardens created by diplomat and author Harold Nicolson and his wife, poet and writer Vita Sackville-West, begun in the 1930s around the remains of the Tudor castle. Sissinghurst's village pub, The Milk House, a 16th-century building with Tudor fireplace, is conveniently located halfway round this figure-of-eight route. The bluebell woodlands traversed in this walk are especially attractive in spring. The return to Cranbrook passes through more beautiful High Weald scenery of orchards and paddocks, fields and copses in the gentle valley of Crane Brook.

Right: Sissinghurst.

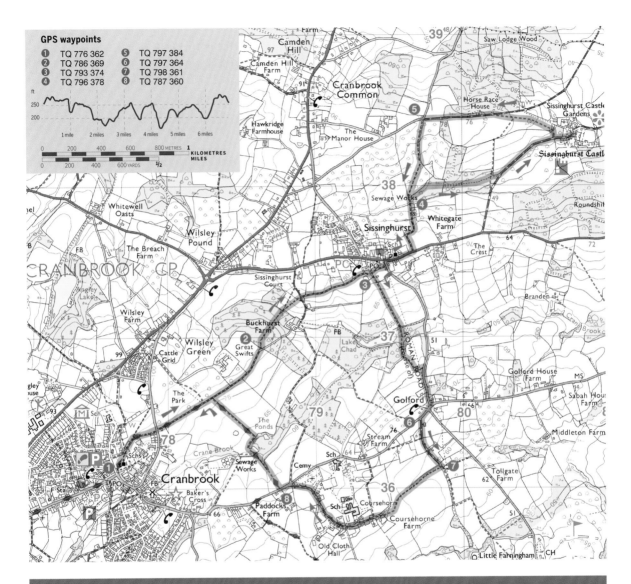

GPS waypoints

①	TQ 776 362	⑤	TQ 797 384
②	TQ 786 369	⑥	TQ 797 364
③	TQ 793 374	⑦	TQ 798 361
④	TQ 796 378	⑧	TQ 787 360

Sissinghurst Castle

Sissinghurst Castle is famous for its gardens, created from the 1930s by Harold Nicolson and his wife, Vita Sackville-West, around the remains of a Tudor tower. A National Trust property since 1967, the castle, gardens and grounds form an estate of 460 acres (186ha). The superb Rose, White, South Cottage and Herb gardens are complemented by the Nuttery (Kentish cobnuts), the Lime Walk, Moat Walk, Orchard and Purple Border.

Freshwater and Tennyson Down

ISLE OF WIGHT AONB

DIFFICULTY ●

START At the top of Highdown Lane

DISTANCE 3¾ miles (6km)

HEIGHT GAIN 475 feet (145m)

APPROXIMATE TIME 2 hours

ROUTE TERRAIN Downland tracks and paths whose gradients are steady and long rather than steep

PARKING National Trust car park at the end of Highdown Lane

OS EXPLORER OL29

OS PATHFINDER Short Walks Isle of Wight

 DETAILED ROUTE DOWNLOAD os.uk/obw

Tennyson's monument marks the high point of the gradual climb over Tennyson Down, a tremendous vantage point over the English Channel on the edge of sheer chalk cliffs 480 feet (147m) above sea level. *Please take care near the unfenced cliff edges.* The walk follows the clifftop path as it descends gently to Freshwater Bay, then continues through Afton Marsh Nature Reserve, passing the island's only thatched church before taking a woodland way to complete the loop.

Tennyson Down was originally called East High Down but was renamed in the poet's honour when the memorial was erected in 1897, after his death. It is now owned by the National Trust, as is much of the West Wight peninsula, including adjacent West High Down and Headon Warren. The area is part of the chalk ridge that forms the island's backbone, culminating in the Needles. This pristine chalk grassland is rich in plants and insects, making it the ideal spot to watch – as it is said that Tennyson did – 'the sunlight glint on a butterfly's wing'.

Right and opposite page left: Freshwater Bay.
Opposite page right: Tennyson's memorial.

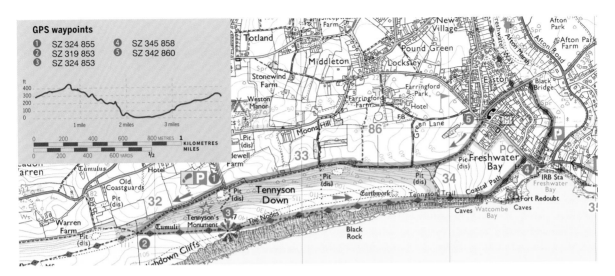

GPS waypoints
1. SZ 324 855
2. SZ 319 853
3. SZ 324 853
4. SZ 345 858
5. SZ 342 860

Tennyson Down

According to a National Trust survey, Tennyson Down came fourth in the list of best places to picnic in Britain. It is also among the best places in the country for spotting butterflies, especially common and chalk hill blues, and the rare Adonis blue. The rabbit- and sheep-grazed, short-cropped chalk grassland and rich mix of downland wildflowers are a memorable sight.

Wye and Crundale Downs

KENT DOWNS AONB

DIFFICULTY ●●●

START Wye, at the church

DISTANCE 8½ miles (13.5km)

HEIGHT GAIN 1,050 feet (320m)

APPROXIMATE TIME 4 hours

ROUTE TERRAIN Field paths, woodland trails and downland byways

PARKING Small car park signed off Churchfield Way in Wye, just west of the church

OS EXPLORER 137

OS PATHFINDER Kent

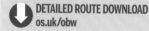 **DETAILED ROUTE DOWNLOAD** os.uk/obw

There are beautiful views to savour on this fine downland route, which starts out from Wye along the Stour Valley Walk, then climbs and follows the ridge of the Crundale Downs before returning along the crest of the North Downs. This last section keeps to the North Downs Way linking the Broad Downs and Wye Downs, both local beauty spots with incredible long-distance Wealden views. At Broad Downs, rare orchids such as Maid of Kent or lady orchid can be found. The North Downs Way passes both the Devil's Kneading Trough, a spectacular steep-sided combe, and the Wye Crown, a hill carving cut into the chalk in 1902 to mark the coronation of Edward VII and restored in the early 1990s. Elsewhere on the walk, there are pleasing and more intimate views of the Kent countryside to be had from Crundale's early Norman church, thanks to its lofty position up on the downs.

Right: North Downs Way signpost.

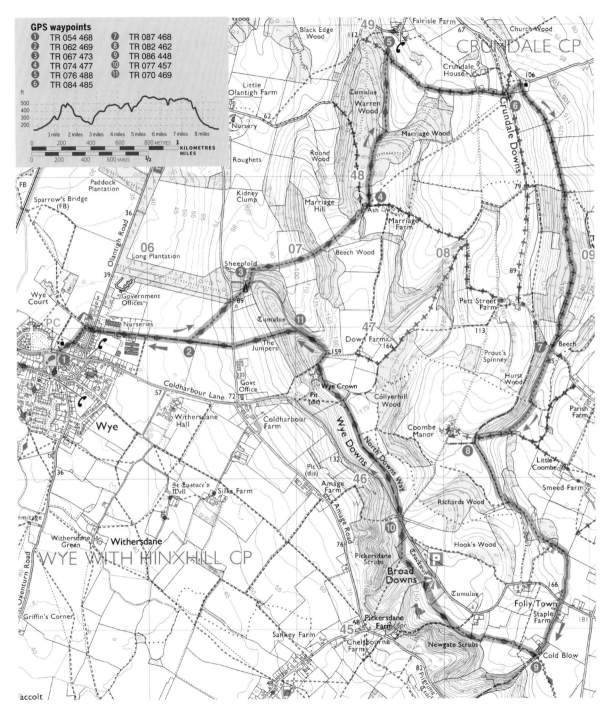

GPS waypoints

1 TR 054 468
2 TR 062 469
3 TR 067 473
4 TR 074 477
5 TR 076 488
6 TR 084 485
7 TR 087 468
8 TR 082 462
9 TR 086 448
10 TR 077 457
11 TR 070 469

Albury Downs and St Martha's Hill

SURREY HILLS AONB

DIFFICULTY ●●

START Newlands Corner

DISTANCE 7 miles (11.2km)

HEIGHT GAIN 985 feet (300m)

APPROXIMATE TIME 3½ hours

ROUTE TERRAIN Downland byways, field paths and farm tracks; there's a steep climb up St Martha's Hill

PARKING Newlands Corner car park

OS EXPLORER 145

OS PATHFINDER Surrey

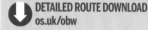
DETAILED ROUTE DOWNLOAD os.uk/obw

This gorgeous walk in the Surrey Hills near Guildford is characterised by open downland frequently interspersed with attractive wooded sections. The route traces a path of dips and rises along the North Downs Way and Pilgrims Way, twice descending below the crest of the downs and twice climbing to regain it. There are superb and extensive views from the highest points of the route at Newlands Corner and St Martha's Church, an isolated hilltop landmark.

The North Downs Way National Trail opened in 1978 and runs the length of the Surrey Hills AONB and Kent Downs AONB between Farnham and Dover. The Pilgrims Way follows an ancient trackway taken by pilgrims between Winchester and Canterbury, but its origins lie in prehistoric paths following the east-west arc of the North Downs. St Martha's Church is of Norman origin but was rebuilt, reusing some of the early stonework, in 1850.

Right and opposite page right: Newland's Corner.
Opposite page left: St Martha's Church.

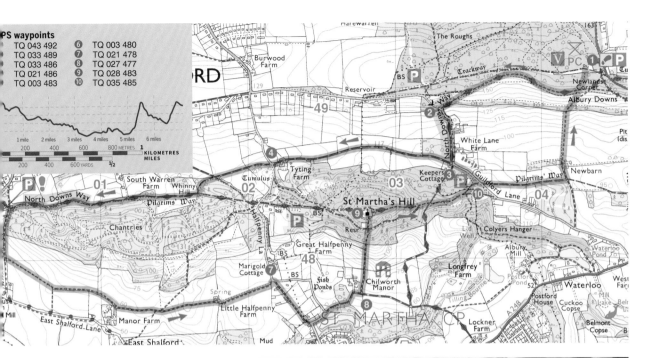

GPS waypoints

●	TQ 043 492	⑥	TQ 003 480
●	TQ 033 489	⑦	TQ 021 478
●	TQ 033 486	⑧	TQ 027 477
●	TQ 021 486	⑨	TQ 028 483
●	TQ 003 483	⑩	TQ 035 485

London

To get the best out of London, avoid trying to do too much, especially in an uncoordinated manner. Focused walking, I've found, is by far the best way to explore the capital, since most of London's key attractions are within walking distance of each other. Moreover, there are far more green oases in London than might be imagined.

However, the emphasis for many visitors is on the centres of power, and a good start would be to amble from Charing Cross, past Trafalgar Square (*left*) and down Whitehall, pausing at Downing Street before

continuing to the Palace of Westminster. Incidentally, the Charing Cross monument is one of twelve 'Eleanor Crosses' (see www.historic-uk.com) erected by order of Edward I in memory of his wife Eleanor of Castile; it is not the original, however, which was destroyed in 1647 during the Civil War.

The stunning Palace of Westminster is the meeting place of the House of Commons and the House of Lords, the two houses of the Parliament of the United Kingdom. It wwas formerly the primary residence of the monarchs of England, until fire destroyed many of the buildings in 1512.

Whitehall

PALACE OF WESTMINSTER AND WESTMINSTER ABBEY (UNESCO)

DIFFICULTY ●

START Charing Cross

DISTANCE ¾ mile (1.4km)

HEIGHT GAIN Negligible

APPROXIMATE TIME 1 hour

ROUTE TERRAIN Pavements

PARKING None; use Charing Cross tube

OS EXPLORER 173

OS PATHFINDER London City Walks

 DETAILED ROUTE DOWNLOAD os.uk/obw

A walk through the corridors of power from Charing Cross to the Palace of Westminster takes in Trafalgar Square and Nelson's Column; Admiralty Arch; Horse Guards Parade and the Household Cavalry; Downing Street; the Cenotaph and Parliament Square.

The old Palace of Westminster, where the Houses of Parliament are located, burnt down in 1834, and Charles Barry, with Augustin Pugin, won the competition to design a replacement. Their brief was to rebuild in the Gothic style, so that the new parliament building would be in harmony with Westminster Abbey. The tower at the north end of the Palace, overlooking Westminster Bridge, is St Stephen's Tower, but is commonly and mistakenly known as Big Ben after the bell inside, which famously tolls the hour.

Right: Admiralty Arch.
Opposite page top: Changing of the Guard.
Opposite page left: Elizabeth Tower, which houses the bell known as Big Ben.
Opposite page right: Downing Street.

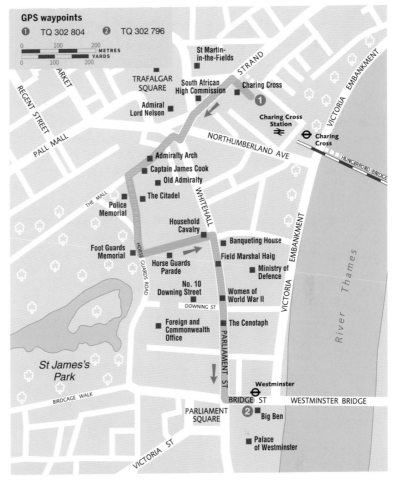

GPS waypoints

❶ TQ 302 804   ❷ TQ 302 796

0   100   200 METRES
0   100   200 YARDS

St Martin-in-the-Fields

TRAFALGAR SQUARE

South African High Commission

Charging Cross ❶

Charing Cross Station

STRAND

Charing Cross

Admiral Lord Nelson

NORTHUMBERLAND AVE

VICTORIA EMBANKMENT

HUNGERFORD BRIDGE

REGENT STREET

ARKET

PALL MALL

Admiralty Arch

Captain James Cook

Old Admiralty

The Citadel

WHITEHALL

THE MALL

Police Memorial

Household Cavalry

Foot Guards Memorial

HORSE GUARDS ROAD

Horse Guards Parade

No. 10 Downing Street

DOWNING ST

Foreign and Commonwealth Office

Banqueting House

Field Marshal Haig

Ministry of Defence

Women of World War II

The Cenotaph

VICTORIA EMBANKMENT

River Thames

St James's Park

BIRDCAGE WALK

PARLIAMENT ST

Westminster

BRIDGE ST

WESTMINSTER BRIDGE

PARLIAMENT SQUARE

❷ Big Ben

Palace of Westminster

VICTORIA ST

DOWNING STREET SW1

CITY OF WESTMINSTER

St James's

PALACE OF WESTMINSTER AND WESTMINSTER ABBEY (UNESCO)

DIFFICULTY ●

START Westminster Underground Station

DISTANCE 2 miles (3.2km)

HEIGHT GAIN Negligible

APPROXIMATE TIME 1½ hours

ROUTE TERRAIN Pavements and parkland pathways

PARKING None; use Westminster tube

OS EXPLORER 173

OS PATHFINDER London City Walks

⬇ **DETAILED ROUTE DOWNLOAD**
os.uk/obw

Starting from Westminster tube station, this walk passes around Parliament Square to Westminster Hall and on to Westminster Abbey, before escaping into the oasis of St James's Park and then on to Pall Mall and concluding at Piccadilly.

Behind a statue of Oliver Cromwell stands Westminster Hall, the only part of the medieval structure of the earlier Palace of Westminster to survive the fire of 1834. Inside, the magnificent oak hammer-beam roof has the widest unsupported span in the country. On the opposite side of the street is Westminster Abbey. St Dunstan established a Benedictine abbey here over 1,000 years ago, but Henry III rebuilt it as a shrine to Edward the Confessor. It was not completed until 1503. Westminster Abbey is used for coronations, royal weddings and funerals, and of all the many tombs of the great and the good inside, the most important is that of the Unknown Warrior 'buried among kings because he had done good toward God and toward his house'.

Right: Buckingham Palace from St James's Park.
Opposite page left: Westminster Abbey.
Opposite page right: Oliver Cromwell.

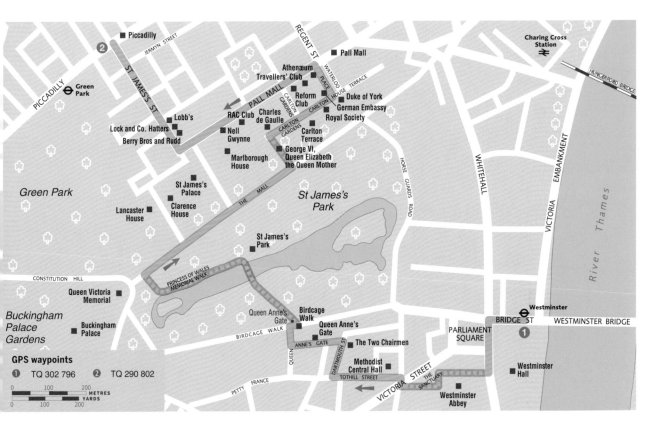

Piccadilly

JERMYN STREET

ST JAMES'S ST

PICCADILLY

Green Park

RAC Club

Pall Mall

Athenæum
Travellers' Club

Reform
Club

Charles
de Gaulle

REGENT ST

WATERLOO

PALL MALL

CARLTON
GARDENS

HOUSE TERRACE

CARLTON

Duke of York
German Embassy
Royal Society

Lobb's

Lock and Co. Hatters
Berry Bros and Rudd

Nell
Gwynne

CARLTON
GARDENS

Carlton
Terrace

Marlborough
House

George VI.
Queen Elizabeth
the Queen Mother

St James's
Palace

THE MALL

St James's
Park

Green Park

Lancaster
House

Clarence
House

St James's
Park

HORSE GUARDS ROAD

WHITEHALL

Charing Cross
Station

HUNGERFORD BRIDGE

VICTORIA EMBANKMENT

River Thames

CONSTITUTION HILL

Queen Victoria
Memorial

PRINCESS OF WALES
MEMORIAL WALK

Queen Anne's
Gate

Birdcage
Walk

Queen Anne's
Gate

Westminster

BRIDGE ST

WESTMINSTER BRIDGE

Buckingham
Palace
Gardens

Buckingham
Palace

BIRDCAGE WALK

ANNE'S GATE

The Two Chairmen

PARLIAMENT
SQUARE

Westminster
Hall

GPS waypoints

① TQ 302 796   ② TQ 290 802

Queen

DARTMOUTH ST

Methodist
Central Hall

TOTHILL STREET

VICTORIA STREET

THE SANCTUARY

Westminster
Abbey

0   100   200
METRES
YARDS
0   100   200

PETTY FRANCE

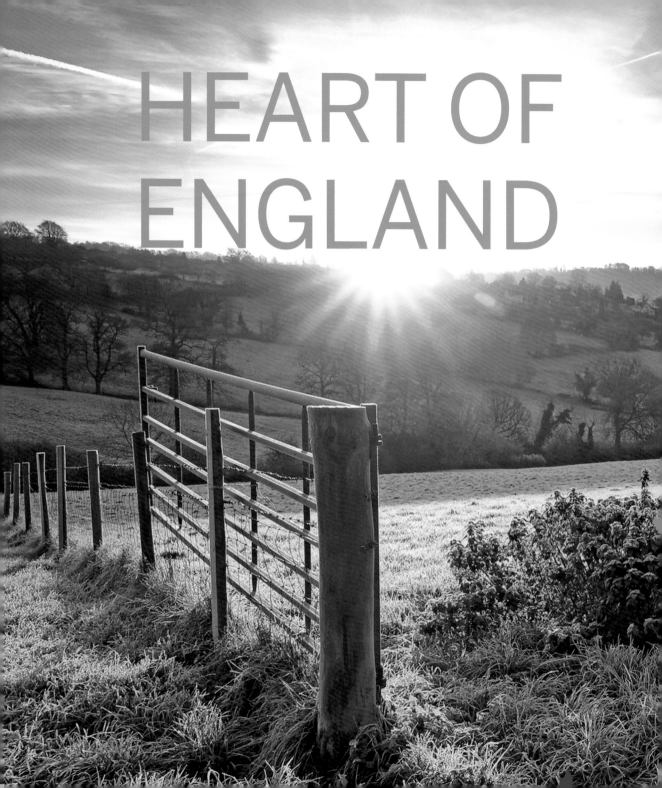

HEART OF
ENGLAND

The Walks

Top: Rolling fields in the Cotswolds.
Bottom: Cannock Chase Forest.
Previous page: Painswick in the Cotswolds.

Areas of Outstanding Natural Beauty

The vision of composer Edward Elgar striding across the Malvern Hills, gaining inspiration and humming quietly to himself as melodic themes invade his thoughts, is an appealing one. There is intricate harmony in these gentle hills that for me has proven hugely relaxing, a juxtaposition of things man-made and things natural to form a perfect blend for the walker.

The region's rich cultural heritage encompasses a sweep of history, from the Iron Age, through medieval times to the Victorian era, in places such as Castlemorton Common, British Camp and Eastnor Park. Yet, there is nothing to surpass the splendid route that traverses the main north–south ridge, then heads over Worcestershire Beacon with unrivalled, wind-tussled views.

The Shropshire Hills are much the same, offering both the energetic ascents of Caer Caradoc and the Cardington Hills, and the gentler beauty of Wenlock Edge. This setting inspired another composer, Ralph Vaughan Williams, as well as the poet A E Housman, who described them as the "blue remembered hills" in 'A Shropshire Lad'. I was enchanted by my time among the Shropshire Hills (*left*) while working on my guide to the Shropshire Way, the most under-appreciated middle-distance trail in Britain. I wandered off-route now and again, following inviting pathways that beckoned impatiently; these detours only confirmed that every step I took in the Shropshire Hills was a joyous one.

Possibly of greater renown are the Cotswolds, a quintessentially English fashion statement of thatched medieval villages, stately homes, rolling hills, incised valleys, ash and beech woodlands and wildflower grasslands, where the distinctive yellow (oolitic) limestone prevails and lends a warm, honey hue to everything. This is the largest of all AONBs, a landscape dotted with Neolithic long barrows, Bronze Age round barrows and Iron Age hill forts that testify to man's presence here for more than 6,000 years. But, for the walker, the fascination of the Cotswolds lies in the narrow western escarpment, which defines the outcrop of Jurassic limestone and runs virtually unbroken for over 50 miles. There are fine outlying hills, too, as the walk from Wotton-under-Edge will demonstrate, while Upper and Lower Slaughter are more idyllic than their names suggest.

AMAZING BUT TRUE ...
A 30-minute game of medieval football has been played at Bourton-on-the-Water every August for over 100 years, with goalposts set up in the River Windrush. Teams play with a standard football, and a referee vainly attempts to keep order.

WALK 33

Shugborough Park and Sherbrook Valley

CANNOCK CHASE AONB

DIFFICULTY ●●

START Milford Common

DISTANCE 7½ miles (12km)

HEIGHT GAIN 670 feet (205m)

APPROXIMATE TIME 3½ hours

ROUTE TERRAIN Good heathland and woodland paths and bridleways, and a section of canal towpath prone to being muddy after wet weather

PARKING Car park off Brocton Road

OS EXPLORER 244

OS PATHFINDER Shropshire and Staffordshire

DETAILED ROUTE DOWNLOAD
os.uk/obw

Plenty of scenic and historic variety can be enjoyed on this walk, which leads through the finest and oldest remaining oak woodlands of Cannock Chase; it also features landscaped parkland, waterside meadows and open heathland, as well as an 18th-century mansion and ancient packhorse bridge.

Cannock, or Cank, Forest originally covered a large area between Stafford in the west and Tamworth in the east and a north-to-south spread between the Trent valley and Wolverhampton. It was originally a royal forest, but, in 1290, Edward I granted part of it to the bishops of Lichfield as their private chase. Ownership passed to the Paget family (later the marquises of Anglesey) in the 16th century, who pioneered the development of the local iron industry. Demands for charcoal for iron-smelting led to the felling of the woodlands, and much of Cannock Chase became bare heathland until the 1920s, when the Forestry Commission began large-scale conifer plantation.

Right: Stag on Cannock Chase.

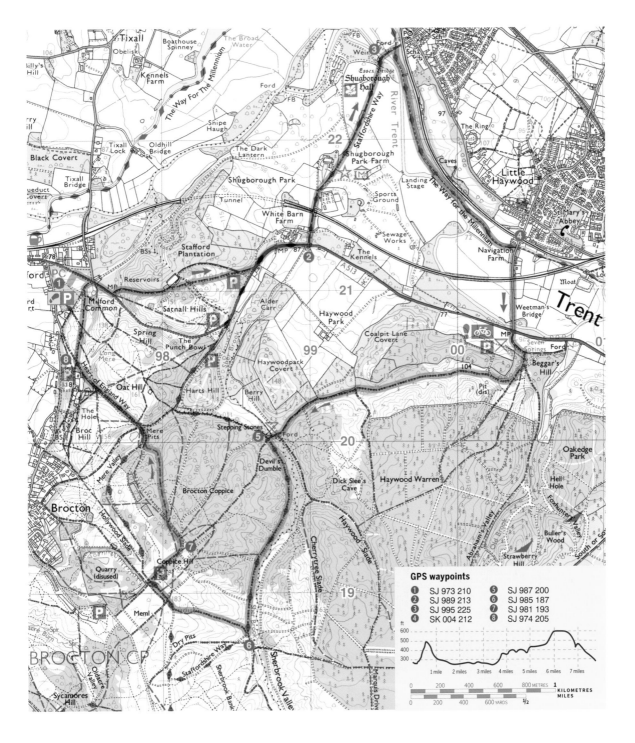

GPS waypoints

1	SJ 973 210	**5**	SJ 987 200
2	SJ 989 213	**6**	SJ 985 187
3	SJ 995 225	**7**	SJ 981 193
4	SK 004 212	**8**	SJ 974 205

Wotton-under-Edge and the Tyndale Monument

COTSWOLDS AONB

DIFFICULTY ●

START Wotton-under-Edge

DISTANCE 4 miles (6.5km)

HEIGHT GAIN 460 feet (140m)

APPROXIMATE TIME 2¼ hours

ROUTE TERRAIN Lanes, field paths and woodland tracks and paths

PARKING Chipping car park, Wotton-under-Edge

OS EXPLORER 167

OS PATHFINDER Cotswolds

DETAILED ROUTE DOWNLOAD os.uk/obw

From Wotton-under-Edge, this delightful short walk explores two of the western outliers of the Cotswolds from where the views – to the west from Nibley Knoll and to the south from Coombe Hill – are truly wonderful. The woodland section is particularly beautiful, especially in spring, when the ground is carpeted with wild flowers, and in autumn, when the canopy itself steals the show. Wotton's name clearly reveals its geographical position under the edge, or at the foot of, the Cotswold escarpment. Passing along the Cotswold Way, the route leads first to the ancient earthworks of Brackenbury Ditches hill fort before going on to the Tyndale Monument. The tower was erected in 1866 in memory of William Tyndale, 'Translator of the English Bible who first caused the New Testament to be printed in the mother tongue of his countrymen. Born near this spot he suffered martyrdom at Vilvorde in Flanders on October 6th 1536'. The views from here are outstanding.

Right:Wotton-under-Edge.
Opposite page top and bottom: Tyndale Monument.

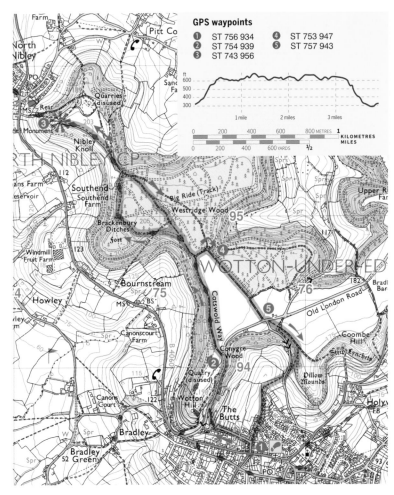

GPS waypoints
1. ST 756 934
2. ST 754 939
3. ST 743 956
4. ST 753 947
5. ST 757 943

Bourton-on-the-Water, the Slaughters and Naunton

COTSWOLDS AONB

DIFFICULTY ●●●

START Bourton-on-the-Water

DISTANCE 10 miles (16km)

HEIGHT GAIN 705 feet (215m)

APPROXIMATE TIME 5 hours

ROUTE TERRAIN Field paths and bridleways

PARKING Bourton-on-the-Water

OS EXPLORER OL45

OS PATHFINDER Cotswolds

 **DETAILED ROUTE DOWNLOAD** os.uk/obw

Opposite page left: River Windrush, Bourton-on-the-Water.
Opposite page right: Bourton-on-the-Water.

One of the classic Cotswolds walks visits four outstandingly attractive and varied villages – bustling Bourton-on-the-Water, idyllic Lower Slaughter, tranquil Upper Slaughter and tucked-away Naunton – all set in the loveliest of woodland landscapes, with expansive views across rolling countryside and through the sheltered valleys of the Eye and the Windrush.

Bourton-on-the-Water is a popular tourist spot. The River Windrush flows through the village, bordered by trees and well-kept lawns and crossed by a number of low, picture-postcard bridges, set against a backdrop of attractive stone buildings. Considerably less commercialised, Lower Slaughter rivals Bourton, thanks to its exquisite composition of fine old houses and cottages with the infant River Eye running between them, little stone bridges and tree-lined greens. Upper Slaughter is rather sleepier than its near neighbour and less obviously picturesque, but it is still a superbly attractive and unspoilt village of cottages grouped around a green. Naunton has a medieval church and a halfway refreshment opportunity in the form of the Black Horse pub.

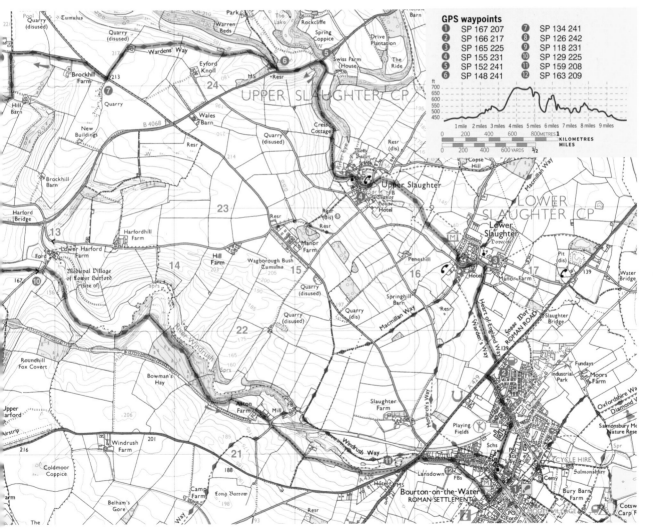

GPS waypoints

❶	SP 167 207	❼	SP 134 241
❷	SP 166 217	❽	SP 126 242
❸	SP 165 225	❾	SP 118 231
❹	SP 155 231	❿	SP 129 225
❺	SP 152 241	⓫	SP 159 208
❻	SP 148 241	⓬	SP 163 209

Great Malvern and the Worcestershire Beacon

MALVERN HILLS AONB

DIFFICULTY ●●

START Great Malvern

DISTANCE 5½ miles (8.9km)

HEIGHT GAIN 1,360 feet (415m)

APPROXIMATE TIME 3 hours

ROUTE TERRAIN Hilly field tracks and paths

PARKING Great Malvern

OS EXPLORER 190

OS PATHFINDER The Malverns to Warwickshire

 **DETAILED ROUTE DOWNLOAD** os.uk/obw

A splendid ramble in Elgar country gives a succession of unbelievable views from the spine of the Malvern Hills. The route climbs from Great Malvern to the highest point, the Worcestershire Beacon, and continues along the ridge, before descending and returning along paths that contour around the Malverns' wooded lower slopes.

Rising abruptly from the flat lands of the Vale of Severn in the east and from the rolling hills of Herefordshire in the west, the Malvern Hills resemble a mountain range, despite reaching only 1,394 feet (425m). The Regency and Victorian hotels and villas that dot their slopes reflect the heyday of Great Malvern as a popular spa and health resort. In the 19th century, buildings were erected over St Ann's Well (visited near the end of the walk) for the use of the increasing number of visitors coming to take the waters in the town. Much older is the grand priory church in the town centre, founded in 1085.

Right: Path from Great Malvern to Colwall.
Opposite page top: Great Malvern Priory.
Opposite page bottom: View from Worcestershire Beacon.

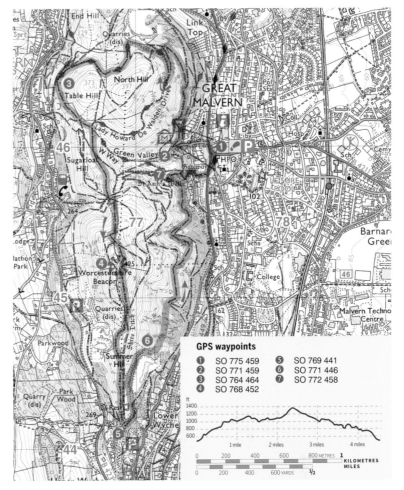

GPS waypoints

① SO 775 459		⑤ SO 769 441	
② SO 771 459		⑥ SO 771 446	
③ SO 764 464		⑦ SO 772 458	
④ SO 768 452			

Worcestershire Beacon

At 1,394 feet (425m) Worcestershire Beacon is the highest point in the Malvern Hills. The toposcope on its summit was erected to commemorate Queen Victoria's Diamond Jubilee in 1897 and, unsurprisingly, the views are immense, including: beyond Birmingham to Cannock Chase, the Shropshire Hills and Welsh borderlands, the Cotswolds and Bristol Channel.

Corvedale and Wenlock Edge

SHROPSHIRE HILLS AONB

DIFFICULTY ●●

START Aston Munslow

DISTANCE 6¾ miles (10.9km)

HEIGHT GAIN 1,000 feet (305m)

APPROXIMATE TIME 3½ hours

ROUTE TERRAIN Field paths, tracks and lanes

PARKING Aston Munslow village car park

OS EXPLORER 217

OS PATHFINDER Shropshire and Staffordshire

 **DETAILED ROUTE DOWNLOAD** os.uk/obw

Commencing in the ancient village of Aston Munslow, the route climbs through the deer-haunted woodlands of Munslow Common to gain the crest of Wenlock Edge, blessed with fabulous views, before returning via the tiny village of Diddlebury with its part-Saxon church.

The Swan Inn at Aston Munslow is 14th century and one of Shropshire's oldest coaching inns; a past guest was the highwayman Dick Turpin. The walk rises gently up the slopes of Wenlock Edge through outcrops of fossil-bearing limestone. Upon gaining the ridge top, grand views are unlocked across verdant Corvedale to the line of the Clee Hills. Later, ever-expanding views sweep across Apedale towards the Long Mynd, and ahead along the ridge the horizon widens to encompass wave-upon-wave of ridges and vales stretching into Mid Wales. St Peter's Church, Diddlebury, is mostly mid-Norman but there are intact remains of some stunning Saxon herringbone brickwork. Also at the church, look out for the Georgian 'Bread Dole' board. Diddlebury has an old ford, just south of the church.

Right: Diddlebury.
Opposite page: View from Wenlock Edge.

Wenlock Edge

Wenlock Edge is a limestone escarpment, 18 miles (29km) in length, in the Shropshire Hills running north-east to south-west between Craven Arms and Ironbridge. Its geology, flower-rich limestone grassland and ancient woodland make it a Site of Special Scientific Interest, and an 8-mile (13-km) stretch is owned by the National Trust.

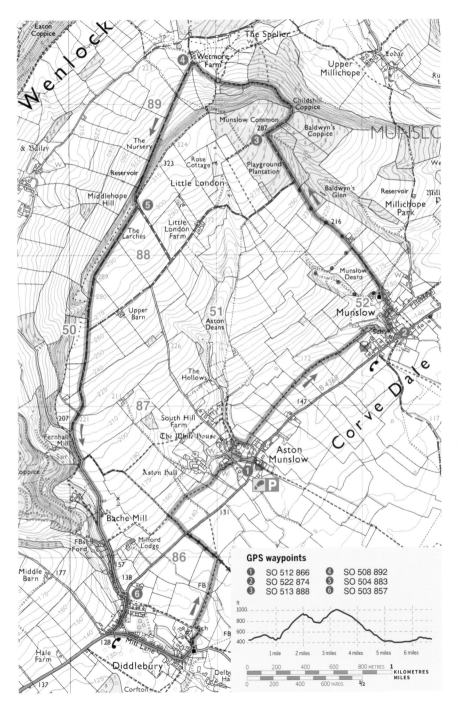

GPS waypoints

❶	SO 512 866	❹	SO 508 892
❷	SO 522 874	❺	SO 504 883
❸	SO 513 888	❻	SO 503 857

WALK 38

Caer Caradoc and Cardington

SHROPSHIRE HILLS AONB

DIFFICULTY ●●●

START Hazler, Church Stretton

DISTANCE 7¼ miles (11.6km)

HEIGHT GAIN 1,720 feet (525m)

APPROXIMATE TIME 4½ hours

ROUTE TERRAIN Field paths, tracks and lanes; the climb up Caer Caradoc Hill is seriously steep; there's also a steep descent and several moderate climbs

PARKING Lay-by at the edge of Hazler on B4371

OS EXPLORER 217

OS PATHFINDER Shropshire and Staffordshire

⬇ DETAILED ROUTE DOWNLOAD
os.uk/obw

A highly energetic walk across the summits of Caer Caradoc and the Cardington Hills is rewarded with entrancing views across the Long Mynd, North Shropshire, Apedale and Wenlock Edge, and a visit to Shropshire's oldest inn, the Royal Oak at Cardington.

The extensive hill fort crowning Caer Caradoc's pyramidal peak dates from around 700BC. It is associated with the tribal chieftain Caradoc, also known as Caractacus, a renowned Celtic warrior during the Roman advance westwards. The final battle between the Celts and the Romans took place in about AD51; Caradoc was captured, but, according to the historian Tacitus, the Roman General Ostorius Scapula was so impressed by the Celt's leadership and bravery that he had Caradoc transported to Rome, where he lived out a good life in exile. Another version has it that Caradoc hid in a cave near the summit, escaped and was later surrendered to the Romans by Cartismandua, queen of the local Brigantes tribe!

Right: Sunset over Caer Caradoc.
Opposite page left: Outcrop at Cardington.
Opposite page left: Long Mynd.

GPS waypoints

❶	SO 468 932	❸	SO 506 951
❷	SO 476 951	❹	SO 488 942

Goodrich Castle

WYE VALLEY AONB

DIFFICULTY ●●

START Goodrich

DISTANCE 8¼ miles (13.3km)

HEIGHT GAIN 310 feet (95m)

APPROXIMATE TIME 3½ hours

ROUTE TERRAIN Riverside field paths, tracks and a quiet lane

PARKING Goodrich Castle car park

OS EXPLORER OL14

OS PATHFINDER Wye Valley and Forest of Dean

 **DETAILED ROUTE DOWNLOAD**
os.uk/obw

Along its length, the sinuous Wye writhes and wriggles between the hills of the southern Welsh borderlands, at times its broad meanders almost meeting themselves. Downstream of Goodrich Castle is an exemplar of this as the river enters a narrowing gorge. This walk follows its splendid course down to the foot of the famous Symonds Yat Rock before gently climbing back over the 'neck' of one of the river's exaggerated meanders.

Goodrich Castle sits atop a rocky spur overlooking the River Wye. It origin is Norman, but it was largely rebuilt in the 13th century. The castle is remarkably intact; massively thick walls connect great buttressed towers set at the cardinal points and enclose a courtyard surrounded by domestic and ceremonial quarters and the castle's original keep. Its near-impregnable defences remained until the Civil War, when, in 1646, Parliamentarian forces laid siege to the fortress. The Royalists held out for four months until 'Roaring Meg' breached the walls with its 200lb (91kg) shot.

Right: Goodrich Castle.

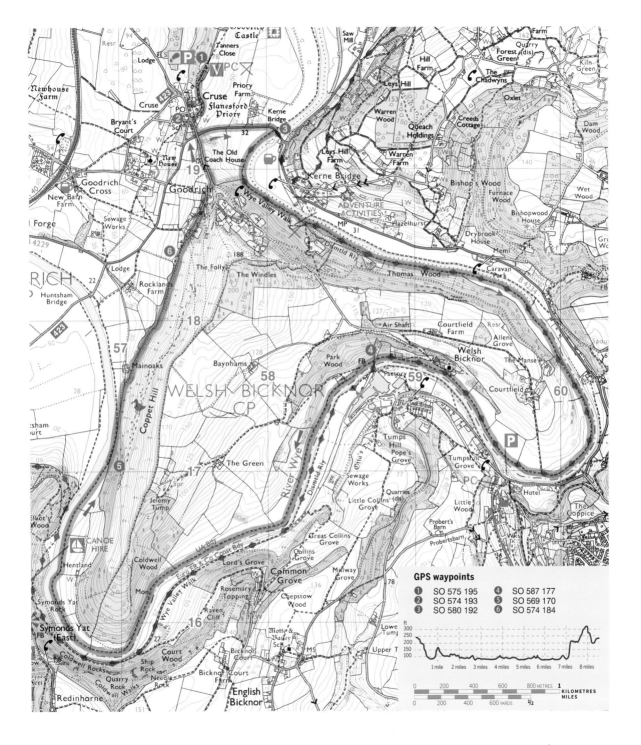

GPS waypoints

①	SO 575 195	④	SO 587 177
②	SO 574 193	⑤	SO 569 170
③	SO 580 192	⑥	SO 574 184

UNESCO World Heritage Sites

The significance of the Ironbridge Gorge (*left*) may not immediately imprint itself on your mind, especially if you are focused on following the Severn Way, the finest riparian walk in Britain. Yet, Ironbridge is renowned as a pioneering symbol of the Industrial Revolution, containing all the elements of progress that contributed to the rapid development of industry in the 18th century, from the mines to the railways.

This area is often described as the 'Birthplace of the Industrial Revolution', due to the fact that, in 1709 in nearby Coalbrookdale, Quaker Abraham Darby perfected the technique of smelting iron with coke, allowing for the much cheaper production of iron. Of course, pinpointing the start of the Industrial Revolution to one event and one place is misleading; nevertheless, Darby's technique marked a turning point in human history that affected almost every aspect of daily life.

A day spent exploring the valley will reveal that many of the historic buildings, structures and urban and rural features have retained their authentic character, not least the Iron Bridge itself, which dates from 1779 and was the first bridge in the world to be constructed from this material.

Blenheim Park, in contrast, is a paragon of English landscaped parkland. The palace is the principal residence of the Dukes of Marlborough and the only non-royal, non-episcopal country house in England to hold the title of palace; Winston Churchill was born here in 1874. Some years ago, I was privileged to be given a private tour of the palace, a building designed in the short-lived English Baroque style. But it is from the freedom of the grounds that the palace is best appreciated.

The catalogue of changes that coalesced into the Industrial Revolution is also apparent in the Derwent valley, upstream from Derby, at the southern extreme of the Pennines. Here, several 18th- and 19th-century cotton mills are part of an industrial landscape of great historical and technological significance, marking the birth of the factory system. This is especially evident in the mill settlement at Cromford, although, even here, nature is not to be overlooked and makes its presence felt throughout the Derwent gorge and in the impressive Black Rocks near Cromford and Wirksworth.

AMAZING BUT TRUE ...
As rent for the land on which Blenheim Palace stands, the Marlboroughs must send a copy of the Blenheim flag to the Queen on the anniversary of the Battle of Blenheim (13 August 1704) to mark the famous victory of the 1st Duke of Marlborough.

Blenheim Park

BLENHEIM PALACE (UNESCO)

DIFFICULTY ●

START Woodstock

DISTANCE 6½ miles (10.5km)

HEIGHT GAIN 360 feet (110m)

APPROXIMATE TIME 3½ hours

ROUTE TERRAIN Field paths and tracks; pavement in Woodstock

PARKING Hensington Road car park, Woodstock

OS EXPLORER 180

OS PATHFINDER Cotswolds

DETAILED ROUTE DOWNLOAD
os.uk/obw

Blenheim Park, designed by Capability Brown, is surely the most superb example of landscaped parkland in the country. It was originally a royal park carved from neighbouring Wychwood Forest by Henry I. Beginning in the small town of Woodstock, an area frequented by England's monarchs from at least the 10th century and once home to a thriving glove-making industry, this walk passes along the course of Akeman Street (a Roman road), climaxing in magnificent views across the lake to Blenheim Palace. The palace, an architectural masterpiece by Vanburgh, was built for John Churchill, first Duke of Marlborough, and named after his greatest military triumph; it was later the birthplace of Winston Churchill. In Blenheim Park, the walk visits Fair Rosamund's Well (Rosamund Clifford was the mistress of Henry II); the impressive Grand Bridge built over the lake, which Brown created by damming the River Glyme, and the Column of Victory – the ultimate monument to Marlborough's victory over the French.

Right: Blenheim Park.
Opposite page left: Duke of Marlborough victory column.
Opposite page right: Blenheim Palace.

PS waypoints

●	SP 446 167	⑤	SP 425 170
●	SP 441 172	⑥	SP 428 163
●	SP 441 186	⑦	SP 432 166
●	SP 417 178	⑧	SP 438 171

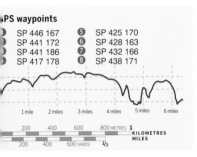

1 mile 2 miles 3 miles 4 miles 5 miles 6 miles

200 400 600 800 METRES 1
                          KILOMETRES
                          MILES
200 400 600 YARDS ½

oodstock

oodstock was synonymous with
ove making for centuries until its
mise in the 1950s. The leather
me from deer in nearby Wychwood
rest and water from the River
yme was used in the tanning
ocess. Both Queen Elizabeth I and,
1956, Queen Elizabeth II were
esented with a pair of gloves upon
iting the town.

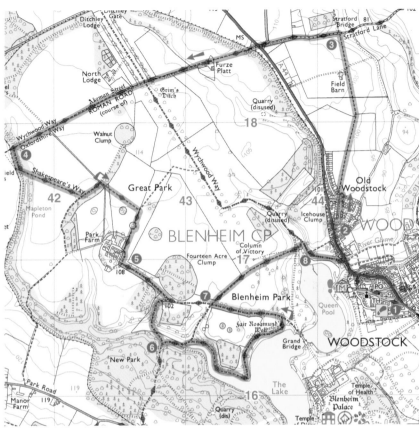

Ironbridge World Heritage Site

WALK 41

IRONBRIDGE GORGE (UNESCO)

DIFFICULTY ●●

START Ironbridge

DISTANCE 7¼ miles (11.6km)

HEIGHT GAIN 525 feet (160m)

APPROXIMATE TIME 3½ hours

ROUTE TERRAIN Mostly good paths, lanes and pavement; one descent down a long, steep flight of 209 steps

PARKING Dale End car park, Ironbridge

OS EXPLORER 242

OS PATHFINDER Shropshire and Staffordshire

DETAILED ROUTE DOWNLOAD os.uk/obw

An undulating walk links a host of museums and points of interest across this World Heritage landscape, which marks the birthplace of the Industrial Revolution. The walk passes over the Iron Bridge itself, which spans a remarkable section of the Severn Gorge.

The old town of Ironbridge climbs steeply up the gorge-side, with alleys and steps offering a chance to explore, before the walk crosses over to the south bank of the river to continue along the Severn Way, following the course of a former railway. The Bedlam Furnaces, the first to be fuelled by coke, were immortalised in a painting by Phillip de Loutherberg and may be glimpsed from a viewing point. Later on, the route takes in the Jackfield Tile Museum, Hay Inclined Plain, Maws Craft Centre, Coalport Pottery Museum, Blists Hill Museum and Abraham Darby's Iron Works, where iron was first smelted with coke in 1709; all are richly diverting heritage features. The belvedere has stunning views to the iron bridge and the distinctive hill profile of The Wrekin.

Right: Disused winding equipment at Blists Hill.

GPS waypoints

❶	SJ 666 037	❸	SJ 697 052
❷	SJ 693 025	❹	SJ 668 049

The Iron Bridge

The Iron Bridge was the first major bridge in the world to be made of cast iron and opened in 1781. It spans just over 100 feet (30m) across the River Severn and was closed to traffic in 1934 when it was designated a Scheduled Ancient Monument.

Designed by Thomas Farnolls Pritchard and made from locally produced cast iron, the bridge is believed to have cost almost twice as much as the £3,250 budget, but toll receipts soon profitably rewarded investors.

Cromford and Matlock Bath

DERWENT VALLEY MILLS (UNESCO)

DIFFICULTY ●●

START Cromford Wharf

DISTANCE 7 miles (11.3km)

HEIGHT GAIN 1,390 feet (425m)

APPROXIMATE TIME 3½ hours

ROUTE TERRAIN Woodland paths and tracks, lanes and canal towpath

PARKING Cromford Wharf

OS EXPLORER OL24

OS PATHFINDER More Peak District

 DETAILED ROUTE DOWNLOAD
os.uk/obw

This absorbing walk is packed with scenic variety and history; natural wonders include the Derwent gorge and the impressive Black Rock above Cromford, but equally striking is the Victorian architecture of Matlock Bath and the fascinating industrial heritage of the mill settlement of Cromford.

In 1771, Sir Richard Arkwright, a Lancashire cotton entrepreneur, established the first successful water-powered cotton mill in the then-scattered farming community of Cromford. This historic event helped transform textile manufacturing from a cottage-based craft into a factory-located industry. The site was chosen because of the power of the River Derwent, but Arkwright lacked labour and transport infrastructure, so he constructed a village to house his workforce and a canal to transport his goods. Unfortunately, Cromford was far from the sea ports through which raw cotton and finished goods were imported and exported, and so was unable to compete effectively with developing centres at Manchester and Bolton. What remains today is a rare example of an early Industrial Revolution textile settlement.

Right: Cromford train station.
Opposite page top: Queen Victoria Jubilee Bridge over River Derwent.
Opposite page bottom: The old mill pond at Cromford.

GPS waypoints

❶	SK 299 570	❻	SK 295 569
❷	SK 300 572	❼	SK 298 561
❸	SK 300 586	❽	SK 293 557
❹	SK 297 583	❾	SK 313 559
❺	SK 293 580		

The old winding house

The old winding house at Sheep Pasture on the former Cromford and High Peak Railway, passed on the walk, was built in 1830 to haul wagons up and down the incline – ¾ mile (1.2km) long with a gradient of one in eight – to High Peak Junction beside the Cromford Canal. Here, at the old railway terminus, restored workshops house an interesting museum.

EAST OF
ENGLAND

The Walks

Top: Dunwich Heath.
Bottom: Flatford Mill, Dedham Vale.
Previous page: Southwold Pier.

The Broads National Park

The Norfolk Broads perfectly demonstrate that National Parks are not just about celebrating and preserving nature's mountains and wild upland areas. Here, the landscape is man-made: shallow lakes formed during medieval times when peat was extracted for fuel – in what is, ironically, one of the driest parts of Britain. And, as for 'mountains', the National Park achieves its greatest elevation in Strumpshaw Hill, barely 147 feet (45m) above sea level, although the wider county does manage 334 feet (102m) in Beacon Hill, and Suffolk, a little more.

Walking in the Broads is a treat for nature-lovers: the region is a wildlife haven for more than a quarter of Britain's rarest species, including birds such as the bittern, crane and marsh harrier, and rare insect and floral species. In fact, a quarter of the National Park – which spans both Norfolk and Suffolk – comprises almost 30 Sites of Special Scientific Interest (SSSI). This is nowhere better exemplified than along the Bure Marshes, a prime example of dense reed beds and wetland woods. Interest in these important conservation expanses is emphasised by a growing number of National Nature Reserves and Local Nature Reserves. Moreover, the entire SSSI portfolio is designated as internationally important for nature conservation under the European Habitats and Birds directives and the Ramsar Convention on Wetlands of International Importance... you get the message.

My own exploration of the Broads has been limited, but only because, on every one of my many visits, I've been side-tracked into birdwatching, waiting patiently for glimpses of bearded tit, black-winged stilt, avocet and an increasingly important winter visitation of Bewick's swan. It's just as bad for botanists – more than 250 plant species – and lepidopterists – Britain's largest butterfly, the swallowtail, can be found here along with the rare Norfolk hawker dragonfly.

Being raised on the heights of Snowdonia and the Lake District, the Norfolk Broads have been a remarkable counterbalance for me; in fact, I learned of the manifold pleasures of low-level walking while working on various Pathfinder guides to this region.

> **AMAZING BUT TRUE ...**
> The Norfolk Broads, were mentioned in David Bowie's song 'Life on Mars', first released in 1971 on the album *Hunky Dory*: *'See the mice in their million hordes From Ibiza to the Norfolk Broads'*.

WALK 43 Horsey

THE BROADS NATIONAL PARK

DIFFICULTY ●

START Horsey Windpump

DISTANCE 3¾ miles (6km)

HEIGHT GAIN Negligible

APPROXIMATE TIME 1½ hours

ROUTE TERRAIN Field paths, dunes and a quiet lane

PARKING National Trust car park at Horsey Windpump

OS EXPLORER OL40

OS PATHFINDER Norfolk

⬇ DETAILED ROUTE DOWNLOAD
os.uk/obw

Horsey drainage mill, perhaps the best-preserved in Norfolk, is an icon of the Broads National Park; this fascinating short walk explores a coastal nature reserve where the lonely beach is home to a large colony of Atlantic grey seals.

Horsey Mere, together with its surrounding marshes and woodland, is an important bird reserve. Bittern and Cetti's warbler are among the rarer species to breed here. The best view of Horsey Mere is to be had from the end of the path that leaves the windpump along the southern bank of the staithe.

The Atlantic grey seal colony on this stretch of coast is one of the largest in the country. There is a viewing platform that can be reached by following a track behind the dunes for some 440 yards (400m) to the right of waypoint 4; from here, pups, born in December and January, can be seen undisturbed, lying above the tide line awaiting the return of their mothers.

Right: Grey seal pup.
Opposite page top: Horsey windpump.
Opposite page bottom: Horsey Mere.

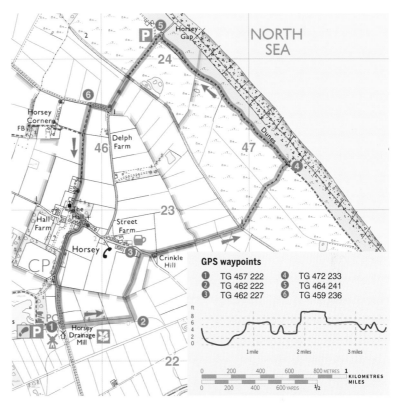

NORTH SEA

24

47

46 Delph Farm

23

Horsey Corner

FB

The Hall

Hall Farm

Street Farm

Horsey

Crinkle Hill

CP

Horsey Drainage Mill

22

Dunes

GPS waypoints

❶	TG 457 222	❹	TG 472 233
❷	TG 462 222	❺	TG 464 241
❸	TG 462 227	❻	TG 459 236

ft
8
6
4
2
0

1 mile   2 miles   3 miles

0   200   400   600   800 METRES   **1**
                                        KILOMETRES
0   200   400   600 YARDS   ½   **MILES**

River Bure and Upton Marshes

THE BROADS NATIONAL PARK

DIFFICULTY ●

START South Walsham Broad, near Pilson Green

DISTANCE 6 miles (9.7km)

HEIGHT GAIN Negligible

APPROXIMATE TIME 2½ hours

ROUTE TERRAIN Riverside and fenland paths and a quiet lane

PARKING Near the moorings on South Walsham Broad

OS EXPLORER OL40

OS PATHFINDER Norfolk

 **DETAILED ROUTE DOWNLOAD** os.uk/obw

The Broads are a crucial haven for wildlife and encompass a wide range of habitats – open water, grazing marsh, dense reed beds and wetland woods – all of which are visited on this outstanding circuit from South Walsham Broad. The walk skirts Upon Fen Nature Reserve, where swallowtail and white admiral butterflies, plus dragonflies, such as the Norfolk hawker, may be seen, as well as reed warblers and yellow wagtails in the fronded margins of the water. In early spring, the woodland bursts into life with a bright show of flowers, including primrose and marsh marigold, followed later by the vivid yellow-topped spikes of flag iris.

Founded in 1020 under the Benedictine Order, St Benet's Abbey was the only monastery established within Norfolk prior to the Norman Conquest. The ruins of the abbey can be seen across the water from the Bure riverside path. The office of abbot is held today by the Bishop of Norwich, who arrives by boat to preach a service in August each year.

Right: Sunset over Upton Marshes.
Opposite page: Ruins of St Benet's Abbey.

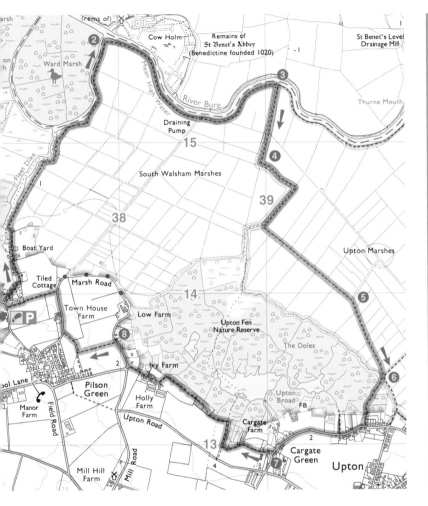

St Benet's Abbey

Founded in 1020 under the Benedictine Order, St Benet's Abbey was the only monastery established within the county prior to the Norman conquest. The monastic buildings stretched along the banks of the River Bure towards the abbey church; the site of the high altar is marked by a tall oaken cross that came from the Queen's Sandringham estate in 1987. Initially surviving Henry VIII's purge, shortly after the Dissolution of the Monasteries the abbey was abandoned. Its last abbot, William Repps, became the Bishop of Norwich in 1536. The office of abbot continues as part of the role of the incumbent bishop. Across the marshes at Thurne, in a small window at the base of the tower of St Edmund's Church, a lantern was placed to signal to the monks in times of danger.

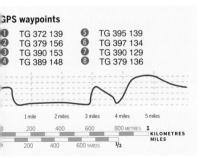

GPS waypoints

1. TG 372 139
2. TG 379 156
3. TG 390 153
4. TG 389 148
5. TG 395 139
6. TG 397 134
7. TG 390 129
8. TG 379 136

The Weavers' Way to the Berney Arms

THE BROADS NATIONAL PARK

DIFFICULTY ●●

START Halvergate

DISTANCE 9 miles (14.5km)

HEIGHT GAIN Negligible

APPROXIMATE TIME 4 hours

ROUTE TERRAIN Fenland tracks and field paths

PARKING Roadside parking in Halvergate

OS EXPLORER OL40

OS PATHFINDER Norfolk

⬇ DETAILED ROUTE DOWNLOAD
os.uk/obw

Experience the full sense of isolation of the Fens on this circuit from Halvergate to the Berney Arms, Norfolk's most remote pub, not reachable by road and standing in the middle of a vast marsh overlooking the confluence of the rivers Yare and Waveney. At low tide the Yare ebbs to a narrow channel running within a huge expanse of mudflat, which, particularly in winter, attracts pink-footed geese, teal, redshank and egret. When the tide comes in, the water can lap the embankment, and a line of green- and red-topped stakes mark the safe channel for watercraft.

The Berney Arms was originally a farmhouse but has been a pub for more than 100 years and is a popular landing for those plying the river between Great Yarmouth and the Broads. Beside the pub stands the tallest windmill on the marshes (70 feet or 21m high), built around 1870 to grind clinker for mortar; it was later converted to a drainage mill, which remained operational until 1951.

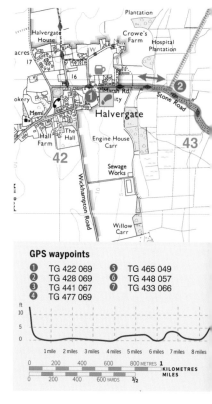

GPS waypoints

❶	TG 422 069	❺	TG 465 049
❷	TG 428 069	❻	TG 448 057
❸	TG 441 067	❼	TG 433 066
❹	TG 477 069		

Right: Teal.
Opposite page: Berney Arms drainage mill.

Halvergate Marshes

Halvergate Marshes is the largest area of traditionally managed grazing marsh in The Broads National Park covering more than 10 square miles (26km²). Much of the land is at or below sea level and criss-crossed by myriad drainage ditches. The wetland habitats are internationally important for plants, insects and birds, such as broad-leaved pondweed, Norfolk hawker dragonfly and Bewick's swan.

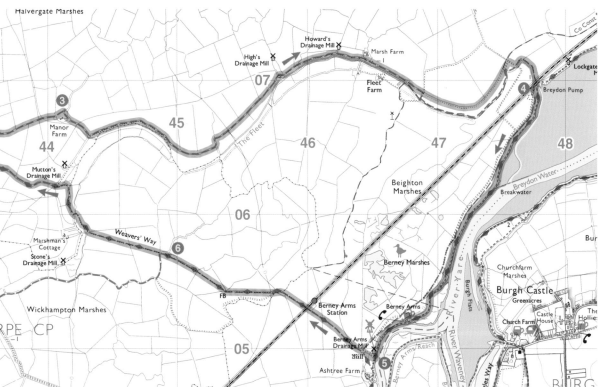

Areas of Outstanding Natural Beauty

Arguably the best-known painter of the English landscape, John Constable was born in East Bergholt and grew up in the Stour valley, a region that is now commonly regarded as 'Constable Country'. If there is an archetypal English lowland landscape, then this is surely it. Any walker who looks at a picture of the Dedham Vale Area of Outstanding Natural Beauty will instantly be drawn to walk into this cherished and increasingly vulnerable pastoral setting.

Much the same captivating impulse applies to the Lincolnshire Wolds AONB (*left*), an area of higher ground than Dedham Vale, reaching 551 feet (168m) at Wolds Top, near the village of Normanby le Wold, south of the Roman town of Caistor. This series of low hills and steep valleys based on chalk, limestone and sandstone, provides important habitats for flowers and wildlife. The AONB is comparatively small, extending from Caistor in the north to Horncastle and Spilsby in the south, just over 200 square miles (518km²).

On a recent visit, I was treated to threefly-bys from the Red Arrows, which reminded me of the military importance of the wider region during World War Two. Indeed, 2017 saw the opening of the new International Bomber Command Centre (www.internationalbcc.co.uk) near the city of Lincoln to remember the men and women who were part of Bomber Command's efforts during World War Two.

To the south, the Norfolk and Suffolk coastlines are hugely popular with birdwatchers; indeed, I once rose at 4am to watch more than 40,000 pink-footed geese take to the dawn air from The Wash. Both coastlines enjoy AONB status, and both are perfect for walks at a range of levels, many of them offering peace and quiet away from the seaside towns. The Suffolk Coast is a landscape rich in history, unspoilt and tranquil, and with extensive heathland, reed beds, ancient woodlands, saltmarsh, estuaries and shingle beaches that provide habitats for flora and fauna not found elsewhere. This is well-demonstrated by the walk through the scrubby grassland of Dunwich Heath and the reedy pools of Minsmere Marsh, but that is singling out one walk from a lavish menu of pleasurable options.

> **AMAZING BUT TRUE ...**
> Petwood Hall at Woodhall Spa (www.petwood.co.uk) flies the RAF flag as a special privilege to mark its role as the Officers' Mess for the 617 'Dambusters' Squadron at the time of the raids on the Ruhr dams in World War Two.

WALK 46

Constable Country – Flatford and East Bergholt

DEDHAM VALE AONB

DIFFICULTY ●

START East Bergholt

DISTANCE 5½ miles (8.9km)

HEIGHT GAIN 230 feet (70m)

APPROXIMATE TIME 2½ hours

ROUTE TERRAIN Quiet lanes, field-edge and paddock paths

PARKING East Bergholt

OS EXPLORER 196

OS PATHFINDER Suffolk

DETAILED ROUTE DOWNLOAD
os.uk/obw

John Constable, probably the best-known painter of the English landscape, grew up in the lovely surroundings of the Stour valley, through which this walk leads from East Bergholt. Although he died more than 150 years ago, much of the countryside he captured on canvas still survives and is instantly recognisable. Several of his classic views can be seen on the route, the first of which appears after an initial gentle climb from Vale Farm looking out over Dedham Vale. On reaching the river, the walk follows the Stour Valley Path for probably the finest riverside ramble in Suffolk to the pretty 16th-century Bridge Cottage, which houses an exhibition on Constable. Then comes Flatford Mill, now a field centre, and Willy Lott's House, both famously depicted in Constable's paintings. Near the end of the walk, do visit East Bergholt's church to see the unique timber Bell House in the churchyard, where the bells are swung by hand cranks rather than traditional bell-ropes.

Right: Flatford Mill.
Opposite page: Flatford Lock.

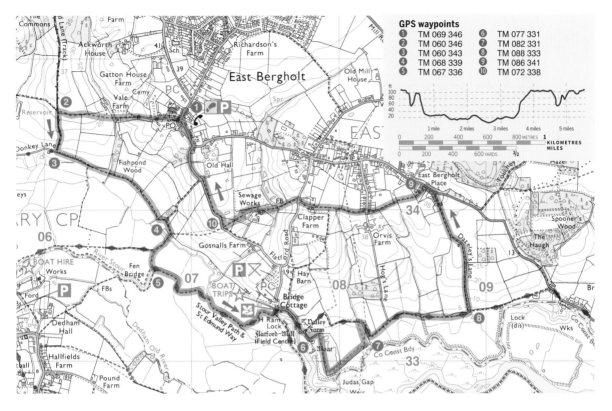

GPS waypoints

1	TM 069 346	6	TM 077 331
2	TM 060 346	7	TM 082 331
3	TM 060 343	8	TM 088 333
4	TM 068 339	9	TM 086 341
5	TM 067 336	10	TM 072 338

The Bell Cage

The Bell Cage in the grounds of St Mary's Church, East Bergholt, is unique in that the bells it houses have to be swung by force of hand, as opposed to pulling on ropes. Building work on a bell tower began in 1525 with support from Cardinal Wolsey, but following his downfall work ceased. The bell cage was erected as a temporary measure in 1531 and the bells have been rung in this unusual way ever since.

Walesby, Claxby and Normanby le Wold

LINCOLNSHIRE WOLDS AONB

DIFFICULTY ●●

START Walesby

DISTANCE 5¼ miles (8.4km)

HEIGHT GAIN 690 feet (210m)

APPROXIMATE TIME 3 hours

ROUTE TERRAIN Undulating tracks, including the Viking Way, and field paths

PARKING Walesby Village Hall car park

OS EXPLORER 282

OS PATHFINDER Lincolnshire and the Wolds

DETAILED ROUTE DOWNLOAD
os.uk/obw

Located in the west of the Lincolnshire Wolds Area of Outstanding Natural Beauty between Caistor and Market Rasen, this excursion is a classic Wolds walk that takes you through an open and rolling countryside of broad ridges and wide valleys, with spectacular and extensive views – as far as Lincoln Cathedral southwards – on the second half of the route. Beginning from Walesby, the route traces a path between the typical Wolds villages of Claxby and Normanby le Wold, from where the 1½-mile (1-km) ridge top finale unfolds. Part of the return leg is along the Viking Way, a 147-mile (237-km) long-distance path joining Barton-upon-Humber, Lincolnshire, to Oakham in Rutland. Walesby has two churches, the oldest and most interesting of which is All Saints, also known as the Old Church and the Ramblers' Church, referring to a stained glass window donated in 1951 by local rambling groups. All Saints' hilltop location makes it the highest church in Lincolnshire and marks the site of a medieval village, which was depopulated by the Black Death in the 14th century and two centuries later abandoned for the present-day village.

Right: Claxby village nestled in the Wolds.
Opposite page: All Saints Church.

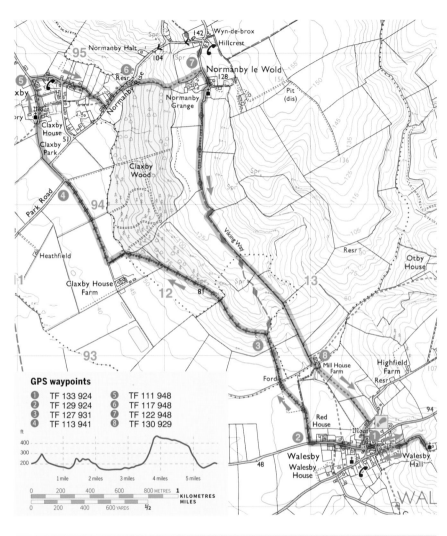

GPS waypoints

①	TF 133 924	⑤	TF 111 948
②	TF 129 924	⑥	TF 117 948
③	TF 127 931	⑦	TF 122 948
④	TF 113 941	⑧	TF 130 929

Normanby le Wold

The highest village in Lincolnshire is Normanby le Wold at approximately 475 feet (145m) above sea level. Really only a hamlet today, Normanby is recorded in the Domesday survey of 1086 as having 37 households, 100 acres of meadow, 40 acres of woodland and two churches. The present church, St Peter's, is built of ironstone and is Grade II listed, and its oldest parts date from the 13th century.

Castle Rising

NORFOLK COAST AONB

DIFFICULTY ●

START Castle Rising

DISTANCE 2¼ miles (3.6km)

HEIGHT GAIN 130 feet (40m)

APPROXIMATE TIME 1 hour

ROUTE TERRAIN Quiet lane, field
and woodland paths

PARKING Castle car park, Castle
Rising

OS EXPLORER 250

OS PATHFINDER Short Walks
Norfolk into Suffolk

DETAILED ROUTE DOWNLOAD
os.uk/obw

Overlooking the vast expanse that was once the tidal estuary of the River Babingley, an old arm of The Wash, Castle Rising is a wonderful example of early Norman military architecture. Founded in 1138 by William de Albini, the castle's spacious keep is set within a massive encircling earthwork. The village itself once prospered as a port, the tide rising along the river throughout the medieval period. This very easy-paced short walk passes through the pretty village, with its ancient church and 17th-century almshouses (Trinity Hospital), to the lazily flowing river, returning by way of pleasant woodlands and gently undulating field paths.

The castle has been home to the widows of two English kings: Adelaide of Louvain, who married William de Albini after the death of Henry II, and then Isabella, formerly the wife of Edward II. The castle was later furnished as a hunting lodge by Isabella's grandson, the Black Prince, and eventually passed to the Howard family, who have held it since 1544.

Right and opposite page right:
Castle Rising.
Opposite page left: Baptism font
detail, St Lawrence's Church, Castle
Rising.

GPS waypoints
1. TF 666 244
2. TF 673 255
3. TF 674 251
4. TF 676 250
5. TF 673 248

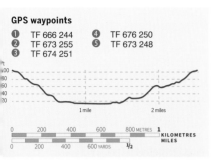

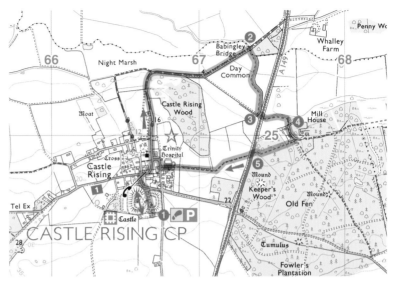

St Lawrence's Church

St Lawrence's Church, Castle Rising, is of Norman origin and built of the highly distinctive carrstone and flint that is local to the Sandringham area. Dating from the 1150s, about the same age as the castle, the church was also founded by William de Albini. While the Norman nave and the church's cruciform style are clear, it has been restored over the centuries, and heavily so in the early Victorian era. The rugged-looking font dates from the 12th century.

West Runton and Beacon Hill

NORFOLK COAST AONB

DIFFICULTY ●●

START East Runton

DISTANCE 7¼ miles (11.7km)

HEIGHT GAIN 575 feet (175m)

APPROXIMATE TIME 3½ hours

ROUTE TERRAIN Field and woodland paths, rocky beach

PARKING East Runton Beach car park

OS EXPLORER 252

OS PATHFINDER Norfolk

DETAILED ROUTE DOWNLOAD os.uk/obw

Climbing to Norfolk's celebrated high point of Beacon Hill, where a signal beacon is known to have existed since the 14th century, this grand walk exploits the fine views overlooking West Runton, but begins along a splendid beach, backed by high cliffs of chalk overlain by crumbling glacial clay that have given up some remarkable fossils. The most spectacular find was made in 1990, when the pelvic bone of a giant mammoth was revealed. Subsequent excavation recovered an almost-complete skeleton, parts of which are displayed at museums in Cromer and Norwich. Known as the West Runton Elephant, it weighed over 1574 stone (10 tons) and, aside from dinosaurs, is the largest land creature yet discovered. Embedded within the chalk are bands of flint nodules which, being harder, remain as the cliff is worn away. Just beyond West Runton Gap are curious formations known as paramoudras or potstones. These doughnut-shaped nodules, some looking like fossilised vertebrae, are plentifully scattered about, while much larger rings lie embedded in the chalk.

Consult tide tables (posted in the car park) before setting off. The 2½-mile (4km) beach between East Runton and Sheringham can become impassible at high tide, with intermediate escape only possible at West Runton and Beeston Regis.

Right: West Runton cliffs and beach.
Opposite page: Sheringham beach and cliffs.

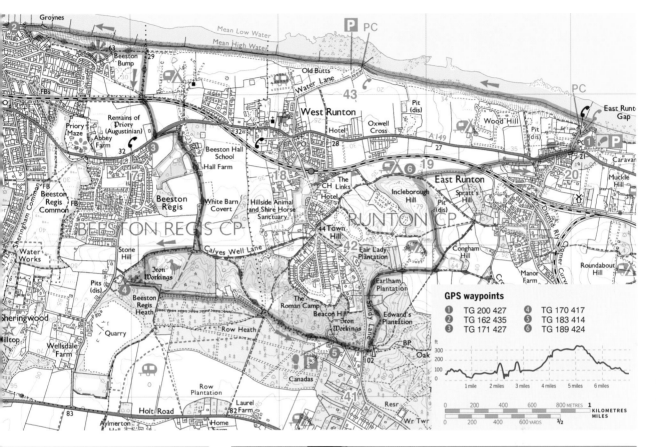

GPS waypoints

❶	TG 200 427	❹	TG 170 417
❷	TG 162 435	❺	TG 183 414
❸	TG 171 427	❻	TG 189 424

Beeston Bump

Beeston Bump, crossed on the route out of Sheringham, is one of the highest points along Norfolk's coast at 207 feet (63m) above sea level. It offers a grand view and was manned as a lookout during World War Two. Geologically known as a kame, as with the rest of the Cromer-Holt Ridge, Beeston Bump is formed of glacial rubble deposited by a retreating ice sheet 15,000–10,000 years ago.

Dunwich Heath and Minsmere Marsh

SUFFOLK COAST AND HEATHS AONB

DIFFICULTY ●

START Dunwich Heath

DISTANCE 5 miles (8km)

HEIGHT GAIN 215 feet (65m)

APPROXIMATE TIME 2 hours

ROUTE TERRAIN Heathland tracks and field paths, with the option of a shingle ridge-top path on the return leg

PARKING National Trust car park at Dunwich Heath

OS EXPLORER 231

OS PATHFINDER Short Walks Norfolk into Suffolk

DETAILED ROUTE DOWNLOAD
os.uk/obw

A walk through two contrasting nature reserves: the first, a sandy heath of scrubby grassland, heather and woodland, and the latter, a watery expanse of reedy pools. The heathland at Dunwich is one of Britain's rarest habitats and entirely man-made. After clearance of the original wild wood at the end of the Neolithic period, the land gradually became acid rich and nutrient poor, with the resultant sparse grassland devoted to sheep grazing. Left untended, birch, bramble and bracken would quickly smother the bedstraw, heather and gorse, destroying the fragile ecosystem that supports adders, grass snakes, slow worms and common lizards. The visitor centre at the RSPB's reserve is well worth the slight detour. The walk's final leg follows the Suffolk Coast and Heaths Path; as an option to the path following the reserve's perimeter fence, you can climb to the top of the shingle ridge. The loose pebbles make walking harder here, but there are splendid views across Minsmere and along the North Sea shore.

Right: Heather on Dunwich Heath.
Opposite page: Drainage dyke, Minsmere Nature Reserve.

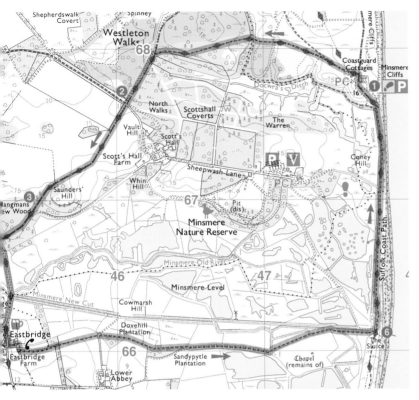

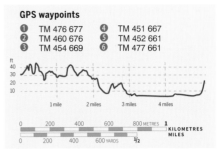

GPS waypoints

1 TM 476 677
2 TM 460 676
3 TM 454 669
4 TM 451 667
5 TM 452 661
6 TM 477 661

Minsmere

One of the best-known RSPB reserves is Minsmere. A public hide is passed on the walk. Look out for avocet, the iconic emblem of the RSPB, distinguished by its long upturned bill and black and white plumage. Other rare birds to watch for are bearded tits and marsh harriers and, in spring, listen for the elusive booming call of the male bittern.

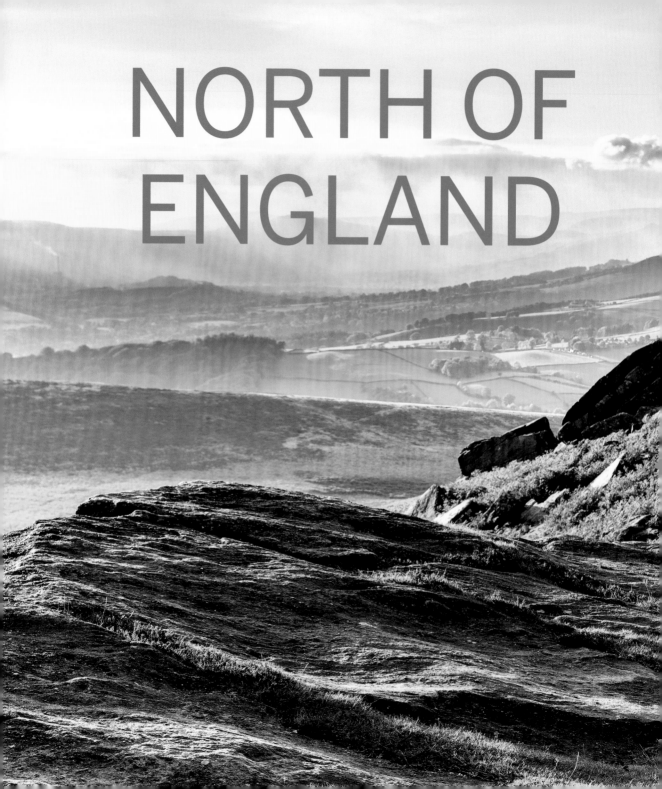

NORTH OF ENGLAND

The Walks

Top: Roseberry Topping.
Bottom: Lose Hill.
Previous page: Stanage Edge in the Peak District.

Berwick-upon-Tweed

Holy Island

Northumberland Coast

R Tweed

69

55

Alnwick   Longhoughton

NORTHUMBERLAND

Kielder Water

54

R North Tyne

Morpeth

72

Frontiers of the Roman Empire, Hadrian's Wall

Haltwhistle

Hexham

R Tyne

Newcastle upon Tyne

Tynemouth

Gateshead

Sunderland

Solway Firth

Solway Coast

Carlisle

R Eden

R South Tyne

North Pennines

R Wear

Durham

71

Durham Castle & Cathedral

Hartlepool

Bishop Auckland

Stockton-on-Tees

R Derwent

Keswick

Penrith

Appleby-in-Westmorland

67

Brough

Darlington

Middlesbrough

R Tees

Whitby

Robin Hood's Bay

Whitehaven

53

LAKE DISTRICT

Ullswater

Scotch Corner

57

R Esk

58

St Bees Head

Wast Water

51

Windermere

Kendal

Coniston Water

Windermere

52

NORTH YORK MOORS

56

Scarborough

64

Bainbridge   Leyburn

Thirsk

Pickering

YORKSHIRE DALES

Howardian Hills

Malton

Flamborough Head

Barrow-in-Furness

Arnside & Silverdale

65

Morecambe Bay

Carnforth

R Lune

63

Settle

68

Nidderdale

Ripon

70

Fountains Abbey & Studley Royal Park

66

Bridlington

Bridlington Bay

Morecambe

Heysham

Lancaster

62

York

R Ouse

R Derwent

Fleetwood

Forest of Bowland

Clitheroe

Skipton

Harrogate

Wetherby

Selby

Kingston upon Hull

Blackpool

R Ribble

Keighley

Saltaire

Leeds

R Aire

Goole

R Humber

Preston

Burnley

Bradford

Spurn Head

Southport

Blackburn

Halifax

Wakefield

Pontefract

Rochdale

Huddersfield

Barnsley

Doncaster

Bootle

Wigan

Bolton

Oldham

Liverpool Maritime Mercantile City

St Helens

Manchester

Stockport

Rotherham

Sheffield

Liverpool Bay

Wallasey

Birkenhead

Liverpool

Widnes

Warrington

Runcorn

60

59

Glossop

Castleton

Buxton

Chesterfield

R Dee

Ellesmere Port

Northwich

Macclesfield

Chester

Congleton

Leek

PEAK DISTRICT

61

Nantwich

Newcastle-under-Lyme

Stoke-on-Trent

Lake District National Park

The knobbly summit of Causey Pike above Derwent Water was the first Lakeland fell I climbed; there is something about its profile when seen from Keswick that is irresistibly enticing. Yet it takes only a few visits to this 'Odd Corner of England', as it was once called, to realise there is an invitation in every one of the fells, big and small. The very name 'fell' holds appeal, too, occurring nowhere in England except the Lake District and the Pennine Dales. It derives from the Old Norse word for a mountain, *fjall*, and highlights the fact that for many years the region was occupied and farmed by people from Scandinavia. In fact, man has been here since the Palaeolithic Period (12,000-8,000 BC), when small bands of hunter-gatherers roamed the tundra-like landscape.

In the 1960s, when my days of mountain-wandering began, there seemed to be few people about, despite the fact that the Lake District has been attracting visitors, writers, artists, scientists, political commentators, tourists and villa-builders for more than 250 years.

Today, contending with over 16 million other visitors annually, you might be forgiven for thinking there was nowhere among the fells to find peace and quiet. But such spots do exist; you just need a good guidebook, a map and a nose for out-of-the-way places. Try, for example, the Back o' Skidda', especially if you make the ascent of Skiddaw first; the ancient Copeland Forest; even around Crummock Water on a quiet day, not to mention that great swathe of land sandwiched between Dunnerdale and the River Esk. You can wander all day in these places and not see another soul... apart from sheep. There is solitude, too, in the far-eastern fells that tumble eastwards from the drowned valley of Mardale towards Shap and its ruined abbey. But time your visit carefully, and you can find the sounds of silence even among the most popular fells: early morning is best, or a summer's evening when the day trippers are heading home.

Today, the Lake District has 'Outstanding Universal Value'; it's a landscape of exceptional beauty, shaped by agro-pastoral traditions that give it special character. Small wonder then that, during 2017, it sought UNESCO World Heritage Status.

AMAZING BUT TRUE ...

There is only one lake in the Lake District – Bassenthwaite Lake; all the other 'lakes' are tarns, waters or meres. Windermere is the longest body of water in England; Wasdale, the deepest. Scafell Pike is England's highest summit, and Seathwaite is the wettest place in England.

Elterwater

LAKE DISTRICT NATIONAL PARK

DIFFICULTY ●

START Elterwater village

DISTANCE 5½ miles (8.9km)

HEIGHT GAIN 310 feet (95m)

APPROXIMATE TIME 3 hours

ROUTE TERRAIN Surfaced riverside paths, tracks, field paths and lanes

PARKING Elterwater car park

OS EXPLORER OL7

OS PATHFINDER Short Walks Lake District

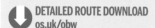 **DETAILED ROUTE DOWNLOAD** os.uk/obw

This delightful and easy-going walk meanders through farm fields and beside tarns, streams and rivers, with exquisite views of the surrounding fells. The going is nowhere difficult, and interest remains high throughout. The opening section follows the River Brathay downstream. Looking back over Elter Water, the Langdale Pikes rise across the tarn and are often reflected on the water's surface, their crags and gullies so vividly etched you could almost reach out and touch them. Highlights include Skelwith Force (pronounced Skel-ith), a tumult of foaming water in rich, green woods that is approached on metal walkways; Colwith Force, one of Lakeland's secret waterfalls; and a superb legacy of quarrying times in the form of the old and almost impossibly photogenic Slater's Bridge. Over the bridge, the way rises to reveal outstanding views to the west over Little Langdale Tarn and Greenburndale beyond. Returning to Elterwater, the village has a pub and a tearoom for post-walk relaxation.

Right: Slater's Bridge.
Opposite page left: Skelwith Falls.
Opposite page right: Elterwater.

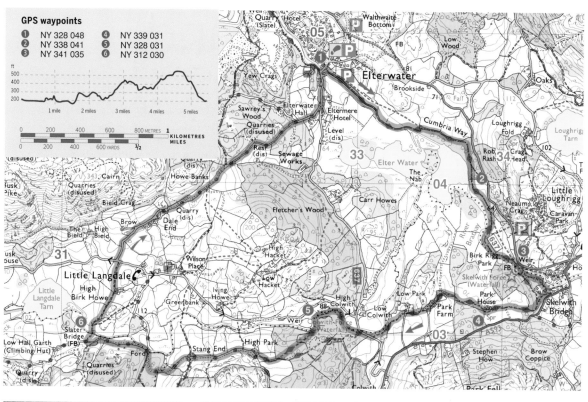

GPS waypoints
1. NY 328 048
2. NY 338 041
3. NY 341 035
4. NY 339 031
5. NY 328 031
6. NY 312 030

Wray Castle and Blelham Tarn

WALK 52

LAKE DISTRICT NATIONAL PARK

DIFFICULTY ●●

START Red Nab, High Wray

DISTANCE 6 miles (9.7km)

HEIGHT GAIN 785 feet (240m)

APPROXIMATE TIME 3 hours

ROUTE TERRAIN Lakeside paths, field and woodland paths and bridleways, and lanes

PARKING Red Nab car park

OS EXPLORER OL7

OS PATHFINDER Lake District

⬇ DETAILED ROUTE DOWNLOAD
os.uk/obw

A chance to walk on the quieter side of Windermere, exploring a landscape that would have been familiar to Beatrix Potter, and which almost certainly sowed seeds in her imagination that later grew into her successful series of books. This walk visits both Wray Castle, where Potter stayed as a child, and the beautifully set Blelham Tarn. Great spotted woodpeckers favour the broad-leaved woodland rising up the slope above Windermere, and it is a rare day when you do not see or at least hear one. At Low Wray Bay, take a short detour to visit the Wray Castle Boathouse, which houses some of the fine steamers that ply the lake. Wray Castle, now owned by the National Trust, is a mid-19th-century mansion with much castle-like architecture; it was the creation of Dr James Dawson, a wealthy Liverpool surgeon. The grounds have many outstanding trees, including Wellingtonia, redwood, weeping lime and ginkgo biloba.

Right: Blelham Tarn.
Opposite page top: Wray Castle.
Opposite page middle: Steamer on Windermere.
Opposite page bottom: View from Wray Castle across Langdale Valley.

Crummock Water

LAKE DISTRICT NATIONAL PARK

DIFFICULTY ●●●

START Scalehill Bridge, above the northern end of Crummock Water

DISTANCE 8½ miles (13.8km)

HEIGHT GAIN 1,050 feet (320m)

APPROXIMATE TIME 4 hours

ROUTE TERRAIN Rough and sometimes rocky and muddy lakeshore path, field and woodland paths and a short section of road

PARKING Scalehill Bridge

OS EXPLORER OL4

OS PATHFINDER More Lake District

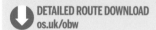
DETAILED ROUTE DOWNLOAD os.uk/obw

Crummock Water is twice the size of Buttermere Lake and boasts just as beautiful a shoreline. Along with Buttermere and nearby Loweswater, it would once have formed one large glacial lake, subsequently split into three by debris washed down from the surrounding fells. The name of the lake derives from the Celtic, 'cromach', a crook. So, it is the crooked lake, forced to bend around the stubby knuckle of Hause Point below Rannerdale. Crummock is one of Lakeland's deepest lakes and was once renowned for char, a deep-water fish that was popular in such delicacies as potted char and char pie. To walk around Crummock Water is no modest undertaking and likely to be damp in places, but it ranks among the finest valley walks in the Lake District. Two-thirds of the way round, Scale Beck tumbles down the fellside into the lake, and a path leads up to Scale Force, the highest waterfall in the Lake District at 125 feet (31m).

Right: Crummock Water.

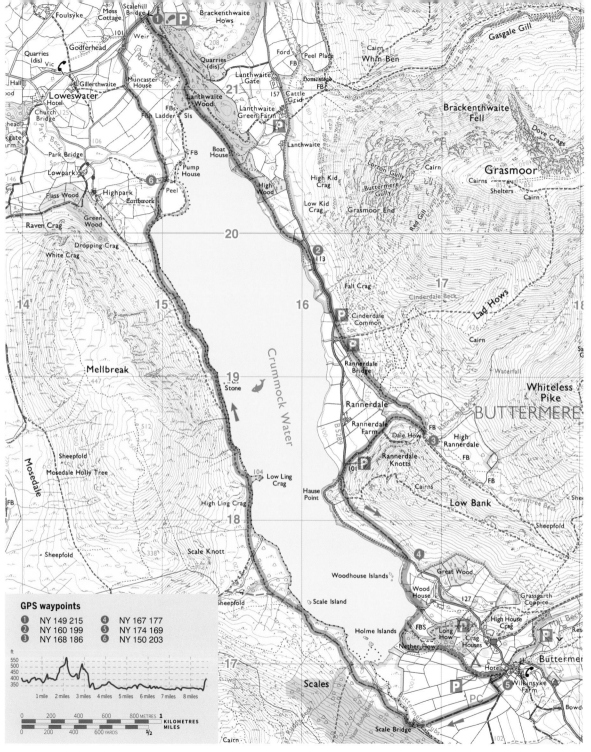

GPS waypoints

❶	NY 149 215	❹	NY 167 177
❷	NY 160 199	❺	NY 174 169
❸	NY 168 186	❻	NY 150 203

Northumberland National Park

Northumberland is the northernmost of the English National Parks, lying between Hadrian's Wall and the Scottish border, and is one of the least visited. This has more to do with geographical remoteness than with any shortcomings in scenic merit, and the isolation brings its own compensation: the hills are quieter and the solitude is more profound. Here, to borrow a phrase used by the late English author Lillian Beckwith, 'Even the sheeps ... on the hills is lonely'.

I've always found it an endearing place, not unlike the Peak District in some of its more glutinous, peaty qualities, but quite heavenly in dry, springy-turf conditions. And 'heavenly' is an apt description, because the National Park, along with Kielder Water and Forest Park, has been granted dark-sky status by the International Dark Skies Association, with potential to benefit from the new trend for astro-tourism. In fact, this is the largest area of protected sky in Europe.

The Northumberland National Park, established in 1956, forms several distinct areas, each with its own unique appeal. In the north are the Cheviots, a range of hills that mark the border between England and Scotland. Moving south, the landscape dips to rolling, forested moorland, notably around Kielder Forest, while the southernmost part of the park embraces that part of Britain occupied by the Romans, today defined by the remains, many of them impressive, of Hadrian's Wall.

Between these areas, the terrain provides walkers with differing challenges, from steady undulations in the south, over Windy Gyle to the peaty clutches of the Cheviots in the north. In my 1989 book, *The Pennine Mountains*, I describe the National Park as a place with '... few orthodox beauty spots or craggy mountainsides, where virtue lies instead in the subtle variety of form and colour among the hills and valleys, and in its richness of flora and fauna.' That remains true today. Visitors find Northumberland uplifting and invigorating; walking here brings a keen sense of wellness, a sense that you're enveloped within the folds of the countryside, and soothed by the sights and sounds of nature.

> **AMAZING BUT TRUE ...**
> On the edge of the park, Sharp's Folly (NU058 009) was one of Britain's earliest job creation schemes, built in the 1720s by the Rector of Rothbury for no other reason than to give work to unemployed men.

Kielder Water and the Bull Crag Peninsula

NORTHUMBERLAND NATIONAL PARK

DIFFICULTY ●

START Leaplish Waterside park

DISTANCE 6¼ miles (10.1km)

HEIGHT GAIN 650 feet (200m)

APPROXIMATE TIME 2½ hours

ROUTE TERRAIN Good paths and tracks

PARKING Visitor centre car park, Leaplish

OS EXPLORER OL42

OS PATHFINDER Northumberland and Scottish Borders

 **DETAILED ROUTE DOWNLOAD** os.uk/obw

Encompassing both Britain's most capacious reservoir and Europe's largest planted woodland, Kielder Forest Park is a superb outdoor activity area. This route can be undertaken as a short stroll that's ideal for families with young children, between Leaplish Waterside Park and the fairytale cabin overlooking Kielder Water, a focus for the tale of Freya and Robin. For a longer ramble, tag on an undemanding loop around the scenic Bull Crag Peninsula. The route follows good forest tracks and clear paths around this picturesquely set tongue of land that protrudes into the reservoir. The Headland, on the peninsula's tip, has a grand view of the reservoir dam.

During the 1920s, planting began on what had been open moorland in the upper reaches of the River North Tyne to create the most extensive man-made forest in England. The woodland is a key stronghold for red squirrels. More recently, Kielder Water has hosted breeding ospreys, the first in Northumberland for more than 200 years.

Right: Kielder dam.
Opposite page left: Kielder Water.
Opposite page right: Kielder Forest.

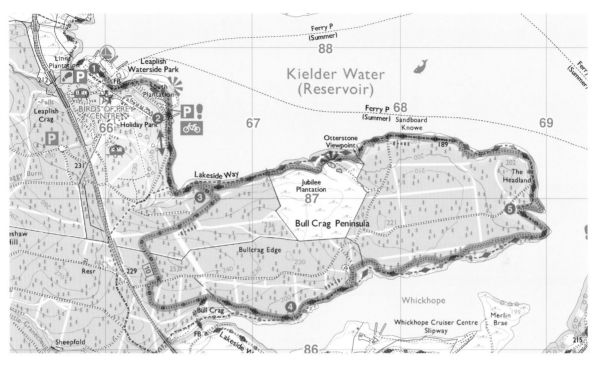

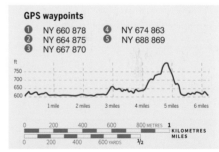

GPS waypoints

1	NY 660 878	**4**	NY 674 863
2	NY 664 875	**5**	NY 688 869
3	NY 667 870		

Hartside, Salter's Road and High Cantle

NORTHUMBERLAND NATIONAL PARK

DIFFICULTY ●●●

START Hartside, 6 miles west of A697, beyond Powburn and Ingram

DISTANCE 8½ miles (13.7km)

HEIGHT GAIN 1,590 feet (485m)

APPROXIMATE TIME 4½ hours

ROUTE TERRAIN Remote moorland tracks and rough paths, not always clear on the ground

PARKING Roadside parking, with consideration, before Hartside Farm

OS EXPLORER OL16

OS PATHFINDER Northumberland and Scottish Borders

 **DETAILED ROUTE DOWNLOAD** os.uk/obw

Opposite page left: Footpath to Linhope Spout.
Opposite page right: Breamish Valley.

Deserted moors often beget forlorn-sounding names, and 'Bleakhope', deep within the folds of the Breamish valley, conjures just such an image. However, take in this area in good weather and a good mood and there is marvellous walking to be had among the vast landscape of undulating hills, deep cleughs and long grassy ridges. The overwhelming characteristic of walks in the Cheviot Hills is the abundant solitude, and this circuit lives up handsomely to that reputation, meandering across the empty moors that encup the River Breamish.

A good part of the walk follows the ancient Salter's Road, used by traders carrying salt, which was vital in the pre-refrigeration centuries for preserving meat and fish, from the coast to inland markets. Salter's Road is also an old drove route used for herding stock from as far afield as the Scottish Highlands for sale in England. Whisky, illicitly stilled in the higher reaches of this remote valley, was much more of a secretive cargo.

For much of the way paths are faint and don't always correspond with those marked on the map, so inexperienced walkers and those less competent in navigating in misty conditions are advised to save this route for a clear day.

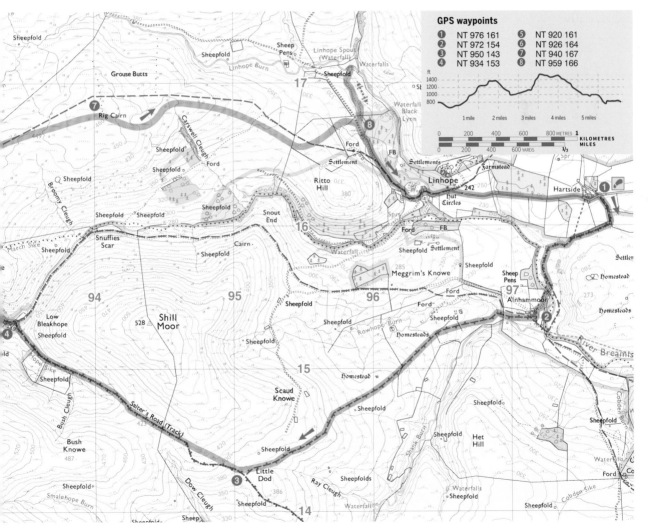

GPS waypoints

❶ NT 976 161		❺ NT 920 161	
❷ NT 972 154		❻ NT 926 164	
❸ NT 950 143		❼ NT 940 167	
❹ NT 934 153		❽ NT 959 166	

North York Moors National Park

There is often a temptation to think that 'moorland' is synonymous with peat bogs, wet, unforgiving conditions and challenging terrain. The North York Moors, a National Park since 1952, beg to differ: these characteristics are present, it is true, but, in spring, Farndale is dazzling with golden daffodils; the pastures around Rievaulx Abbey, bright with flowers; the legendary Hole of Horcum – in reality a valley 400 feet (120m) deep and just under a mile (1.6km) across – is lush and inviting, and the northern escarpment of the Cleveland Hills, as fine a walking canvas as any in Britain. Not without good reason do the Lyke Wake Walk, the Cleveland Way and the Coast-to-Coast Walk all share the same stretches of the hills.

Not until I was working on my own guide to the Coast-to-Coast Walk did I visit the Moors, but I came speedily to realise what I'd been missing: broad farmland dales; one of the largest expanses of high, heathery moorland in the United Kingdom; shaded forests and dramatic coastline (perfect for a beach-combing walk). Even on an inclement day, there is a cheerfulness about the North York Moors. And, when the uplands are shrouded in mist, the woodlands offer superb walking. There's more woodland here, in fact, than in the New Forest; it covers more than 20% of the National Park in the form of ancient woodland, bluebell woodland and tree-lined avenues on the great estates.

The scenic variations are self-evident and are the result of the underlying geology, which not only supports differing wildlife communities, but also allows walkers to enjoy contrasting terrain, almost all of which is Open Access Land. The highest part of the National Park is Urra Moor at 1,489 feet (454m), although the name applies to the whole moor, of which Round Hill is the highest point. This area is noted for its prehistoric remains, which include carved rocks, cup and ring carvings and barrows.

Yet, it's not all about the high ground, or even the moors. On a recent visit, I stayed at the Black Swan in Helmsley and set off up Ash Dale following a stretch of the Tabular Hills Walk; it didn't matter where I was heading, or how long I was going to be; this simple wooded dale was more than enough to satisfy me.

> **AMAZING BUT TRUE ...**
> The Kilburn White Horse, to the south of Sutton Bank, was finished in 1857 and is believed to be the most northerly and, possibly, the largest white horse in Britain, being 318 feet (97m) long and 220 feet (67m) high.

WALK 56 Farndale

NORTH YORK MOORS NATIONAL PARK

DIFFICULTY ●

START Low Mill

DISTANCE 3½ miles (5.6km)

HEIGHT GAIN 245 feet (75m)

APPROXIMATE TIME 2 hours

ROUTE TERRAIN Field paths and quiet lanes

PARKING Low Mill

OS EXPLORER OL26

OS PATHFINDER North York Moors

DETAILED ROUTE DOWNLOAD
os.uk/obw

This is an enchanting ramble at any time of the year, but, in spring, this walk in the heart of the North York Moors National Park takes on an added beauty. A short and leisurely circuit from Low Mill, it follows the upstream course of the River Dove through meadows, open pastures and small woodland copses to Church Houses. The path is known as the 'daffodil walk', because early in the year, before the trees come into leaf, the ground is carpeted in a glorious riot of yellow, as countless wild daffodils open their bright trumpets to the sun; at this time of year, it is difficult to conceive of a finer stretch of countryside walking. The return is along field paths on the eastern side of Farndale, from where there is a superb panorama to the heights of Rudland Rigg, whose flanks in late summer are tinged purple by flowering heather.

Right: Church Houses graveyard.
Opposite page left: Fields of Farndale.
Opposite page right: Country lane in Farndale.

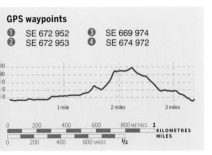

Farndale

Farndale is a valley drained by the River Dove, which rises on the remote and wild moorland of Farndale Moor near the highest point of the North York Moors' watershed, running southwards between the higher ground of Rudland Rigg to the west and Blakey Ridge to the east. It is a scattered agricultural community with the hamlets of Church Houses and Low Mill popular centres during the daffodil season.

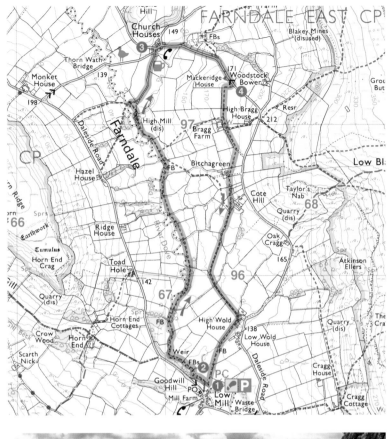

WALK 57

The Cook Monument and Roseberry Topping

NORTH YORK MOORS NATIONAL PARK

DIFFICULTY ●●

START Gribdale Gate, 2½ miles (4km) east of Great Ayton

DISTANCE 6½ miles (10.5km)

HEIGHT GAIN 1,315 feet (400m)

APPROXIMATE TIME 3½ hours

ROUTE TERRAIN Woodland and field paths, lanes and moorland tracks

PARKING Gribdale Gate

OS EXPLORER OL26

OS PATHFINDER North York Moors

DETAILED ROUTE DOWNLOAD
os.uk/obw

To the east of Great Ayton lie two of the most prominent landmarks of the Cleveland Hills: the monument to Captain Cook on Easby Moor and the pyramidal peak of Roseberry Topping (1,051 feet, 320m), whose unique and distinctive profile is visible from many vantage points over a wide stretch of the moors and from the plain below. This walk incorporates both features, as well as the village of Great Ayton. The climb is gradual and easy-paced to the Cook Monument; it was erected in 1827 to commemorate the life and extraordinary achievements of navigator and explorer Captain James Cook, who attended the local school at Great Ayton. In contrast, the ascent of Roseberry Topping is much steeper and more strenuous. Early prints show that the hill once had a perfect conical shape, but subsidence, caused by tunnelling into the hill for iron ore led to the collapse of the western face, creating the abrupt scar by which it is distinguished today.

Right: The view to Roseberry Topping.
Opposite page: The Cook Monument.

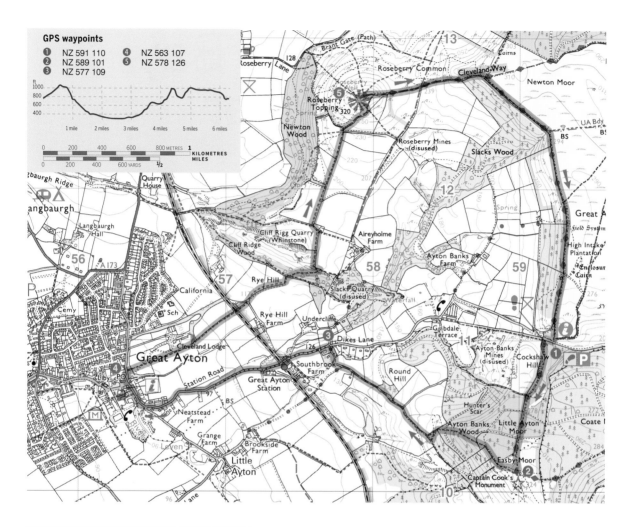

GPS waypoints

1. NZ 591 110
2. NZ 589 101
3. NZ 577 109
4. NZ 563 107
5. NZ 578 126

Great Ayton

Great Ayton was the boyhood home of the navigator and explorer Captain James Cook. The museum in the village devoted to Cook is housed in the former Postgate School, where he attended. The cottage occupied by the Cook family was dismantled in 1934 and now stands in Fitzroy Park in Melbourne, but in its place is an obelisk made from stone quarried from Point Hicks, Australia. The 12th-century All Saints Church, where the Cook family worshipped, is also worth a visit.

Robin Hood's Bay and Ravenscar

NORTH YORK MOORS NATIONAL PARK

DIFFICULTY ●●●

START Robin Hood's Bay

DISTANCE 9 miles (14.5km)

HEIGHT GAIN 605 feet (185m)

APPROXIMATE TIME 4½ hours

ROUTE TERRAIN Old railway trackbed, field paths and clifftop coastal path along the Cleveland Way

PARKING Robin Hood's Bay

OS EXPLORER OL27

OS PATHFINDER North York Moors

DETAILED ROUTE DOWNLOAD
os.uk/obw

A jumble of red-roofed cottages, clustered below steep cliffs, with narrow winding lanes, passages and stepped paths leading down to the sea, make up the enchanting fishing village of Robin Hood's Bay. Once remote and inaccessible, it was, not surprisingly, a notorious haunt for smugglers. Utilising the track of the disused Whitby to Scarborough Railway creates a splendid circular coastal walk that links Robin Hood's Bay and Ravenscar, formerly a centre for alum manufacturing. The inland, outward leg along the old railway line to Ravenscar offers up magnificent, far-reaching views over the bay. The walk becomes even better on the way back, joining the Cleveland Way to follow the broad sweep of Robin Hood's Bay along a particularly spectacular section of the North Yorkshire coastal path, which, although rather more energetic, has its own special delights. If the tide is safely out, you can follow the shore for the finale.

Right: Robin Hood's Bay.

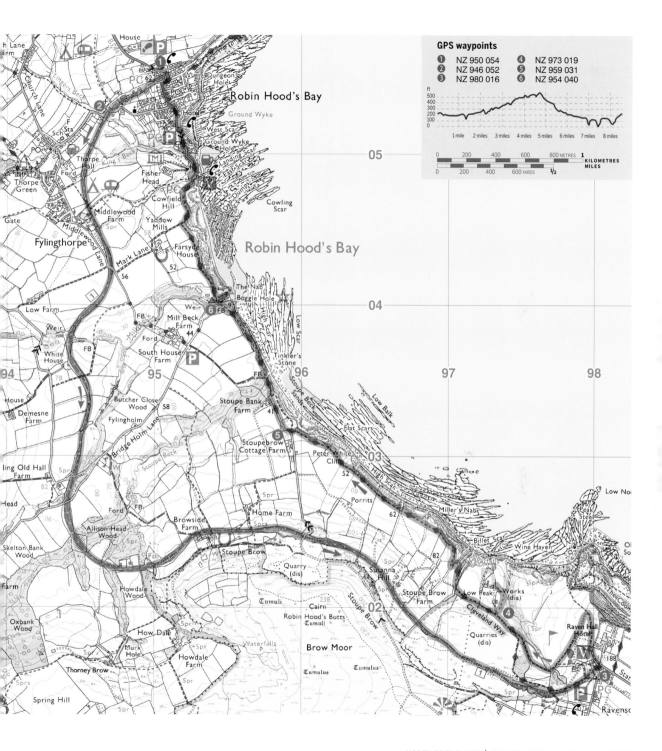

GPS waypoints
①	NZ 950 054	④	NZ 973 019
②	NZ 946 052	⑤	NZ 959 031
③	NZ 980 016	⑥	NZ 954 040

Robin Hood's Bay

Robin Hood's Bay

Fylingthorpe

Brow Moor

Peak District National Park

The history of walking has a strong association with the Peak District, memorably in the Kinder Scout mass trespass of April 1932, and the region has been regarded by many as a national heritage landscape since the 1880s. Yet, anyone charged with promoting the region for walkers might wonder how to make a start, given the decades of dispirited writing about the region: 'unpleasant and disgustful to the imagination' (James Pilkington in *A view of the present state of Derbyshire*, 1789); a region with 'no features and no landmarks, where the earth lays snares for you' (Mrs Humphrey Ward in *The History of David Grieve*, 1906).

Melanie Tebbutt, Professor in History at Manchester Metropolitan University, has explored how masculine values became identified with particular kinds of landscape and has identified portrayals of the Peak District as a place that defines manliness. This gendering of an upland landscape is difficult to appreciate in the context of the Peak's softer southern section, known as the 'White Peak', where limestone dales and glittering streams entice the walker into exploration. But the moment you set foot on the millstone grit peat landscapes of the Dark Peak to the north, then a new range of perspectives come into play.

The White Peak is a limestone theatre of flat plateaux, incised by steep-sided valleys, or dales, with wedges of broadleaved woodland and clear, fast-flowing streams. The Dark Peak, in contrast, is a gritstone landscape characterised by vast, peaty plateaux, rocky ridges and edges, sheltered valleys and cloughs. If you plan to head for the Dark Peak, choose a clear, settled day and good company. Then there is the less well-known South West Peak, a setting that blends wild moorland and heathery hill tops, with valleys of hay meadows and lush pasture. But here, too, gritstone appears in isolated ridges, such as The Roaches, where the uplands slip away into lower hills and widening valleys.

The Peak District thus provides a diversity of landscape that will appeal to walkers of all persuasions: opt for the gentle embrace of the White Peak, test your mettle on the challenging terrain of the Dark Peak, or, better still, try them all.

AMAZING BUT TRUE ...

The much-hyped Kinder Trespass of April 1932, described as the most significant event in the fight for the right to roam, came 40 years after similar battles on the Darwen and Bolton moors of Lancashire.

Stanage Edge and Higger Tor

PEAK DISTRICT NATIONAL PARK

DIFFICULTY ●

START Upper Burbage Bridge

DISTANCE 3½ miles (5.6km)

HEIGHT GAIN 375 feet (115m)

APPROXIMATE TIME 1½ hours

ROUTE TERRAIN Clear but occasionally rugged moorland paths

PARKING Upper Burbage Bridge car park

OS EXPLORER OL1

OS PATHFINDER Short Walks Peak District

DETAILED ROUTE DOWNLOAD
os.uk/obw

Heather and gritstone moors are a distinct feature of the Dark Peak, and this undemanding walk gives a taste of their wild and rugged character, making it a perfect introduction to Peak District walking. This route follows the dramatic gritstone 'Stanage', meaning simply 'Stone Edge', which is a popular haunt for rock climbers and is part of the long escarpment bounding the eastern rim of the Derwent Valley. Easily attained, this superb high-level stroll is full of visual interest, visiting the Cowper Stone, a massive detached outcrop of gritstone, and Robin Hood's Cave, one of many local natural features with supposed connections to the folk hero. The cave was used surreptitiously by Sheffield-based climbers as an overnight shelter on climbing expeditions, during times when public moorland access was forbidden. On this airy section of the route, there are fine views across the valley to Eyam and Offerton moors as well as the more distant profiles of Win Hill, Lose Hill, Mam Tor and Kinder Scout.

Right: Discarded mill stones at Stanage Edge.
Opposite page left: Upper Burbage Bridge East.
Opposite page right: Stanage Edge.

GPS waypoints

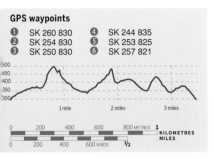

❶	SK 260 830	❹	SK 244 835
❷	SK 254 830	❺	SK 253 825
❸	SK 250 830	❻	SK 257 821

Carl Wark

Carl Wark (also known as Carl's Wark), a rocky promontory of millstone grit approximately 755 feet (230m) long by 197 feet (60m) wide, can be observed well from Higger Tor, lying just ¼ mile (400m) to the south. Although lower than Higger Tor, it stands proud of the surrounding expanse of heathery Hathersage Moor. The low natural cliffs are surrounded by a high wall of massive boulders, suggesting a defensive encampment, but Carl Wark's purpose and date of construction is uncertain. It may date from the Iron Age, or possibly have Bronze Age origins, but there is no evidence of any permanent settlement.

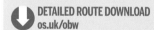

Lose Hill

WALK 60

PEAK DISTRICT NATIONAL PARK

DIFFICULTY ●●

START Edale

DISTANCE 6 miles (9.7km)

HEIGHT GAIN 1,650 feet (505m)

APPROXIMATE TIME 3½ hours

ROUTE TERRAIN Generally good moorland tracks, field paths and lane

PARKING Car park south of the village by Edale station

OS EXPLORER OL1

OS PATHFINDER Peak District

⬇ **DETAILED ROUTE DOWNLOAD** os.uk/obw

Lose Hill was gifted to G.H.B. Ward, one of the prime activists for access to the Peak District moorland and participant in the mass trespass of Bleaklow, a forerunner of the Kinder Scout mass trespass. Lose Hill has since assumed iconic status and marks the culmination of a classic Peak District walk. The route begins from Edale and climbs to the long ridge of high ground separating the Vale of Edale from Castleton, which nestles at the head of the Hope Valley; there are stunning views almost every step of the way. The high points of Mam Tor and Hollins Cross are traversed along the ridge, and the route doubles back to Hollins Cross from Lose Hill to drink in views in the opposite direction, before descending to cross the River Noe and return to Edale. Hollins Cross stands on a high pass at a junction of ancient paths, one of which was a medieval coffin route along which mourners from Edale carried their dead for burial in Castleton.

Right: Mam Tor and Great Ridge.
Opposite page left: Old Roman Road at Win Hill.
Opposite page left: Misty morning in Hope Valley.

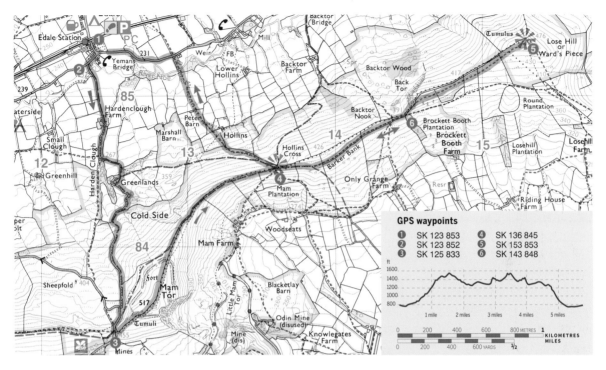

GPS waypoints

❶	SK 123 853	❹	SK 136 845
❷	SK 123 852	❺	SK 153 853
❸	SK 125 833	❻	SK 143 848

The Manifold Valley

PEAK DISTRICT NATIONAL PARK

DIFFICULTY ●●

START Wetton

DISTANCE 6½ miles (10.5km)

HEIGHT GAIN 1,420 feet (435m)

APPROXIMATE TIME 3½ hours

ROUTE TERRAIN Field paths, with one steep descent into Ecton, and a valley trail along the trackbed of a former railway

PARKING Village-edge car park at Wetton

OS EXPLORER OL24

OS PATHFINDER More Peak District

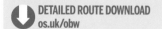 **DETAILED ROUTE DOWNLOAD** os.uk/obw

The Manifold is one of the lesser-known valleys of the White Peak area and is aptly named, since the River Manifold forms a whole series of folds or loops through attractive limestone scenery along its length. From Wetton, the walk takes an undulating course across the fields, passing the ruins of abandoned copper mines and eventually climbing to a most dramatic and expansive viewpoint overlooking the Manifold valley. After a steep descent into the dale at Ecton, there is a lovely walk along the Manifold Track, a disused railway line that keeps alongside the winding river. Created in 1937 by Staffordshire County Council, the Manifold Way follows the disused Leek and Manifold Light Railway, a single-track line that had a brief 30-year career but is now a splendid passage for walkers and cyclists. Later, the walk passes the mightily impressive Thor's Cave, inhabited during prehistoric times and, without doubt, the dominant feature of the surrounding landscape.

Right: River Manifold at Wetton.
Opposite page top: Manifold Trail.
Opposite page bottom: Manifold and Dove valleys.

Yorkshire Dales National Park

The predominantly Carboniferous limestone geology of the Yorkshire Dales creates scenery that is unlike most parts of Britain: a place of few soaring crags – although Malham Cove is a notable exception – but blessed with a labyrinth of caverns formed by long-gone subterranean rivers; these are topped by gleaming spreads of limestone pavement.

The Dales were fashioned by glaciers, ancient rivers and waterfalls; today, broadleaved woodlands stand in stark contrast to stone-built villages and the legacy of mine workings and rural industries. This is a traditional farming landscape of field barns, drystone walls and hay meadows that, in spring, are flower-rich, aromatic and loud with bird-song.

The principal dales – Wharfedale, Wensleydale, Swaledale, Ribblesdale and Airedale – are well known, but there are more than 50 dales in total to explore, including Barbondale in the north-west, added to the National Park only in 2016; Lonsdale, shaped by the River Lune on its journey to Lancaster, and the lush farmlands of Langstrothdale at the top end of Wharfedale, through which the Dales Way middle-distance trail finds a way. Curiously, the stunning scenery and green meadows of Nidderdale were not included in the National Park when it was formed in 1954, and so this dale has had to settle for AONB status, but that makes it no less eminently walkable.

Limestone isn't the only characteristic rock here; in places, darker millstone grit outcrops can be seen above the landscape, capping the summits of the famous 'Three Peaks' (Ingleborough, Whernside and Pen-y-ghent) and forming bizarre collections of boulders, such as the Brimham Rocks near Pateley Bridge. Elsewhere, near Ingleton, stand groups of isolated granite boulders, known as the Norber Erratics, carried here by long-retreated glaciers.

For the walker, the Dales are an easy-going wonderland – although bad weather can inspire darker moments – and offer endless trails, many along ancient highways and drove roads, and all with a stunning sense of openness, of big skies and rippling moorlands. Such is the attraction of the Dales for walkers, that three nationally important trails pass through them: the Pennine Way, the Dales Way and the trans-England Coast-to-Coast walk, each exposing differing aspects of the region and offering the scope to return and explore more widely.

AMAZING BUT TRUE ...
Parts of the film *Harry Potter and the Deathly Hallows Part 1* were filmed on the limestone pavement at the top of Malham Cove. This is the rocky camp where Harry and Hermione hide from Voldemort.

Malham Cove, Gordale Scar and Janet's Foss

YORKSHIRE DALES NATIONAL PARK

DIFFICULTY ●●

START Malham

DISTANCE 5 miles (8km)

HEIGHT GAIN 640 feet (195m)

APPROXIMATE TIME 2½ hours

ROUTE TERRAIN Field paths, Pennine Way track, lanes and one steep, stepped path

PARKING Village-edge car park, south of Malham

OS EXPLORER OL2

OS PATHFINDER Short Walks Yorkshire Dales

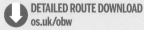 **DETAILED ROUTE DOWNLOAD**
os.uk/obw

This justifiably popular walk offers spectacular scenery with breathtaking views above Malham Cove's huge amphitheatre, a sharp contrast to the darker confines of Gordale, where a lusty waterfall cascades into the gorge. Lower down, it is the same stream that tumbles picturesquely over Janet's Foss, from where a delightful return stroll beckons through woodland and meadows. Malham Cove is the finest limestone cirque in Britain, 250 feet (76m) high and extending 1,000 feet (305m) around the head of the valley. It is part of the Craven Fault, which is revealed in the lines of sheer scars that dominate the area. At one time, a waterfall cascaded over its lip, fed by Malham Tarn, 1¼ miles (2km) to the north. The water now falls into a swallow hole, just south of the lake, leaving this fascinating example of a dry valley. Janet's Foss is interesting for its tufa formation, a residue of fragile limestone left behind by evaporating water collecting on the mosses around the lip of the fall.

There is one steep, stepped path to negotiate on this route; you should also take care on unguarded cliff edges and slippery rocks.

Right: Janet's Foss waterfall.
Opposite page top: Malham Cove and Malham Beck.
Opposite page bottom: Gordale Scar.

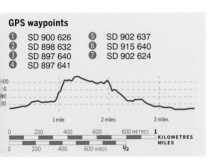

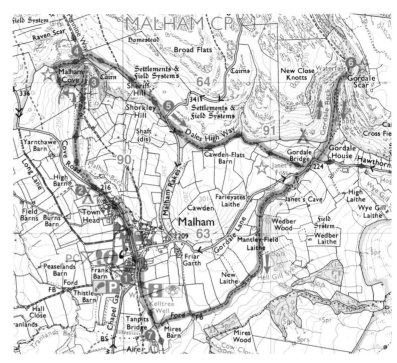

Pen-y-ghent

WALK 63

YORKSHIRE DALES NATIONAL PARK

DIFFICULTY ●●

START Horton-in-Ribblesdale

DISTANCE 6 miles (9.5km)

HEIGHT GAIN 1,610 feet (490m)

APPROXIMATE TIME 3½ hours

ROUTE TERRAIN Good moorland paths and tracks, including the Pennine Way

PARKING Horton-in-Ribblesdale

OS EXPLORER OL2

OS PATHFINDER Yorkshire Dales

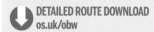

DETAILED ROUTE DOWNLOAD os.uk/obw

Like an ancient galleon, Pen-y-ghent's two-tiered prow sails purposefully across the surrounding countryside, drawing thousands to its top each year. This highly distinctive summit is the lowest of the Yorkshire 'Three Peaks', but it is the only one on the Pennine Way, used here on the climb up. As the crow flies, it lies barely two miles (3.2km) from the valley of the Ribble, which it overlooks, and its ascent need occupy little more than half a day. Midway to Pen-y-ghent, there's a chance to visit a magnificent pot hole called Hull Pot. In dry weather, no water enters the pot, but, when it is wet, with upstream sinks constricted, the resulting waterfall in Hull Pot is a splendid sight. Despite its massive size, there are times, perhaps only once or twice a year, when the pot fills up completely. Normally all the water sinks beneath the boulders, but, in times of full flood, the water overflows down the dry valley.

Right: Hull Pot.
Opposite page left: Path to Pen-y-ghent.
Opposite page right: View from Pen-y-ghent.

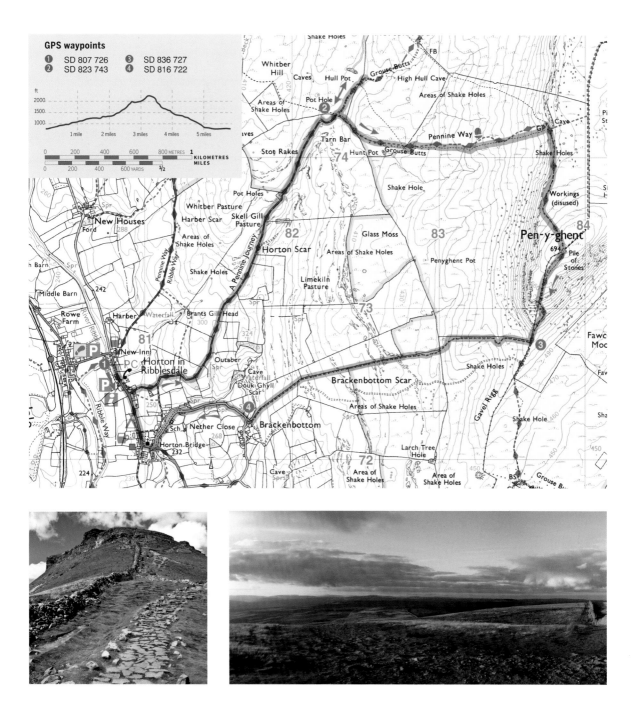

GPS waypoints

① SD 807 726 ③ SD 836 727
② SD 823 743 ④ SD 816 722

Gunnerside, Kisdon and Muker

YORKSHIRE DALES NATIONAL PARK

DIFFICULTY ●●●

START Gunnerside

DISTANCE 11¼ miles (18km)

HEIGHT GAIN 1,790 feet (545m)

APPROXIMATE TIME 6 hours

ROUTE TERRAIN Moorland, field and riverside paths, and a lane

PARKING Parking area at Gunnerside

OS EXPLORER OL30

OS PATHFINDER Yorkshire Dales

DETAILED ROUTE DOWNLOAD
os.uk/obw

Opposite page: River Swale.

Linking three of upper Swaledale's delightful villages, this lengthy walk is relatively easy and most agreeable. With the River Swale a near-constant companion, the route explores one of the most outstanding regions of the Yorkshire Dales. It affords magnificent high- and low-level views of Swaledale, taking in a great variety of riverside meadows, moorland fringes, woods, waterfalls and a taste of the Pennine Way long-distance trail.

The village of Gunnerside dates from the time the dale was settled by the Vikings; its name derives from 'Gunner's saetr', meaning 'Gunner's dwelling place'. In the 19th century, the village was at the centre of an important lead-mining industry largely concentrated in Gunnerside Gill to the north of the settlement, which still bears the resulting scars and remains. Today, Gunnerside enjoys all the appeal of a typical Dales village: attractive stone cottages clustered around and radiating from a central square, exquisitely positioned above the River Swale.

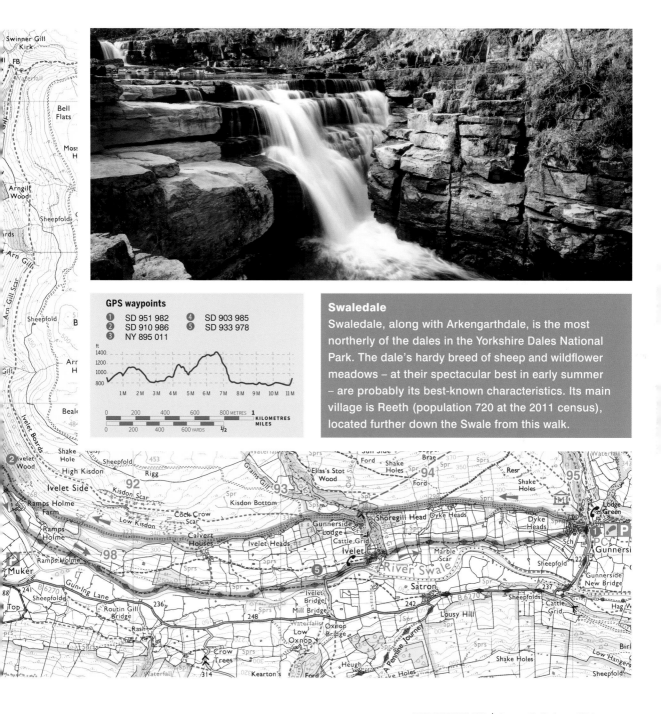

GPS waypoints

1. SD 951 982
2. SD 910 986
3. NY 895 011
4. SD 903 985
5. SD 933 978

Swaledale

Swaledale, along with Arkengarthdale, is the most northerly of the dales in the Yorkshire Dales National Park. The dale's hardy breed of sheep and wildflower meadows – at their spectacular best in early summer – are probably its best-known characteristics. Its main village is Reeth (population 720 at the 2011 census), located further down the Swale from this walk.

Areas of Outstanding Natural Beauty

Among the Areas of Outstanding Natural Beauty in the north of England, Arnside and Silverdale, and the Forest of Bowland are closest both to my heart and my home. Arnside is a gem, a place of panoramic views, stunning sunsets and the vastness that is Morecambe Bay. This daunting expanse draws thousands of people annually, who join one of the guided walks across the bay.

Arnside and Silverdale offer a delectable walker's habitat of limestone pavements, flower-rich meadows and easy-going ways across farmland that has retained the traditional practices of drystone walling and hedge laying. The RSPB reserve at Leighton Moss draws visitors throughout the year, and there are woodlands to explore too.

The Forest of Bowland, in contrast, is a gritty place of rocky outcrops, open heather moorland and peaty hollows. But it is far from being a dismal place; rather its deeply incised cloughs and semi-natural wooded valleys are a draw for walkers, botanists and birdwatchers. From the M6 motorway, Bowland doesn't present its best face, but closer investigation reveals myriad joys, tangled trails and endless airy rambles.

Nidderdale lies out with the Yorkshire Dales National Park, but no self-respecting walker should ignore it on that count. Here deep, wooded dales, reservoirs and the long dale of the Nidd itself are captivating. Millstone grit dominates the geology, giving a solemn appearance to buildings and walls, but, in summer, the heather moorlands and lush grasslands make such a difference, bringing colour and animation.

This flamboyant beauty repeats itself in the unspoilt scenery of the North Pennines, the second largest of all the AONBs. High Cup Nick and Cross Fell draw walkers from the west, while High Force (*left*), Upper Teesdale and lead-mining Allendale are easily accessible from the east. It was on Cross Fell, the highest of the Pennine mountains, that I first saw dotterel, a lovely, delicate bird of the uplands; all the more pleasing to spot due to its rarity.

> **AMAZING BUT TRUE ...**
> The north of England AONBs are host to red squirrels, otters, bittern, marsh harriers, rare Arctic plants and 80% of England's black grouse population. They are also where you'll find England's highest single-drop waterfall, Hardraw Force.

Leighton Moss

WALK 65

ARNSIDE AND SILVERDALE AONB

DIFFICULTY ●

START Yealand Storrs

DISTANCE 4½ miles (7.3km)

HEIGHT GAIN 345 feet (105m)

APPROXIMATE TIME 2½ hours

ROUTE TERRAIN Woodland and field paths and nature reserve trails

PARKING Limited roadside parking near the start

OS EXPLORER OL7

OS PATHFINDER Lancashire

⬇ DETAILED ROUTE DOWNLOAD
os.uk/obw

The Arnside and Silverdale AONB fully deserves its designation for it is indeed outstanding, natural and beautiful. There's plenty of evidence in this short, circular walk from Yealand Storrs, which makes its way through undulating limestone landscapes and visits the popular bird-watching arena of Leighton Moss, noted for bittern, marsh harrier and bearded tit. Leighton Moss is the largest remaining reed bed in north-west England, with shallow meres and fringing sedge and woodland that, in addition to birds, attract roe and red deer. The diverse flora, butterflies and other insect life seen en route make this a walk to be savoured on a warm, sunny day. In sharp contrast is the former Trowbarrow Limeworks, which is passed half way round this circuit, where tarmacadam was invented around 1898. Originally called 'quarrite', the mix of graded limestone chippings and hot tar was found to produce an ideal road surface.

Right: Eurasian bittern.
Opposite page left: Marsh harrier.
Opposite page right: Bird hide at Leighton Moss RSPB.

GPS waypoints

1. SD 493 761
2. SD 483 765
3. SD 476 766
4. SD 480 755
5. SD 492 746

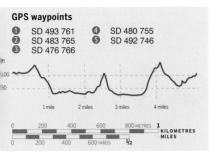

Leighton Hall

Leighton Hall, passed near the end of the walk, is the historic seat of the Gillow family. There has been a fortified manor here since 1246 and the present Adam-style house dates from 1763, when the parkland was also laid out and woodlands planted. The nationally rare high brown fritillary butterfly is found here. Violets, the food plant of the butterfly larvae, grow in the actively coppiced woodland and in the cracks of the naturally occurring limestone pavements on the estate.

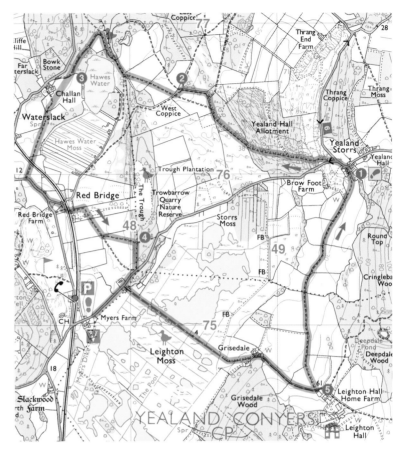

Kirkham Priory and the River Derwent

HOWARDIAN HILLS AONB

DIFFICULTY ●

START Kirkham

DISTANCE 4¾ miles (7.6km)

HEIGHT GAIN 280 feet (85m)

APPROXIMATE TIME 2½ hours

ROUTE TERRAIN Woodland and field paths, lanes and riverside path

PARKING Kirkham Priory car park

OS EXPLORER 300

OS PATHFINDER Vale of York and Yorkshire Wolds

 **DETAILED ROUTE DOWNLOAD** os.uk/obw

The extensive ruins of Kirkham Priory stand in a lovely position above the River Derwent and date from 1125. The priory was founded for Augustinian canons by Walter l'Espec, who held Helmsley Castle to the north. Legend has it that he endowed the land in memory of his only son, whose untimely death followed a riding accident here. Parts of the church and monastic buildings remain, but the most impressive feature of the ruin is the ornate late 13th-century gatehouse. From the priory, the walk crosses Kirkham Bridge and ascends through Oak Cliff Wood, before falling across the fields and lanes on the west side of the Derwent valley to return along the riverside path. The high ground affords excellent views across the Vale of York to the Yorkshire Wolds and over the Howardian Hills; towards the end of the walk, the ruins of Kirkham Priory make a fine picture on the opposite bank of the Derwent.

Right and **opposite page left**: Ruins at Kirkham Priory.
Opposite page right: Bridge over River Derwent.

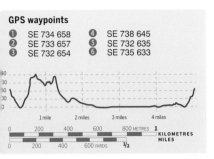

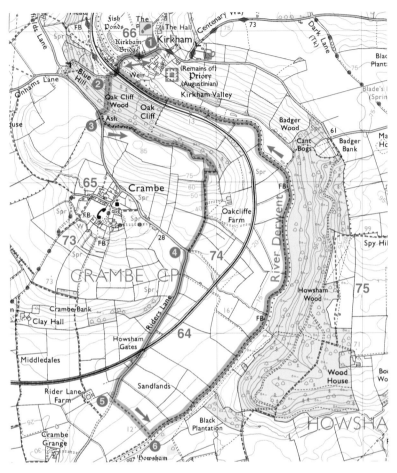

Kirkham Bridge

The Grade II-listed Kirkham Bridge, spans the River Derwent. Constructed in gritstone ashlar, it was built by John Carr in 1806. The bridge has one pointed arch and two segmental arches, the supports of which carry refuges for pedestrians. It was repaired in 2018 following damage caused by a heavy goods vehicle.

High Cup Nick

NORTH PENNINES AONB

DIFFICULTY ●●●

START Dufton

DISTANCE 8 miles (12.9km)

HEIGHT GAIN 1,445 feet (440m)

APPROXIMATE TIME 4 hours

ROUTE TERRAIN Lane, surfaced track and well-defined moorland track that's part of the Pennine Way

PARKING Dufton

OS EXPLORER OL19

OS PATHFINDER Durham, North Pennines and Tyne and Wear

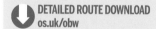
DETAILED ROUTE DOWNLOAD
os.uk/obw

The deep, narrow and almost perfectly geometrically U-shaped chasm of High Cup Gill is one of the great natural wonders of the Pennines. This there-and-back route walks along the Pennine Way from Dufton to High Cup Nick at the head of the chasm. For the whole descent back to the village, there are unbelievable views ahead across the Eden valley to the Lakeland fells on the horizon, with the conically shaped Dufton Pike nearer at hand and the village nestling below. The climb is steady and unremitting, but there are no steep or especially strenuous sections, and the route is along generally clear and well-defined tracks. The village of Dufton, its pub and red sandstone cottages grouped around a wide green with a Victorian drinking fountain, lies between two of the wildest, loneliest and most challenging sections of the Pennine Way.

There are precipitous drops along the higher sections of the walk, and the Helm wind blowing through the gap at High Cup Nick can be very strong, even on a seemingly still summer's day.

Right: High Cup Nick.
Opposite page: Cottages in Dufton.

Helm Wind

Helm Wind is a striking
enomenon in the Dufton
a and one of Britain's best
mples of a 'local wind',
ated by the area's topography
ng rise to atmospheric
ulence. In an easterly air flow
oss the UK, the Cross Fell
nge of the Pennine uplands
es the air to rise, cooling
Subsequently this colder air
cends steeply into the Eden
ey, displacing warmer air and
ding to local turbulence, which
es rise to the Helm Wind. In
n, the ascending warmer air
ls, leading to formation of
Helm Cloud, rising over the
nnine tops.

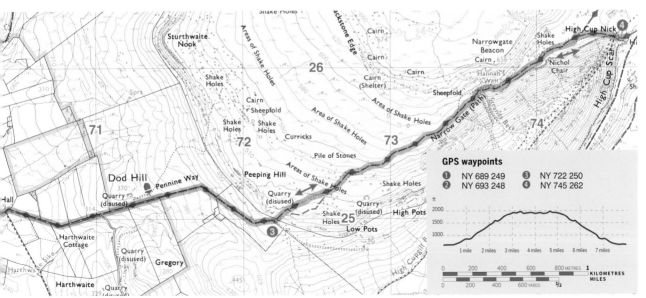

GPS waypoints

❶	NY 689 249	❸	NY 722 250
❷	NY 693 248	❹	NY 745 262

How Stean Gorge and Upper Nidderdale

NIDDERDALE AONB

DIFFICULTY ●

START Lofthouse

DISTANCE 4¼ miles (7km)

HEIGHT GAIN 670 feet (205m)

APPROXIMATE TIME 2½ hours

ROUTE TERRAIN Field and riverside paths and lanes

PARKING Small car park at Lofthouse; alternative car park at How Stean

OS EXPLORER OL30

OS PATHFINDER Yorkshire Dales

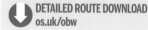
DETAILED ROUTE DOWNLOAD
os.uk/obw

How Stean Beck makes an impressive display as it bullies its way through a narrow gorge bound for the River Nidd, which it joins below the village of Lofthouse. This walk leaves Lofthouse to push through the dramatic How Stean Gorge. There's an outdoor activities centre here catering for rock climbers, canoeists and cavers, and there is an admission charge to see the narrow chasm close up. The walk then saunters up-dale along the Nidderdale Way to reach Middlesmoor. The village's hilltop churchyard is a place to pause and take in the beautiful views down the length of Nidderdale. The final section of the walk explores the course of the River Nidd, once more on the Nidderdale Way. This follows a track called Thorpe Lane, which crosses the Nidd (which does not always have water in it), and then mirrors its southbound line to run on a slightly elevated course along the valley slope above, leading directly back to Lofthouse.

Right: The village of Lofthouse.
Opposite page top: Middlesmoor church.
Opposite page bottom: View towards Middlesmoor in Nidderdale.

GPS waypoints

1. SE 101 735
2. SE 088 735
3. SE 092 743
4. SE 095 755
5. SE 099 758

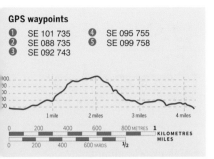

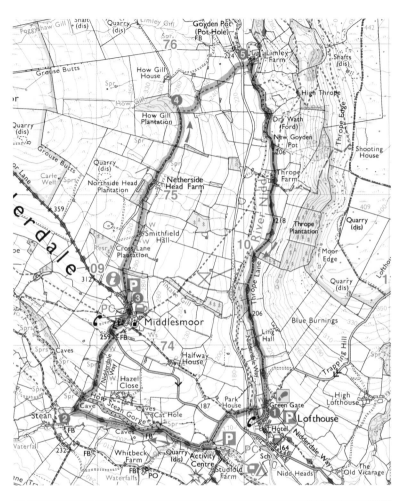

Lofthouse

Lofthouse is seemingly miles from anywhere, but a railway, which was laid at the beginning of the 20th century, once passed through the village. It carried construction materials to the Angram and Scar House Reservoirs being built at the head of Nidderdale, damming the headwaters of the River Nidd, but also brought passengers as far as Lofthouse. The line closed in 1936 when Scar House, the second of the two dams, was completed. There's a third reservoir, Gouthwaite, the largest of the trio, downstream of Lofthouse and north of Pateley Bridge.

Craster and Dunstanburgh Castle

NORTHUMBERLAND COAST AONB

DIFFICULTY ●

START Craster

DISTANCE 4¾ miles (7.6km)

HEIGHT GAIN 380 feet (115m)

APPROXIMATE TIME 2 hours

ROUTE TERRAIN Well-used tracks and field paths

PARKING Large car park on the village outskirts at Craster

OS EXPLORER 332

OS PATHFINDER Northumberland and Scottish Borders

DETAILED ROUTE DOWNLOAD
wos.uk/obw

Dunstanburgh Castle is an iconic feature of the Northumberland coast, reached here on a popular walk from the picturesque village of Craster. The aroma from Robson's smokehouse, famous for its oak-smoked Craster kippers, pervades the tiny harbour. The North Sea coast between Craster and Dunstanburgh is wild and scenically rough-hewn, and the coastal path is justifiably popular. Early mornings or late evenings are quiet, when misty light and long shadows add their own special quality, but the castle will be closed to visitors at such times. Begun around 1313 by Thomas, Earl of Lancaster, Dunstanburgh sits imposingly upon an outcrop of the Great Whin Sill volcanic intrusion. The castle's curtain walls enclose some 9 acres (3.6ha), heightening the natural defences of the sea cliffs and steep inland bank that protect it on three sides. The fortification remained impregnable until the Wars of the Roses, when it succumbed to the Ear of Warwick's pounding cannon. The walk cuts back cross-country over the fine vantage point of The Heughs.

Right: Dunstanburgh Castle.
Opposite page top: Rusted artefact on Craster harbour wall.
Opposite page bottom: Craster harbour.

Craster kippers

Craster kippers are famous the world over. Tucked away behind the small fishing harbour is Robson's smokehouse. The original smokehouses here have been in continuous use for 130 years and the traditional method of oak smoking kippers and salmon has been a family-operated business for four generations. Freshly caught herring are firstly split, a task undertaken in times past by 'herring girls' but now done by machine. Then the herring are soaked in a specially prepared brine solution and hung on hooks in the smokehouses, where fires of whitewood shavings and oak sawdust smoulder away for up to 16 hours.

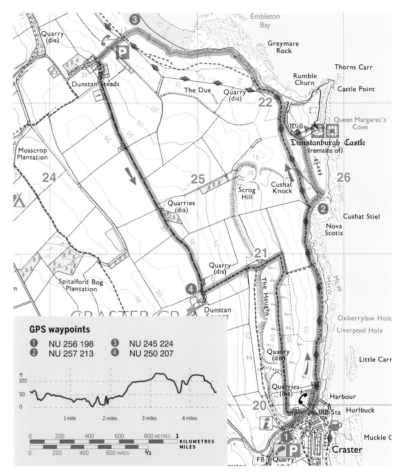

GPS waypoints

❶	NU 256 198	❸	NU 245 224
❷	NU 257 213	❹	NU 250 207

UNESCO World Heritage Sites

The need to keep barbarians at bay was the incentive behind the building of the Romans' epic coast-to-coast wall across northern England. But the legionaries who manned the wall could never have imaged that, 2,000 years or so later, their handiwork would prove an attraction in itself. Or, indeed, that the entire length of the wall would become a popular long-distance walk, as well as providing feeder circuits into the countryside to both the north and the south.

Contrary to popular belief, this was not the northernmost border in Roman Britain. Around the year AD142, the Roman Emperor Antoninus Pius ordered the construction of a wall across the central belt of Scotland, from the Firth of Forth to the Clyde. Together, both walls are included within UNESCO World Heritage citation for the international 'Frontiers of the Roman Empire'. At a more prosaic level, Birdoswald, Housesteads, Chester and Corbridge serve as perfect bases for radiating trails.

Of more recent design, Studley Royal Park, which includes the ruins of the 12th-century Fountains Abbey (*left*), provides several excellent rambles both within and around the deer park. There are no mountain heights here, but the surroundings are every bit as pleasurable for walking, featuring an 18th-century landscaped garden and canal, some of the largest Cistercian ruins in Europe, an Elizabethan/Jacobean mansion and the Victorian (St Mary's) church, one of the finest Gothic works of William Burges. Studley is among the few great 18th-century gardens to survive in its original form, an outstanding example of the development of the English style of garden, whose influence spread to parts of western Europe.

A far cry from the rural landscapes of Hadrian's Wall and Studley Royal Park, the castle in the city of Durham, easily visited as part of a town walk, was the stronghold and residence of the Prince-Bishops of Durham, who were granted virtual autonomy in return for protecting the northern boundaries of England. Within the precinct of the castle, Durham Cathedral, built under the orders of William the Conqueror to house the bodies of St Cuthbert and the Venerable Bede, is testimony to the importance of the early Benedictine monastic community. Today, it is the largest and finest example of Norman architecture in England.

> **AMAZING BUT TRUE ...**
> Hadrian's Wall took around 15,000 legionaries – the citizen-soldiers of the Roman army – about six years to build. Auxiliary soldiers from across the Roman Empire were garrisoned here, far away from their homelands.

WALK 70 Fountains Abbey

STUDLEY ROYAL PARK (UNESCO)

DIFFICULTY ●

START Fountains Abbey

DISTANCE 5¾ miles (9.3km)

HEIGHT GAIN 550 feet (165m)

APPROXIMATE TIME 3 hours

ROUTE TERRAIN Parkland and field paths and tracks

PARKING Visitor centre car park, Fountains Abbey

OS EXPLORER 298

OS PATHFINDER North East England Heritage Walks

DETAILED ROUTE DOWNLOAD
os.uk/obw

Although roofless, the great Fountains Abbey is still a splendid sight, tucked in a valley below the eastern fringe of the Pennines. It was founded in 1132, when 13 dissident monks from the Benedictine abbey of St Mary's in York sought the simpler life originally envisaged by St Benedict. Medieval monks tamed the surrounding landscape, but the parkland and water gardens seen today are an aesthetic creation undertaken in the 18th century by John Aislabie and his son William. John Aislabie was Chancellor of the Exchequer under Prime Minister Robert Walpole. He inherited Studley Royal in 1693 and began transforming the Skell valley into a visionary water garden. William continued his father's work, incorporating the ruins of the neighbouring abbey after purchasing the Fountains estate in 1768. This picturesque parkland walk crosses the deer park to meander its way through the lower valley on the return; it crosses higher ground to the south giving views over the abbey and Fountains Hall.

Right: Benedictine monks at Fountains Abbey.
Opposite page top: River Skell with Fountains Abbey in the distance.
Opposite page bottom: Fountains Abbey.

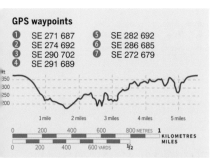

GPS waypoints

①	SE 271 687	⑤	SE 282 692
②	SE 274 692	⑥	SE 286 685
③	SE 290 702	⑦	SE 272 679
④	SE 291 689		

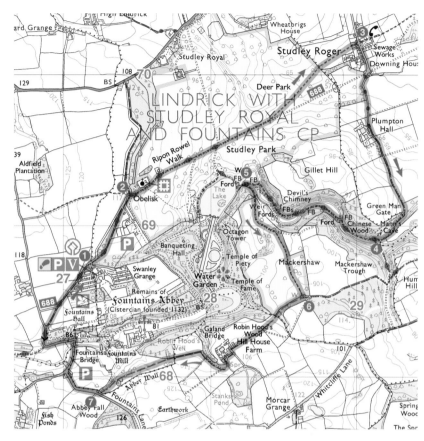

Durham – Riverside and Woods

DURHAM CASTLE AND CATHEDRAL (UNESCO)

DIFFICULTY ●

START Market Place, Durham

DISTANCE 5 miles (8km)

HEIGHT GAIN 215 feet (65m)

APPROXIMATE TIME 2½ hours

ROUTE TERRAIN Roads and pavements, surfaced riverside track, field and woodland paths

PARKING Durham

OS EXPLORER 308

OS PATHFINDER Durham, North Pennines and Tyne and Wear

 DETAILED ROUTE DOWNLOAD os.uk/obw

Although it passes through much attractive riverside and woodland scenery, it is the magical finale of this walk that makes it so special: the classic view of the towers and walls of Durham Cathedral and Castle rising majestically above the wooded cliff of the River Wear; this must surely rank as one of the grandest scenes in the country. Durham Cathedral is a masterpiece of Norman architecture, widely regarded as among the finest in Europe. The Galilee Chapel at the west end is the burial place for the Venerable Bede. Although it has been much altered over the centuries, Durham Castle retains its basic Norman plan. Together they symbolise the twin powers of the medieval bishops of Durham, military as well as spiritual, for they were the prince bishops, entrusted by the king to protect the area from Scottish invaders. The walk passes Maiden Castle, a prehistoric fort, and the University Botanic Garden and City Boathouse.

Right: Framwellgate Bridge with Durham Castle and Cathedral above.
Opposite page: Durham Cathedral.

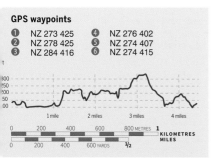

GPS waypoints

1. NZ 273 425
2. NZ 278 425
3. NZ 284 416
4. NZ 276 402
5. NZ 274 407
6. NZ 274 415

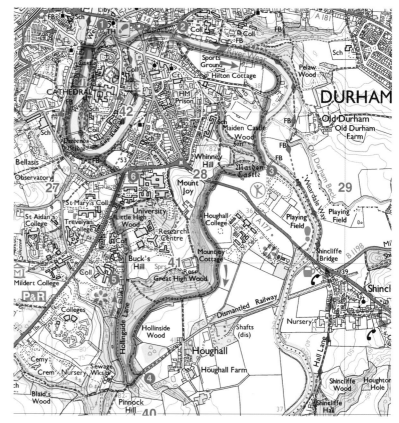

Durham World Heritage Site

Durham World Heritage Site was added to the UNESCO List in 1986. The site includes the Cathedral, among the finest Norman cathedrals in Europe; the Shrine of St Cuthbert, the final resting-place of this most revered of English saints inside the Cathedral; and Durham Castle, more than 900 years old and still retaining the basic plan of the original Norman castle, but internally transformed when it became part of Durham University from 1840.

WALK 72

Hadrian's Wall at Walltown and Thirlwall Castle

FRONTIERS OF THE ROMAN EMPIRE (UNESCO)

DIFFICULTY ●●

START Walltown Quarry, signed from Military Road (B6318), 1 mile (1.6km) east of Greenhead

DISTANCE 7¾ miles (12.5km)

HEIGHT GAIN 1,020 feet (310m)

APPROXIMATE TIME 3½ hours

ROUTE TERRAIN A section of Hadrian's Wall Path, rugged moorland paths, field paths and lanes; Tipal Burn's stepping stones may occasionally be flooded

PARKING Walltown Quarry car park

OS EXPLORER OL43

OS PATHFINDER Northumberland and Scottish Borders

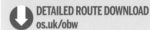
DETAILED ROUTE DOWNLOAD
os.uk/obw

Right: Hadrian's Wall above Walltown Quarry.
Opposite page: Thirlwall Castle.

Those following Hadrian's Wall from the west get their first appreciation of its awesome scale at Walltown. This walk allows exploration of the Roman wall at first hand and the opportunity to call in at the Greenhead Roman Army Museum to learn about the lives of the men stationed along this distant frontier of the Roman Empire. The route follows one of the most rugged sections of the wall; a century of quarrying the Whin Sill dolerite has added extra drama to the scene by creating an abrupt cliff at the end of the crag. The walk passes King Arthur's Well, reputedly the spot where Paulinus baptised King Edwin prior to his marriage with Princess Ethelberga of Kent in AD596. In addition, this walk takes in some of the countryside on both sides of the wall, visits medieval Thirlwall Castle, constructed from stone repurposed from the Roman wall, and goes past the industrial remains of a limekiln near Walltown.

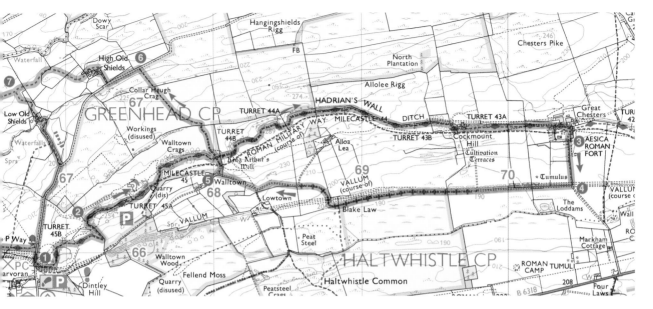

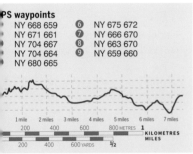

eat Chesters

Great Chesters stand the ruins
a Roman infantry fort, which is
aller and with fewer remains above
und than at Housesteads. Much
the perimeter wall can be seen
d outlines of many of the buildings
hin the compound. A stone arch,
t of the vaulting for a strong room,
vell and a pedestal altar are of
rticular interest.

WALES

The Walks

Top: Waterfalls Walk.
Bottom: Saundersfoot
and Tenby.
Previous page: Snowdonia
National Park.

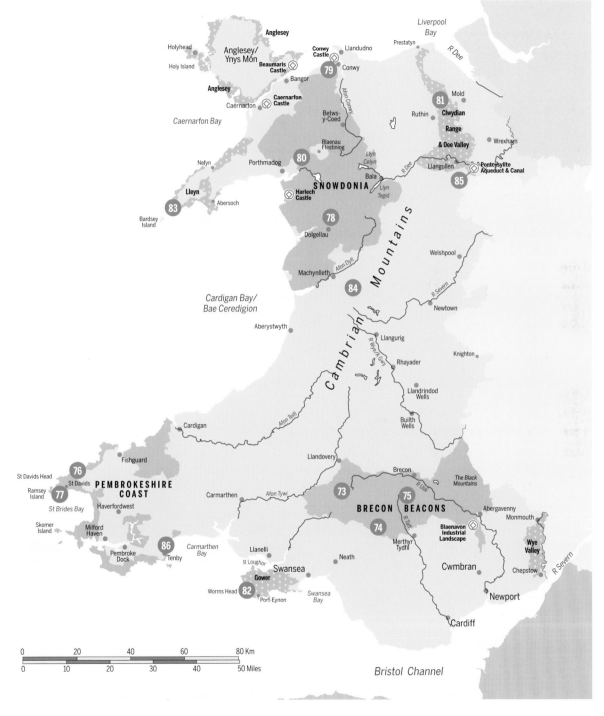

Liverpool
Bay

Holyhead

Anglesey

Anglesey/
Ynys Môn

Holy Island

Anglesey

Caernarfon

**Caernarfon
Castle**

Caernarfon Bay

Nefyn

Lleyn

Abersoch

Bardsey
Island

Llandudno

**Conwy
Castle**

Prestatyn

R Dee

Conwy

Bangor

**Beaumaris
Castle**

79

81

Mold

Betws-
y-Coed

Ruthin

Clwydian

Range

Blaenau
Ffestiniog

Afon Conwy

& Dee Valley

Wrexham

80

Llyn
Celyn

R Dee

Llangollen

**Pontcysyllte
Aqueduct & Canal**

Porthmadog

SNOWDONIA

Bala

85

**Harlech
Castle**

Llyn
Tegid

78

Dolgellau

83

St Davids Head

Ramsey
Island

Skomer
Island

Welshpool

Afon Dyfi

84

Machynlleth

Cardigan Bay/
Bae Ceredigion

C
a
m
b
r
i
a
n

M
o
u
n
t
a
i
n
s

Newtown

R Severn

Aberystwyth

Llangurig

R Wye/A Gwy

Knighton

Rhayader

Llandrindod
Wells

Afon Teifi

Cardigan

Builth
Wells

Fishguard

St Davids

76

77

**PEMBROKESHIRE
COAST**

St Brides Bay

Haverfordwest

Milford
Haven

86

Pembroke
Dock

Tenby

Carmarthen Bay

Llandovery

Carmarthen

Afon Tywi

73

Brecon

R Usk

The Black
Mountains

75

BRECON BEACONS

Abergavenny

Monmouth

74

**Blaenavon
Industrial
Landscape**

**Wye
Valley**

Llanelli

R Loughor

Neath

Merthyr
Tydfil

R Taff

Cwmbran

Chepstow

R Severn

Swansea

82

Gower

Worms Head

Port-Eynon

Swansea
Bay

Newport

Cardiff

Bristol Channel

0	20	40	60	80 Km

0	10	20	30	40	50 Miles

Brecon Beacons National Park

Anyone wandering up the easy slopes to Corn Du and Pen y Fan from the Storey Arms Outdoor Centre to the south may wonder what is so special about these mountains that brings the military to train here. But when you see the steep escarpments of Craig Cwm Sere and Craig Cwm Cynwyn and the great spread of steep-sided valleys reaching northwards like stubby fingers you gain an altogether different impression. Tackle them from Brecon and the River Usk to the north, and it becomes possible to fashion quite a few horseshoe circuits – up one ridge and down another.

The National Park contains four distinct upland areas. The Brecon Beacons (Bannau Brycheiniog) per se are roughly in the middle, with Pen y Fan as their highest point. To the west lies Fforest Fawr, the Great Forest, and, beyond that but arguably still within Fforest Fawr, lies Mynydd Du, the Black Mountain, of which the most prominent feature is the long escarpment running north from Glyntawe to Fan Brycheiniog and Bannau Sir Gaer. I walked that escarpment one hot and memorable day, and concluded it by skinny dipping in Llyn y Fan Fach.

AMAZING BUT TRUE ...
Llangorse Lake (Llyn Syfaddan) has a man-made island in the middle of it; it is Wales' only crannog and is believed to have been the home of Welsh royalty for over 1,000 years.

Amid this broad expanse of rolling mountains, a dedicated walker can find endless trails, some easy, some more demanding. There are lakes, forests, beauty spots and secret places; there are long trails, such as the Beacons Way, and short walks to mountain waterfalls and hidden lakes. Indeed, water is a feature everywhere, not least at the southern edge of Fforest Fawr, where a spread of rivers – Mellte, Hepste, Pyrddin and Nedd Fechan – provide a seemingly endless display of waterfalls.

One of my fondest memories, however, doesn't involve a particularly high summit. It came at the end of a superb day crossing Hay Bluff and Twmpa, when I spent an hour watching the sun go down, as I dangled my feet over the escarpment of Pen Rhos Dirion, while buzzards and gliders fought for airspace, and wild ponies placidly munched their way across the moorland just a few feet behind me. As darkness fell, it soon became clear why, many years later, the Brecon Beacons would become the world's fifth International Dark Sky Reserve, attracting hikers keen to indulge in the current vogue for walking on clear, star-filled nights.

Llyn y Fan Fach and the Carmarthen Fans

BRECON BEACONS NATIONAL PARK

DIFFICULTY ●●●

START Near Llanddeusant

DISTANCE 6 miles (9.7km)

HEIGHT GAIN 2,130 feet (650m)

APPROXIMATE TIME 4 hours

ROUTE TERRAIN Mountain and moorland paths, sometimes faint, sometimes pathless, and steep-going in places; return from Llyn y Fan Fach on a broad track

PARKING Off a track leading on from the dead-end lane east from Llanddeusant

OS EXPLORER OL12

OS PATHFINDER Brecon Beacons

 **DETAILED ROUTE DOWNLOAD**
os.uk/obw

The Black Mountain, the western-most massif of the Brecon Beacons National Park, is often described as its last surviving wilderness. This route ascends to walk along the crest of the sweeping, craggy escarpments known as the Carmarthen Fans, which tower commandingly above glistening Llyn y Fan Fach and its surrounding peaty upland plateau. It links a spectacular ridge-top path with a good waterworks track to create an extremely rewarding circuit, the high points being the cairned summits of Fan Foel and Bannau Sir Gaer.

Llyn y Fan Fach is associated with a mythical story about a lady of the lake who appeared to a shepherd named Rhiwallon. He fell in love with her, and she agreed to marry him, but only on the condition that he should never strike her with iron. Alas, he did not keep his promise. This long-told tragic tale of love and loss may have its origins in early Iron Age Britain, where there was mistrust of the new iron-working settlers by Bronze Age people.

Right: Llyn y Fan Fach.
Opposite page: Welsh Mountain ponies.

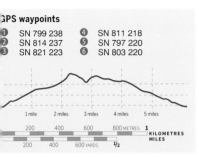

GPS waypoints

1	SN 799 238	**4**	SN 811 218
2	SN 814 237	**5**	SN 797 220
3	SN 821 223	**6**	SN 803 220

Llyn y Fan Fach

Llyn y Fan Fach is often referred to as the magic lake after a mythical story of a lady of the lake with healing powers. The story may well have its origins in the Iron Age period as it is likely that a Bronze Age lady would have had a good understanding of healing using natural medicines. But what is particularly interesting about this version of the tale is that from the mid-12th century there actually was a line of successful herbalist physicians operating from nearby Myddfai.

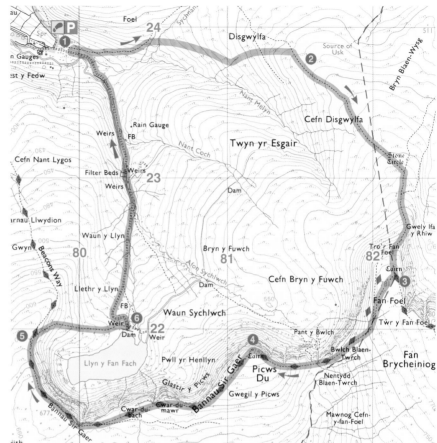

Waterfalls Walk

BRECON BEACONS NATIONAL PARK

DIFFICULTY ●●●

START Cwm Porth

DISTANCE 9 miles (14.5km)

HEIGHT GAIN 2,100 feet (640m)

APPROXIMATE TIME 5 hours

ROUTE TERRAIN Clear but rough paths with some very steep and exposed sections and a slippery section around the back of a waterfall

PARKING Car park on minor road, 1 mile (1.6km) south of Ystradfellte

OS EXPLORER OL12

OS PATHFINDER Brecon Beacons

DETAILED ROUTE DOWNLOAD
os.uk/obw

There can be few more exhilarating and satisfying walks than this. On the southern edge of Fforest Fawr, where the sandstone that underlies most of the National Park gives way to limestone, the rivers Mellte, Hepste, Pyrddin and Nedd Fechan plunge over a series of waterfalls, forming the highest concentration of falls in Wales. All are spectacular, but probably the most exciting part of the walk comes when you walk behind the great sheet of water at Sgŵd yr Eira. The walk is lengthy and quite energetic, with plenty of ascents and descents and some fairly difficult sections over rocky terrain and muddy paths, some above very steep drops. Take your time and watch your step, for this is a walk to be enjoyed to the full and worth taking slowly. Half way round, the circuit runs into the village of Pontneddfechan, where the Angel Inn is ideally placed for a mid-walk refreshment break.

Right: Sgŵrd yr Eira.

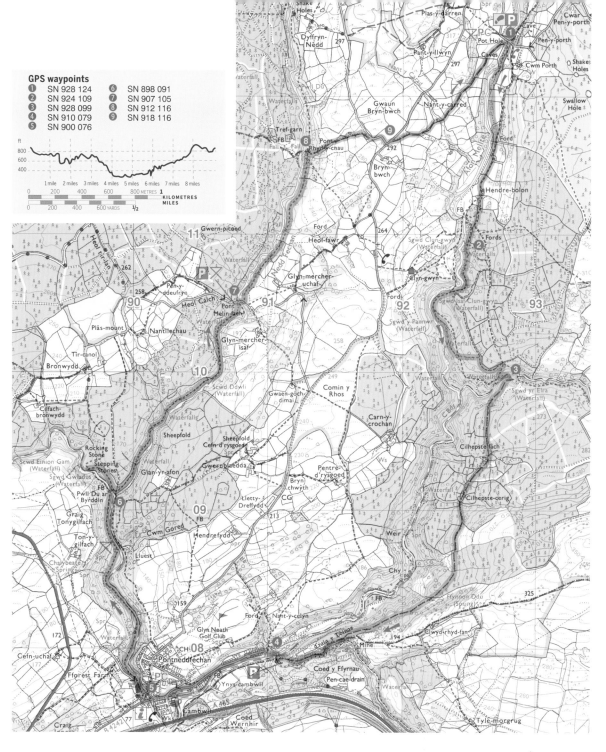

GPS waypoints
1 SN 928 124   6 SN 898 091
2 SN 924 109   7 SN 907 105
3 SN 928 099   8 SN 912 116
4 SN 910 079   9 SN 918 116
5 SN 900 076

Brecon Beacons Horseshoe

BRECON BEACONS NATIONAL PARK

DIFFICULTY ●●●

START Cwm Gwdi

DISTANCE 8½ miles (13.7km)

HEIGHT GAIN 2,890 feet (880m)

APPROXIMATE TIME 5 hours

ROUTE TERRAIN Mainly good paths over high mountains but one short untracked section and some steep climbs and drops; the return leg follows quiet, narrow lanes

PARKING Car park in Cwm Gwdi

OS EXPLORER OL12

OS PATHFINDER Brecon Beacons

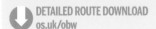

DETAILED ROUTE DOWNLOAD
os.uk/obw

This is, quite simply, the finest mountain walk in South Wales and one of the best in Britain. A lengthy, gradual, steadily ascending approach leads to Cribyn, then the final climb up to its summit (2,608 feet, 795m) is steep and exhausting. A descent into a col is followed by another steep, though short, pull up to Pen y Fan (2,907 feet, 886m), the highest point in the Brecon Beacons and the most elevated in Britain south of Snowdonia. A much gentler descent and ascent leads on to the distinctive flat summit of Corn Du (2,863 feet, 873m). The return route drops down to the beautiful little lake of Llyn Cwm Llwch, and this is followed by a relaxing walk through the lovely valley of Cwm Llwch. *This is a walk worth taking plenty of time over; the approach and return are every bit as enjoyable as the three peaks themselves and the views are magnificent. Do not attempt in poor visibility, unless you are experienced in navigation in such conditions, using a map and compass.*

Right: View from Pen y Fan.

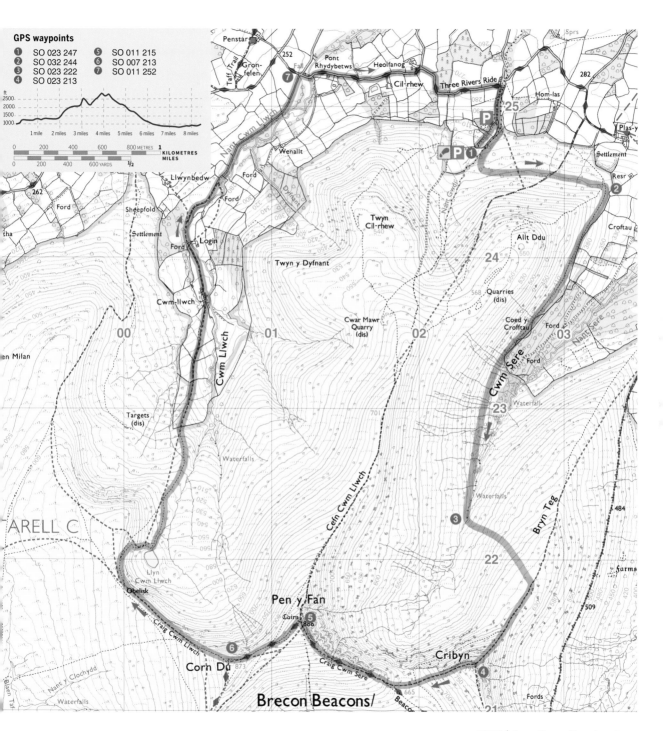

GPS waypoints

1. SO 023 247
2. SO 032 244
3. SO 023 222
4. SO 023 213
5. SO 011 215
6. SO 007 213
7. SO 011 252

Pembrokeshire Coast National Park

It was the coastline – a wild landscape of rugged cliffs, wooded estuaries, sandy beaches and windswept inland hills – that was the key factor in the establishment of this National Park in 1952; it remains Britain's only coastal National Park.

My introduction to the Pembrokeshire coast came north of St David's, parked up at Abereiddi beach and walking along the coast to Porthgain. The reason for the visit escapes me, but the walk, albeit brief, was a splendid circuit of seascapes and industrial archaeology – slate was quarried here, which is typical of the area. Arguably there is no view that better sums up this coastline than that of the boulder-strewn rough pastures from Penllechwen, near St David's Head.

What makes the National Park especially important is that it embraces many sites of national or international conservation significance, including seven Special Areas of Conservation, a Marine Nature Reserve, six National Nature Reserves, 75 Sites of Special Scientific Interest, and almost 40 beaches recommended by the Marine Conservation Society.

Although it is branded as a 'coastal' park, it has inland attractions, too. In the north, Carn Llidi, Pen Beri and Garn Fawr, backed by the moorlands on Mynydd Carningli and Mynydd Preseli, give a mountainous feel to the landscape. To the south, the Castlemartin Peninsula, west of Pembroke, is a place of limestone plateaux and cliffs, steep-sided wooded valleys and lakes. And, for a day of easy, urban walking, a visit to the cathedral and medieval buildings of St David's combines historical and architectural appeal in a way that is hard to better in Wales.

Dotted about the landscape you will find evidence of its fascinating past: burial mounds, Celtic crosses, Iron Age hill forts, Norman castles, medieval churches and Victorian forts. And with over 595 miles (950km) of public footpaths and bridleways, there is no shortage of places to go.

Porthgain and Abereiddi

PEMBROKESHIRE COAST NATIONAL PARK

DIFFICULTY ●

START Porthgain

DISTANCE 3½ miles (5.6km)

HEIGHT GAIN 260 feet (80m)

APPROXIMATE TIME 2 hours

ROUTE TERRAIN Pembrokeshire Coast Path, field paths and farm tracks prone to mud

PARKING Porthgain

OS EXPLORER OL35

OS PATHFINDER Pembrokeshire and Carmarthenshire

 DETAILED ROUTE DOWNLOAD os.uk/obw

This delightful strip of coastline has to be among the most stunningly scenic on the whole of the Pembrokeshire Coast Path. Porthgain is both quaint and fascinating in equal measure, and Abereiddi, with its eye-catching turquoise pool (known as the 'blue lagoon', slate quarry ruins and Gothic-looking folly, offers plenty of opportunity for exploration. Between the two, there is a section of typically rugged coast, interspersed with beautiful and often deserted beaches.

Porthgain was once a thriving centre for brick-making and for quarrying. Evidence of this industrial past is plain to see, with the tall red-brick ruins of the old storage hoppers towering above the quay, the visible remains of a dismantled railway and ruined buildings up on the hill above the village.

Steps give easy access to the beach at Traeth Llyfn. At the next headland, Carn Lwyd, there are wonderful views to Trwyn Castell and Abereiddi Tower; the rocks on its summit make a great place to take a rest.

Right: Blue lagoon, Abereiddi.
Opposite page left: Derelict brick hoppers at Porthgain.
Opposite page right: Porthgain harbour.

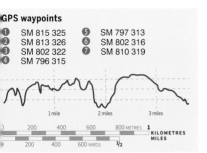

1 mile   2 miles   3 miles

| 200 | 400 | 600 | 800 METRES | 1 |
200   400   600 YARDS   ½

KILOMETRES
MILES

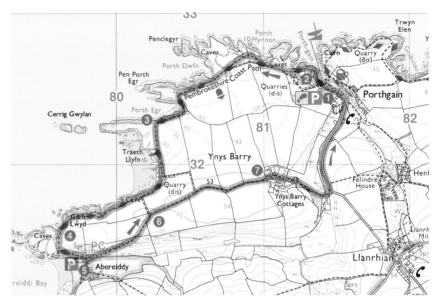

he Pembrokeshire Coast Path

he Pembrokeshire Coast Path, walked
etween Porthgain and Abereiddi,
as opened in 1970 as a National
rail following the establishment of
e Pembrokeshire Coast National
ark in 1952. Its course follows
e coastline of Pembrokeshire
with a few inland detours) for 186
iles (almost 300km) between
oppit Sands, near St Dogmaels on
ardigan Bay in the north, to Amroth
Carmarthen Bay in the south. The
oastal scenery is wide ranging and
unning, including rugged limestone
iffs, volcanic headlands, sheltered
d sandstone coves, drowned
acial river valleys and more than 50
aches and a dozen harbours.

St David's, Porth Clais and Ramsey Sound

PEMBROKESHIRE COAST NATIONAL PARK

DIFFICULTY ●●●

START St David's

DISTANCE 9 miles (14.5km)

HEIGHT GAIN 770 feet (235m)

APPROXIMATE TIME 4½ hours

ROUTE TERRAIN Pembrokeshire Coast Path, farmland tracks and lanes

PARKING Main car park on the eastern outskirts of St David's

OS EXPLORER OL35

OS PATHFINDER Pembrokeshire and Carmarthenshire

 DETAILED ROUTE DOWNLOAD os.uk/obw

The cathedral and medieval buildings nestling in St David's, the smallest city in Britain, add immense historical and architectural appeal to a coastal walk of the finest scenic quality. This is a long but relatively easy-going walk on an outstandingly wild and beautiful coastline between St Non's Bay and Porthstinian, beginning from the home of the Welsh patron saint and the holy city of Wales. Although seemingly remote, St David's was an important centre of the Celtic world in the Dark Ages, lying at the crossing of routes linking Wales, Ireland, England and Brittany. St David references abound. St Non, mother of St David, is traditionally associated with St Non's Chapel (the ruins of which can be visited upon reaching the coast path). This was the birthplace of St David around AD500; the adjacent well is alleged to have sprung up at the same time. Later, the walk visits St Justinian's Chapel, built on the site of a Celtic chapel founded by St Justinian, friend and colleague of St David.

Opposite page left: St David's Cathedral.
Opposite page right: Porthclais harbour.

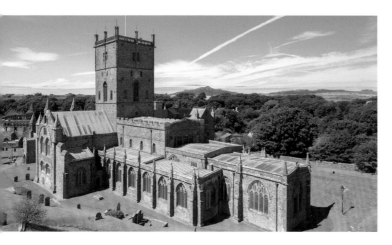

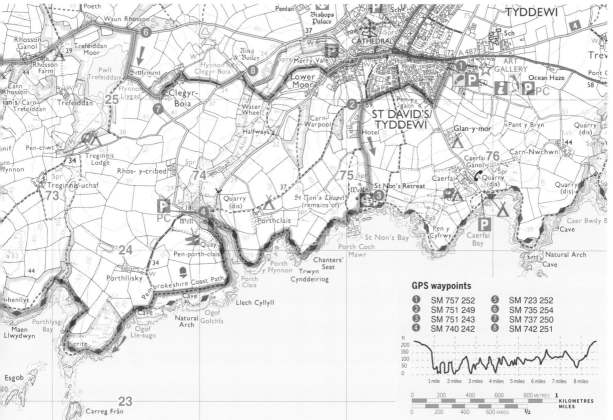

GPS waypoints

① SM 757 252 ⑤ SM 723 252
② SM 751 249 ⑥ SM 735 254
③ SM 751 243 ⑦ SM 737 250
④ SM 740 242 ⑧ SM 742 251

Snowdonia National Park

It was in Snowdonia that I found my mountain feet and took the first steps that have since led me on numerous winding trails. From my living room in Bangor, the heights of Eryri, as the northern part of today's Snowdonia was once known, ranged across the southern skyline, throwing down a challenge it was impossible to resist. Within three months I had somehow threaded my way through the rugged and broken ranges to reach the top of all of them – and lost my way more than once, for good measure.

From the Cantilever on Glyder Fach, the view southwards is across a rippling, tormented landscape of exquisite appeal, a scene of fecund greenness held in place by gaunt, rocky peaks, looking like a crumpled blanket hung out to dry, from which all the water is draining away.

Yet the mountainous characteristics of Snowdonia, used as a training ground by those with ambitions to reach the top of the world, is disproportionate to the height of its mountains; although Yr Wyddfa (Snowdon) is the highest peak in England and Wales, few others exceed 3,000 feet (914m). The distorted impression of height is due to the fact that most of the mountain uplands are bare of trees and offer no measure of scale. Between the fury of the wind and the attentions of sheep, trees are unable to survive, and so, the lonely grey lakes, harsh boulder-strewn slopes and tundral heights stand bare and elemental. Gone are the great fastnesses of ancient oak, ash, rowan and birch that once covered the slopes; gone, too, are the eagles that once flew among these mountains.

Despite the ruggedness of much of Snowdonia – there are places where you really do feel the power of the rocky landscape, there is also scope for less demanding, low-level leisure walks, suitable for all the family and for those less able, too. Nor should it be assumed that 'Snowdonia' means just the area around the mountain: this vast National Park reaches from the shores of the Conwy Estuary to the mouth of the River Dovey (Dyfi), south-west of Machynlleth, offering the walker a variety of contrasting landscapes and an essential, primordial beauty that it is hard to match elsewhere.

AMAZING BUT TRUE ...

The Snowdon lily (*Lloydia serotine*) is a delicate Arctic–Alpine flowering plant that can be found in only one place in Britain: Snowdonia. Here they grow in inaccessible cracks and crevices on north-facing cliffs.

Precipice Walk

SNOWDONIA NATIONAL PARK

DIFFICULTY ●

START National Park car park, 2½ miles (4km) north of Dolgellau

DISTANCE 3½ miles (5.5km)

HEIGHT GAIN 705 feet (215m)

APPROXIMATE TIME 2 hours

ROUTE TERRAIN Rugged and uneven hill paths

PARKING National Park car park

OS EXPLORER OL18

OS PATHFINDER Snowdonia

DETAILED ROUTE DOWNLOAD
os.uk/obw

This is one of the classic short walks of Snowdonia and is entirely on courtesy paths owned by the Nannau Estate, which permits public access. *It is important that the Countryside Code is observed, in particular that walkers keep to the waymarked paths and close gates.* Nannau House was built in 1693 and belonged to the Vaughan family, owners of the estate, until the 1960s. The views on this walk are magnificent, constantly changing as the route follows a circuit around the slopes of Foel Cynwch and Foel Faner; every bend reveals new vistas over the Arans, Coed y Brenin Forest, the Mawddach valley and estuary, and Cadair Idris. The precipice itself is the western section of the walk, high above the Mawddach, along a path believed to have been made by sheep. The final section is along the lovely shores of Llyn Cynwch. The path surfaces are often uneven – watch your footing as well as the scenery.

Right: View from Precipice Walk.
Opposite page: Llyn Cynwch.

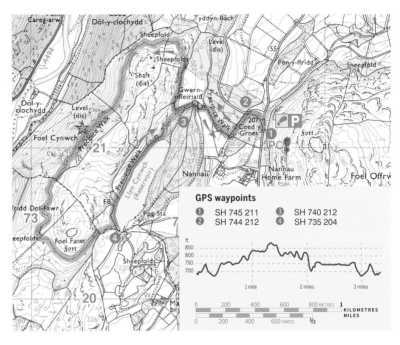

GPS waypoints

❶	SH 745 211	❸	SH 740 212
❷	SH 744 212	❹	SH 735 204

Afon Mawddach

Magnificent views of the Mawddach river and over the Mawddach estuary are to be gained along the Precipice Walk. Rising high in the Snowdonia National Park near Dduallt, the river is 28 miles (45km) long. Downstream of Penmaenpool the Mawddach opens out into a broad, sandy estuary, and the small town of Barmouth is located at its mouth on Barmouth Bay. The 18th century saw the peak of ship building on the estuary, but very little evidence remains of this once important activity. Today the river sustains a salmon and trout fishery.

On the estuary's north bank is the village of Bontddu. It is set against hills that were at the centre of a goldrush in the 19th century. Prospectors discovered gold in the area in 1834 while digging for copper. Dolgellau, the main town of the area, enjoyed a brief boom as miners and fortune seekers flooded into the area from 1860 until the turn of the 20th century, but by the 1920s the industry had all but disappeared. The gold is renowned for its light colour and has been used to fashion royal wedding rings.

Conwy Mountain and Sychnant Pass

SNOWDONIA NATIONAL PARK

DIFFICULTY ●●

START Conwy town centre

DISTANCE 6 miles (9.5km)

HEIGHT GAIN 1,215 feet (370m)

APPROXIMATE TIME 3 hours

ROUTE TERRAIN Field and moorland paths and tracks, lanes and pavement

PARKING Conwy

OS EXPLORER OL17

OS PATHFINDER North Wales and Snowdonia

DETAILED ROUTE DOWNLOAD
os.uk/obw

Conwy is an ancient market town and possibly one of the best medieval walled towns in Europe. Highlights include the castle, a 13th-century merchant's house, a 14th-century church, two 16th-century buildings – the town house, Plas Mawr, and the Quay House – and the smallest house in Britain, which has been lived in since the 16th century. This route ascends from King Edward I's castle on to the panoramic heights of Conwy mountain, the grandstand views including Conwy Bay, Great Orme and the eastern summits of Snowdonia National Park. There are numerous pathways across its breezy, gorse- and bracken-laden slopes, offering a range of delights such as ease of access, clear paths and easy-paced walking, allowing visitors to create many route variations. This walk rises to the top of the mountain, following a broad grassy way along its spine, before dropping to the Sychnant Pass (Bwlch Sychnant) and returning to Conwy through farmland pastures. The top of Conwy mountain is occupied by the remnants of over fifty Neolithic hut circles and by Castell Caer Seion, an Iron Age stone-walled hill fort.

Right: Conwy Castle.
Opposite page left: The smallest house in Britain.
Opposite page right: Heather and gorse on Sychnant.

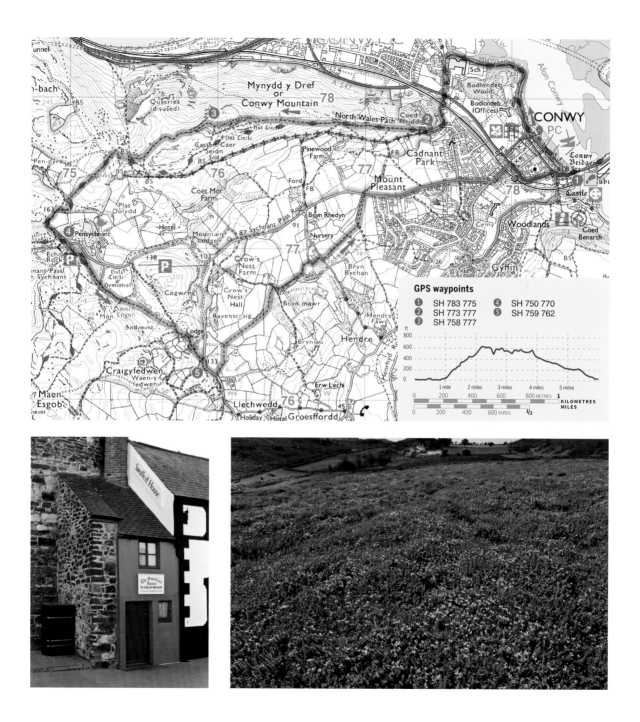

GPS waypoints

1	SH 783 775	4	SH 750 770
2	SH 773 777	5	SH 759 762
3	SH 758 777		

Cnicht

Rising to 2,265 feet (690m), Cnicht is possibly the most distinctive of all the Snowdonia peaks. The ascent from Croesor is rewarding and challenging, a deceptively easy initial section culminating in a steep scramble above sheer drops to gain the bristly summit. From this modest top are fabulous views to the Glyders, Snowdon, Moel Hebog, Cardigan Bay and the Lleyn Peninsula. Leaving Cnicht, a springy turf path falls towards Llyn yr Adar, and, at a large cairn, the route swings south-eastwards to reach evocative slate-quarrying remains, including the Rhosydd Incline. This gravity-operated incline opened in 1864 to link the slate quarry with the end of the Croesor Tramway, which carried slates to Porthmadog. On the return leg, there are splendid views along Cwm Croesor, a superb glaciated valley, towards the Hebogs, with Cnicht standing out prominently on the right.

This walk is best undertaken on a fine day, both for the remarkable views and to allow line-of-sight navigation near Llyn Cwm-corsiog. Some sections will be slippery underfoot in wet or cold weather; gradients are steep near the summit, and, between waypoints 4 and 5, the route may be boggy and is easy to lose.

Right: The slopes of Cnicht at Croesor.

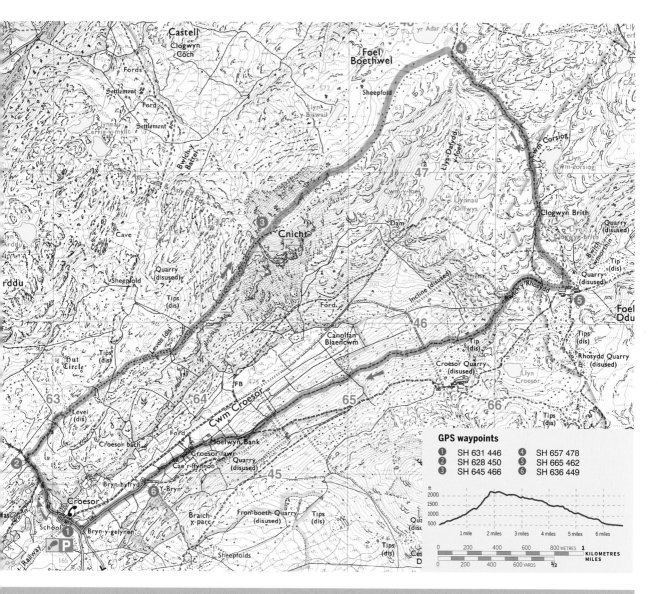

GPS waypoints

①	SH 631 446	④	SH 657 478
②	SH 628 450	⑤	SH 665 462
③	SH 645 466	⑥	SH 636 449

oesor

oesor is a small welsh-speaking village in Cwm Croesor,
g at the head of the valley road at the foot of Cnicht.
m Croesor is an example par excellence of a U-shaped,
aciated valley. Slate mining here dates back to the 1840s

with Croesor Quarry, a large underground slate mine,
coming into operation in 1865. This was productive until
closure in 1930. The main adit can still be seen, as can the
line of the Croesor Tramway, which is crossed in the walk.

Areas of Outstanding Natural Beauty

It was not until I was working on my Pathfinder guide to North Wales and Snowdonia that I reacquainted myself with Moel Famau, although I'd never forgotten the stirring sight, long ago, of an osprey migrating north to Speyside in Scotland, as I plodded up a stretch of Offa's Dyke Path to the summit.

Moel Famau is the highest point of the Clwydian Range and Dee Valley Area of Outstanding Natural Beauty (AONB) and is easily seen from the West Pennine Moors near my home. It is such a delightful and popular hill to amble up and offers a splendid view across Snowdonia, North Wales and back into my homeland beyond the Dee and the Mersey.

The 21-mile Clwydian Range, which rises above the Dee valley (*left*), is a stunning gathering of hills, forests and heathlands, with a history that reaches almost to the dawn of time. Designated an AONB in 1985, the area was extended in 2011 to embrace the Dee valley and the rocky plateau of Mynydd Eglwyseg, the Horseshoe Pass and Mynydd Esclushamnorth of Llangollen. The delight for walkers is that, while visitors from England head for Snowdonia, the bosom of the Clwydian Hills is left to the locals.

It wasn't until the 1980s that I 'discovered' the hills of the Lleyn Peninsula, large parts of which have been an AONB since 1956. I had an artist friend who lived in the Nantlle valley, and he would often show me his paintings of the sweeping slopes of Yr Eifl and Bwlch Mawr, so, I knew they were there; moreover, they were plainly visible from Anglesey, where I lived for a while.

But, sadly, in those days I had elevated altitude to an importance it doesn't deserve, and so the 1,850-foot (564-m) summit of Yr Eifl fell below my radar. That was a mistake. There are days of delectable wandering to be had here, even on the diminutive hills of Mynydd Ystum and Mynydd Rhiw and, especially, around the coastline near Aberdaron.

My introduction to the Gower Peninsula came at the behest of my first editor, who lived on the coast there. I was supposed to be interviewing her (for a change), so we walked as we talked, out to Llangennith Burrows and then looped northwards to Whiteford Sands. What a stunning eye-opener this stretch of coastline proved to be: I was talking about it for days.

Wales is also blessed with the stunning AONBs of the Isle of Anglesey and the Wye Valley – each wildly different, but both offering a wealth of outdoor pleasure.

> **AMAZING BUT TRUE ...**
> Despite all the places that might seem more suitable, the National Welsh Language Centre is based in a secluded Victorian quarrying village at Nant Gwrtheyrn on the Lleyn Peninsula (www.nantgwrtheyrn.org).

Moel Famau

CLWYDIAN RANGE AND DEE VALLEY AONB

DIFFICULTY ●●

START Woodland car park, Moel Famau

DISTANCE 5¼ miles (8.25km)

HEIGHT GAIN 1,265 feet (385m)

APPROXIMATE TIME 3 hours

ROUTE TERRAIN Offa's Dyke Path across heather moorland, woodland paths and forest tracks

PARKING Woodland car park, Moel Famau

OS EXPLORER 265

OS PATHFINDER North Wales and Snowdonia

DETAILED ROUTE DOWNLOAD
os.uk/obw

Moel Famau is the highest hill in the Clwydian Range and, at 1,817ft (554m), ranks as a Marilyn for hill-baggers. The hill gives its name to the country park here and is the centrepiece of the Clwydian Range and Dee Valley Area of Outstanding Natural Beauty. This walk has two distinct parts, beginning and finishing through woodland and plantations, but with a fine stretch of the 'Offa's Dyke Path National Trail between the two, ultimately giving access to the summit. This section offers fine far-reaching views of the rolling Denbighshire moorlands and to the distant mountains of Snowdonia. Looking back to the south on the ascent, Foel Fenlli is prominent, with Bron-y-felin to the west, both sites of Iron Age hill forts. The walking is gentle and invigorating, easing steadily upwards in easy stages to a final pull to the Jubilee Tower that crowns the top of Moel Famau. Built in 1810 in the style of a three-tiered Egyptian obelisk, it commemorates the Golden Jubilee of George III.

Right: Sunset at the top of Moel Famau.
Opposite page: Woodland at the base of Moel Famau.

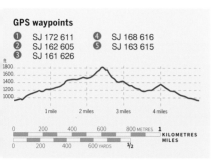

Bwlch Penbarra

Bwlch Penbarra is the first waypoint reached on the walk after a gradually rising climb from the start. 'Bwlch' in Welsh means 'pass' and is a common prefix in place names throughout the hilly and mountainous countryside of Wales.

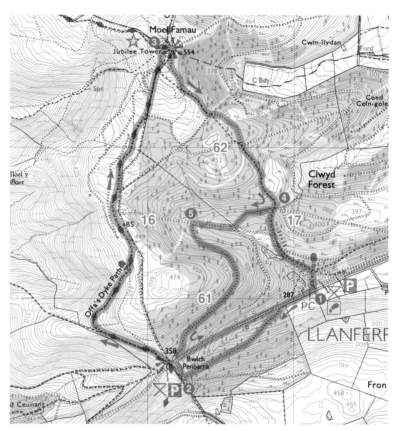

Llanmadoc Hill

GOWER AONB

DIFFICULTY ●●

START LLanmadoc

DISTANCE 6½ miles (10.5km)

HEIGHT GAIN 1,000 feet (305m)

APPROXIMATE TIME 3½ hours

ROUTE TERRAIN Field and hillside paths and tracks

PARKING Whiteford Beach car park

OS EXPLORER 164

OS PATHFINDER Gower, Swansea and Cardiff

DETAILED ROUTE DOWNLOAD
os.uk/obw

Llanmadoc is tucked away in the north-west corner of the Gower Peninsula, sheltered to the south by Llanmadoc Hill and overlooking the Loughor Estuary to the Carmarthenshire coast. Setting out from the village the walk passes around the National Trust's Cwm Ivy estate with views to the limestone crag of Cwm Ivy Tor and following the Wales Coast Path between Cwm Ivy Marsh and the woodland and dunes of Whiteford Burrows, a national nature reserve noted for its exceptional dune system which supports rare plants such as dune gentian. The second half of the walk ascends Llanmadoc Hill. At 610 feet (186m) above sea level it is not the highest point in Gower, but its relative isolation lends it an impressive grandeur. The fairly steep climb ends at a large Iron Age hill fort occupying the eastern end of the hill. Such forts were usually sited on the highest land, but this one stands at the lower end of the hill's spine, probably all the better for watching over the Loughor Estuary. There are 14 Bronze Age burial mounds across the hill.

Right: Whiteford Burrows.
Opposite page top: Llanmadoc church.
Opposite page middle: Cwm Ivy Woods.

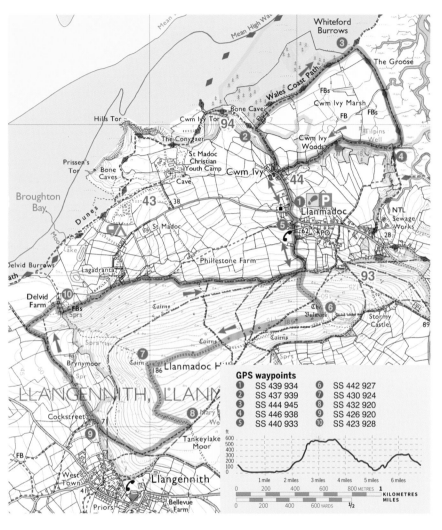

GPS waypoints			
① SS 439 934		⑥ SS 442 927
② SS 437 939		⑦ SS 430 924
③ SS 444 945		⑧ SS 432 920
④ SS 446 938		⑨ SS 426 920
⑤ SS 440 933		⑩ SS 423 928

Llanmadoc church

Llanmadoc church, dedicated to St Madoc, is the smallest church on the Gower Peninsula. The building is mostly 13th century. Two features of particular interest are the oak reredos, carved by the Reverend J. D. Davies, and a 6th-century inscribed stone. Madoc, the son of a Celtic king, studied in Ireland before coming to Wales, where he followed St David. He became Abbott of Glyn Rhosyn, founding the church here and monasteries in Ireland. His bones were laid to rest in Ireland in 626.

WALK
83

Aberdaron and Land's End

LLEYN AONB

DIFFICULTY ●●●

START Aberdaron

DISTANCE 7½ miles (12km)

HEIGHT GAIN 1,280 feet (390m)

APPROXIMATE TIME 4½ hours

ROUTE TERRAIN Clifftop path, sometimes rocky; field paths and lane

PARKING Aberdaron

OS EXPLORER 253

OS PATHFINDER North Wales and Snowdonia

 **DETAILED ROUTE DOWNLOAD** os.uk/obw

Follow in the footsteps of medieval pilgrims on their way to Bardsey Island on this fantastic coastal walk from Aberdaron around the tip of the Lleyn Peninsula, with breathtaking views to Bardsey Island and inland towards Snowdonia. *This walk is not recommended in strong winds; although it is not strenuous, there are a few places where the coastal path is narrow and slippery with sheer drops, and care is needed.* Aberdaron was the last stopping place for medieval pilgrims to Bardsey Island, and the 14th-century Y Gegin Fawr (The Old Kitchen), which gave them food and shelter, appropriately retains a similar function as a café for visitors today. The highest point on the walk is Mynydd Mawr, where there is an old coastguard lookout station. On fine days, there are immense views along the Lleyn Peninsula, across to the heart of Snowdonia and down the sweep of Cardigan Bay; on very clear days, the Wicklow mountains in Ireland can be seen.

Right: Lleyn Peninsula.
Opposite page left: Y Gegin Fawr.
Opposite page right: Bardsey Island.

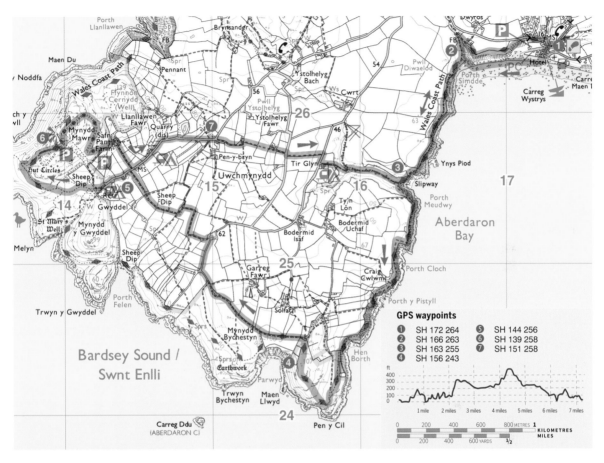

GPS waypoints

❶	SH 172 264	❺	SH 144 256
❷	SH 166 263	❻	SH 139 258
❸	SH 163 255	❼	SH 151 258
❹	SH 156 243		

Bardsey Sound /
Swnt Enlli

Aberdaron
Bay

UNESCO World Heritage Sites & National Trails

As the narrowboat edged its way across the Pontcysyllte Aqueduct (*left*; inscribed as a World Heritage Site in 2009), I was convinced we were doomed: there was no way the boat was going to fit. I was wrong, of course; boats have been successfully navigating this pioneering piece of engineering since 1805. Yet, even when I returned a few years later, having walked along the canal from Llangollen and then continued to the Ty Mawr Country Park, I was even less sure that the boat trip had been a good idea; we must have squeezed through by the skin of the boat's teeth.

At the time, I showed little appreciation for the handiwork of the aqueduct's creator, the seemingly ubiquitous Thomas Telford, but whether or not you are impressed by his monumental metal masterpiece, there can be no doubt that its setting is splendid. Small wonder then that those visitors who prefer to keep their feet on dry land choose to stroll along the canal – if you start in Llangollen, there is a bus back – test their mettle on a nearby stretch of the Offa's Dyke Path, or opt for something rather more gentle in Ty Mawr.

Along this stretch, the Vale of Llangollen is blessed with soaring and very steep-sided heights that give a stunning view not only of the valley, but also of the much-neglected Berwyn Hills to the south and the Clwydian Range to the north.

Offa's Dyke was an earthwork constructed in the late 8th century by King Offa of Mercia. Just as the earthwork closely follows the Anglo-Welsh border, so the National Trail – the Offa's Dyke Path – tries to maintain faith with the earthwork. From north to south, it runs from the seaside resort of Prestatyn to the Sedbury Cliffs on the River Severn, almost in the shadow of Chepstow's 11th-century castle.

This stunning walk is not the only long-distance trail in Wales. Near Welshpool, the Offa's Dyke Path joins forces with the Severn Way – a route I commend to everyone – and, at Knighton, it meets up with the Glyndŵr Way National Trail, which commemorates the 15th-century Welsh prince and folk hero Owain Glyndŵr. This, too, links with the Severn Way at various points. But the foremost of the Welsh National Trails is surely the Pembrokeshire Coast Path, 186 miles (299km) of undulating cliff-top scenery that now forms part of the Welsh Coast Path.

> **AMAZING BUT TRUE ...**
> With around 35,000 feet (11,000m) of height gain, the Pembrokeshire Coast Path matches the ascent of Everest. Fortunately, however, the highest point is 574 feet (175m), so altitude sickness is unlikely to be a problem.

Wynford Vaughan Thomas' Viewpoint

GLYNDŴR'S WAY NATIONAL TRAIL

DIFFICULTY ●●

START Aberhosan

DISTANCE 6 miles (9.7km)

HEIGHT GAIN 1,605 feet (490m)

APPROXIMATE TIME 3½ hours

ROUTE TERRAIN Clear tracks and lanes

PARKING Aberhosan, near the post bus stop

OS EXPLORER 215

OS PATHFINDER Mid Wales

 **DETAILED ROUTE DOWNLOAD** os.uk/obw

Rising along the finger-like ridge of Foel Fadian from the isolated hamlet of Aberhosan, this walk has as its objective the viewpoint and memorial toposcope dedicated to writer and broadcaster Wynford Vaughan Thomas, from where Snowdon is visible on a clear day. The walk passes beneath Foel Fadian's summit to return via Glyndŵr's Way.

One of Wynford Vaughan Thomas's favourite spots, the viewpoint lies beside the mountain road running between Machynlleth and Staylittle. An incongruously well-dressed crowd gathered at the unveiling of the memorial in May 1990. Its sculptured panel shows Wynford Vaughan Thomas in walking gear pointing to Snowdon.

Glyndŵr's Way is a 135-mile National Trail across Mid Wales, joining Welshpool, Machynlleth and Knighton. It is named after the last native-born Prince of Wales, Owain Glyndŵr, who at the turn of the 15th century led an initially successful revolt against the English, gaining control over much of Wales. Driven from his last remaining stronghold in 1409, he spent the last five years of his life in hiding.

Right: Wynford Vaughan Thomas's Viewpoint.
Opposite page: Wynford Vaughan Thomas.

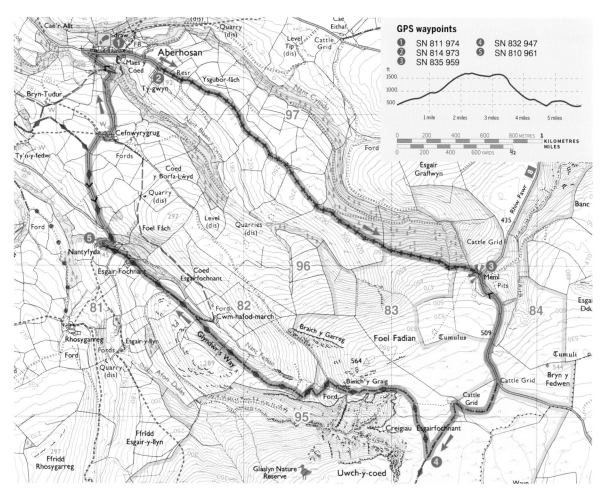

GPS waypoints

1	SN 811 974	4	SN 832 947
2	SN 814 973	5	SN 810 961
3	SN 835 959		

Wynford Vaughan Thomas

Wynford Vaughan Thomas 1908–87, was born in Swansea and after graduating in Modern History at Oxford University rose to prominence at the BBC. His rich and distinctive Welsh accent became synonymous with broadcasting commentaries from 1937.

He became famous as a war correspondent during World War Two, after which he broadcast on various nationally important events. He left the BBC to found a forerunner of ITV Wales and later became President of the Council for the Protection of Rural Wales.

Ty Mawr and the Pontcysyllte Aqueduct

PONTCYSYLLTE AQUEDUCT AND CANAL (UNESCO)

DIFFICULTY ●

START Ty Mawr Country Park

DISTANCE 5½ miles (9km)

HEIGHT GAIN 500 feet (150m)

APPROXIMATE TIME 3 hours

ROUTE TERRAIN Riverside path, field paths, lanes, pavement and canal towpath

PARKING Ty Mawr Country Park car park

OS EXPLORER 256

OS PATHFINDER North Wales and Snowdonia

 **DETAILED ROUTE DOWNLOAD** os.uk/obw

This offers agreeable and easy-paced walking beside the River Dee and along the towpath of the Llangollen branch of the Shropshire Union Canal. The visual highlight of the walk is the dramatic and towering Pontcysyllte Aqueduct spanning the Dee Valley. Designed by engineers Thomas Telford and William Jessop, it opened in 1805 following a 10-year construction period. Pontcysyllte Aqueduct crosses the River Dee at a height of 127 feet (38m) and is 1,007 feet (307m) long, a true marvel of the canal age and a giant technological feat in the early Industrial Revolution. It is the oldest and longest navigable aqueduct in Britain and the highest in the world. The iron trough containing the canal is supported by 18 stone columns. In season, public narrowboat trips are available from Llangollen along a 5-mile (8km) length of the Llangollen Canal World Heritage Site in the beautiful Vale of Llangollen. The aqueduct and canal received World Heritage Site status in 2009.

Right: Pontcysyllte Aqueduct.
Opposite page: Llangollen Canal.

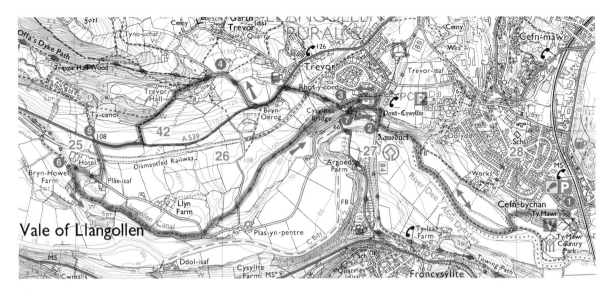

GPS waypoints

1. SJ 283 414
2. SJ 270 420
3. SJ 268 421
4. SJ 259 423
5. SJ 251 419
6. SJ 249 417
7. SJ 268 421

The River Dee

The River Dee (Afon Dyfrdwy in Welsh) flows through the Vale of Llangollen. The Llangollen Canal crosses over it on the soaring Pontcysyllte Aqueduct. The Dee rises in the Snowdonia National Park and flows for 68 miles (110km), draining eastwards to Chirk, swinging northwards to Chester and passing the Wirral into the Irish Sea. Historically it was the boundary of the Kingdom of Gwynedd.

Saundersfoot and Tenby

**PEMBROKESHIRE COAST PATH
NATIONAL TRAIL**

DIFFICULTY ●

START Saundersfoot

DISTANCE 4 miles (6.5km)

HEIGHT GAIN 1,085 feet (330m)

APPROXIMATE TIME 2½ hours

ROUTE TERRAIN Coastal path with woodland, field-edge, clifftop, shore and lane sections

PARKING Car park, Saundersfoot

OS EXPLORER OL36

OS PATHFINDER Pembrokeshire and Carmarthenshire

 **DETAILED ROUTE DOWNLOAD**
os.uk/obw

A linear walk between the two most popular and picturesque resorts on the south Pembrokeshire coast, Saundersfoot and Tenby. It starts in Saundersfoot and follows a sheltered, highly scenic and well-wooded section of the Pembrokeshire Coast Path to North Beach at Tenby. Public transport could be used for the return to Saundersfoot, as there is a bus service linking the two resorts. But the walk is a relatively modest undertaking and, if time permits, reversing the route to make the return (a total distance of 8 miles, 13km) and enjoying the coast path views from south to north is an attractive proposition.

Tenby was important in the Middle Ages as a busy port and staging-post between Bristol and Ireland. It has the largest parish church in Wales, dating from the 13th century and enlarged in the 15th century, reflecting the town's prosperity at that time. On the north side of Tenby's headland, attractive colour-washed Regency and Victorian houses overlook the harbour and glorious curving sandy beach.

Right: Tenby harbour.
Opposite page top: View from Monkstone Point.
Opposite page bottom: Rock pools on Saundersfoot beach.

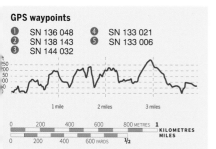

SCOTLAND

The Walks

Top: Falls of the Glasallt, Lochnagar.
Bottom: Loch an Eilein.
Previous page: Loch Lomond.

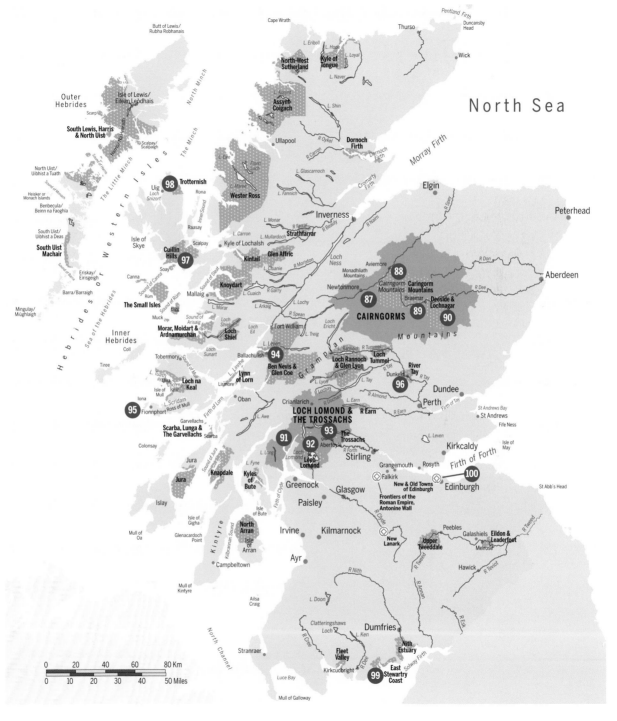

North Sea

Outer Hebrides

Butt of Lewis/
Rubha Robhanais

Cape Wrath

Pentland Firth

Thurso

Duncansby Head

Wick

North-West Sutherland

Kyle of Tongue

L. Hope

L. Loyal

L. Eriboll

L. Naver

Isle of Lewis/
Eilean Leòdhais

Scarp

98 Trotternish

Rona

Assynt-Coigach

L. Assynt

L. Shin

Ullapool

R Oykel

Dornoch Firth

L. Glascarnoch

Dornoch Firth

Morray Firth

Elgin

R Spey

Peterhead

South Lewis, Harris & North Uist

Taobh Tuath/Northton

Scalpay/
Scalpaigh

The Minch

L. Maree

Fionn Loch

Wester Ross

L. Fannich

L. Fannich

Cromarty Firth

Aberdeen

R Don

North Uist/
Uibhist a Tuath

Uig

Loch Snizort

Inner-Sound

L. Monar

L. Mullardoch

Strathfarrar

R Farrar

R Beauly

Inverness

Aviemore

R Nairn

Cairngorm Mountains

88

Cairngorm Mountains

R Dee

Heisker or
Monach Islands

Benbecula/
Beinn na Faoghla

South Uist/
Uibhist a Deas

Isle of Skye

Raasay

Scalpay

Kyle of Lochalsh

L. Carron

R Moriston

Loch Ness

Monadhliath Mountains

87

Cairngorm Mountains

89

Deeside & Lochnagar

Braemar

90

South Uist Machair

Cuillin Hills

97

Soay

Canna

Kintail

L. Cluanie

R Garry

Newtonmore

CAIRNGORMS

Mountains

Eriskay/
Eirisgeigh

Knoydart

Rùm

L. Cuaich

R Spean

Fort William

L. Ericht

Barra/Barraigh

The Small Isles

Muck

Eigg

Sound of Arisaig

R Arkaig

L. Lochy

L. Treig

Mingulay/
Miùghlaigh

Hebrides
or Western Isles

Sea of the Hebrides

Mallaig

L. Morar

L. Garry

L. Laggan

Grampian

L. Rannoch

R Tummel

Morar, Moidart & Ardnamurchan

L. Shiel

Loch Shiel

L. Eil

94

L. Leven

Loch Rannoch & Glen Lyon

Loch Tummel

R Tay

R Tummel

Inner Hebrides

Tobermory

Coll

Sound of Mull

Ben Nevis & Glen Coe

R Lyon

Dunkeld

River Tay

R Tay

Dundee

Tiree

Loch na Keal

Isle of Mull

Lynn of Lorn

Ballachulish

L. Lochy

L. Tay

96

Lismore

R Almond

Perth

Iona

Ross of Mull

Sound of Mull

Oban

Crianlarich

R Dochart

L. Earn

R Earn

St Andrews Bay

St Andrews

95

Fionnphort

Garvellachs

Scarba, Lunga & The Garvellachs

Scarba

LOCH LOMOND & THE TROSSACHS

R Earn

Fife Ness

Colonsay

Jura

Jura

L. Awe

91

Aberfoyle

93

The Trossachs

L. Leven

Kirkcaldy

Isle of May

92

Loch Lomond

Stirling

R Forth

Firth of Forth

Knapdale

Kyles of Bute

L. Fyne

Loch Lomond

Grangemouth

Falkirk

Rosyth

100

St Abb's Head

Islay

Greenock

Paisley

Glasgow

Clyde

New & Old Towns of Edinburgh

Edinburgh

Isle of Gigha

Isle of Bute

Irvine

Kilmarnock

Frontiers of the Roman Empire, Antonine Wall

Peebles

Galashiels

Eildon & Leaderfoot

R Tweed

Mull of Oa

Glenacardoch Point

North Arran

Isle of Arran

Ayr

New Lanark

Upper Tweeddale

R Tweed

Melrose

Kintyre

Kilbrannan Sound

Campbeltown

R Nith

Hawick

R Teviot

Mull of Kintyre

Ailsa Craig

L. Doon

Dumfries

R Annan

R Esk

North Channel

Stranraer

Clatteringshaws Loch

R Cree

R Ken

Fleet Valley

Nith Estuary

Solway Firth

Luce Bay

Kirkcudbright

R Dee

East Stewartry Coast

99

Mull of Galloway

0   20   40   60   80 Km

0   10   20   30   40   50 Miles

Cairngorms National Park

About 30 years ago, I was perched near the top of Cairnwell, a fine summit south of Braemar, eating a sandwich, when five of the nearby rocks got up and walked away. They were ptarmigan, in fact, and I hadn't seen them until they moved, but that memory has clearly stayed with me for a long time.

The Cairngorms are a haven for wildlife, and the high mountains, ancient forests, fields and moorlands are nationally and internationally important conservation areas. There are wildcats in the woods and osprey fishing the lochs. High-altitude birds, such as dotterel, golden plover, snow bunting and ptarmigan, are found here, as are others that hide themselves across the moors and in the forests: capercaillie, red grouse and black grouse.

The National Park is hugely diverse, a living, working landscape that embraces magnificent forests, wetlands, rivers and glens, heathered moorlands, farms and crofts. Yet, perhaps more so than any other place in Britain, the high Cairngorms pose a threat for walkers that cannot be ignored: their seemingly benign uniform slopes succumb easily to a steady plod, and, on a fine day, there is no better setting. But, many have died on these mountains and continue to do so; in winter, there is a tundral bleakness here that is Arctic in its intensity.

For the mountain-bagger, 43 Munros await, including five of the six highest mountains in Britain. But the process of becoming an all-round walker means knowing when to opt for low-level alternatives to mountain heights. Fortunately, the National Park is more than the sum of its parts, and the scope for enjoyable walks through glens and forests far outweighs the temporary inaccessibility of the Cairngorm plateau in poor conditions. There are many waymarked walks through the Rothiemurchus Forest and wild walks in Glen Feshie, for example, and competent map readers will have no difficulty picking out the ancient drove roads and passes by which cattle were brought to Lowland markets for sale.

And, in this wild and rugged setting, a contemplative walker will also see how the landscape is constantly changing and evolving: some of the forests present today barely existed 100 years ago, while the great Caledonian forest of old, which would have covered hundreds of square miles, is now all but gone.

> **AMAZING BUT TRUE ...**
> In his excellent book, *Feral*, George Monbiot argues the case for the reintroduction of lynx, beaver and wolf into the Scottish Highlands, for what he sees as rewilding.

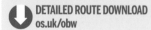

Glen Feshie

WALK 87

CAIRNGORMS NATIONAL PARK

DIFFICULTY ●

START Near Achlean on the east side of Glen Feshie

DISTANCE 3½ miles (5.5km)

HEIGHT GAIN 415 feet (125m)

APPROXIMATE TIME 2 hours

ROUTE TERRAIN Lane, moorland and woodland paths

PARKING Car park 4½ miles (7.2km) south of Feshiebridge on a single-track road signposted 'Lagganlia' and 'Achlean'

OS EXPLORER OL57

OS PATHFINDER Cairngorms

⬇ **DETAILED ROUTE DOWNLOAD**
os.uk/obw

Set amid the tranquillity of wild Glen Feshie, this route is initially over the floodplain of the dynamic River Feshie before climbing through pine woods to one of the National Park's most attractive waterfalls, where the Allt Fhearnagan cascades down water-sculpted pink granite. While the scenery is distractingly beautiful, take care here as the path runs close to the drop. *The route fords the Allt Fhearnagan twice; it should be fordable in all but severe spates, but crossing dry-shod may be tricky when river levels are above average.* As they tumble down to their confluence with the River Spey between Kingussie and Aviemore, the waters of the River Feshie are continually carving into the banks and depositing fresh gravel with every flood to create a braided river channel. Glen Feshie is home to many old 'granny' pines. These are splendid individual Scots pine trees of considerable age, which provide a contrast to the ranks of pines typically seen in forestry plantations.

Right and opposite page left: Glen Feshie.
Opposite page right: Pine marten.

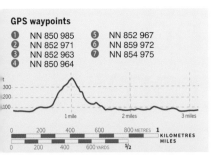

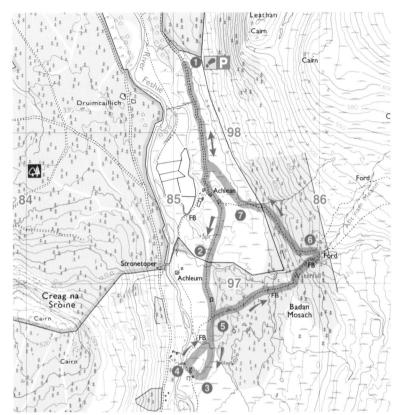

The Lily Loch and Loch an Eilein from Inverdruie

CAIRNGORM MOUNTAINS NSA

DIFFICULTY ●

START Inverdruie

DISTANCE 6 miles (9.7km)

HEIGHT GAIN 445 feet (135m)

APPROXIMATE TIME 3 hours

ROUTE TERRAIN Surfaced access drives, good paths and tracks

PARKING Car park at Inverdruie

OS EXPLORER OL57

OS PATHFINDER Cairngorms

 **DETAILED ROUTE DOWNLOAD** os.uk/obw

Lochan Mor is one of the scenic gems of the Cairngorms. Known as the Lily Loch by locals, it forms an enchanting setting in summer, with its abundance of water lilies, pine-fringed shore and backdrop of mountains in the distance. This walk makes a pleasant evening stroll (though you will likely need anti-midge precautions) and is an undemanding circuit with no taxing gradients. The Lily Loch is first encountered as an enticing glimpse of brilliant blue water through the trees; in summer, the lilies appear in all their glory. It is an idyllic spot to linger.

Inverdruie was an important centre for timber. Felled pines from the Rothiemurchus Forest were brought to the village to be sawn into planks. Each spring timber was heaped on to rafts made of logs and launched into the Spey to float downriver guided by two men, both wielding oars to manoeuvre the raft and prevent it from going aground.

Right: The ruined castle at Loch an Eilein.
Opposite page: Scots pine.

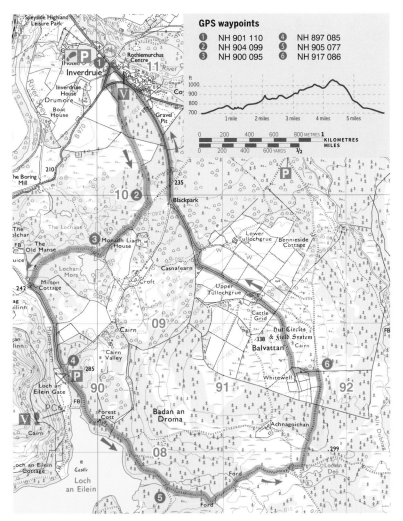

GPS waypoints

①	NH 901 110	④	NH 897 085
②	NH 904 099	⑤	NH 905 077
③	NH 900 095	⑥	NH 917 086

Rothiemurchus

Rothiemurchus means 'the grand plain of the fir trees' and the walk's approach to Lochan Mor, the Lily Loch, is a lovely part of the route through the old and stately pines of the Rothiemurchus Forest. This land has been in the Grant family since 1574. The seat of this sept of the clan is at the Doune, a mansion about 1 mile (1.6km) south-west of Inverdruie. Fittingly, the emblem of Clan Grant is a sprig of Scots Pine.

The Scots pine (Pinus sylvestris) can grow to a height of 115 feet (35 metres) and, in favourable conditions, can live for 700 years.

WALK 89 Morrone

DEESIDE AND LOCHNAGAR NSA

DIFFICULTY ●●●

START The duck pond at the end of Chapel Brae, on the west side of Braemar

DISTANCE 7 miles (11.3km)

HEIGHT GAIN 2,015 feet (615m)

APPROXIMATE TIME 4 hours

ROUTE TERRAIN Mountain paths and tracks, quiet road, woodland and field paths

PARKING The car park is reached from Braemar along the Linn of Dee road, forking left at Airlie House and climbing to the end of the road at Chapel Brae

OS EXPLORER OL52

OS PATHFINDER Cairngorms

⬇ **DETAILED ROUTE DOWNLOAD** os.uk/obw

Lying just south of Braemar, Morrone ('the big nose') is unmistakeable. At 2,815 feet (859m), it is a fair way from being a Munro, yet it is still a considerable hill, if only in terms of its bulk, and affords staggering views over the town and surrounding Deeside. Geologically, Morrone is mainly of quartzite, though there is also an outcrop of limestone. The bare moorland supports good flocks of grouse; look out for mountain hares too. The vista back to Braemar on the way up takes in the famous Games Park, where the Highland Gathering is held during the first week in September each year. At the summit, the major peaks of the Cairngorms are arrayed to the north-west; Ben Avon, with its distinctive tors is obvious to the north; to the east is the River Dee and, farther to the right, the magnificent face of Lochnagar; while Loch Callatar lies to the south.

Right: Braemar Castle.
Opposite page: Traditional games at the annual Highland Gathering.

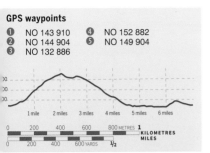

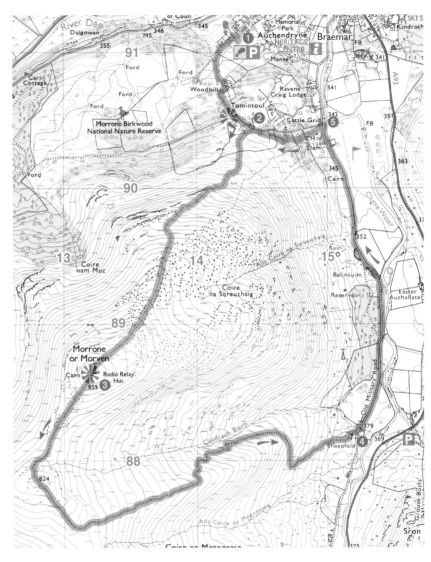

Braemar

Braemar is famous all over the world for its Highland Gathering in late summer, but the village is also a UK meteorological record holder. Being one of the highest villages in Scotland, situated at over 1,000 feet (305 metres), its altitude, combined with the surrounding hills which trap cold air, have bestowed on Braemar the unenviable record of having experienced the lowest temperature recorded in Britain ... twice! A bone chilling -27.2°C (-17°F) was reached on 11 February 1895, and the mercury plummeted to this level again on 10 January 1982.

WALK 90
Lochnagar and Loch Muick

DEESIDE AND LOCHNAGAR NSA

DIFFICULTY ●●●

START Spittal of Glenmuick

DISTANCE 14 miles (22.4km)

HEIGHT GAIN 2,790 feet (850m)

APPROXIMATE TIME 8 hours

ROUTE TERRAIN Mountain paths and tracks

PARKING The car park is at the end of the public road through Glen Muick from Ballater

OS EXPLORER OL53

OS PATHFINDER Cairngorms

DETAILED ROUTE DOWNLOAD
os.uk/obw

This full-day walking bonanza in the Lochnagar massif is a challenging undertaking in terms of both distance and ascent, and should only be attempted in favourable weather, but, on the best of days, the walking memories made here will be treasured for a lifetime. Lochnagar is a monarch among mountains, and the view from the summit (a clear day is essential) takes in the grandest of all corries and a landscape that comprises nearly half of Scotland. Cac Carn Beag is the true summit and politely translates as 'the cairn of the little heap of manure'. The toposcope here indicates points including Ben Nevis, Ben Lomond, the Caithness Hills and the Pentlands. On a really clear day you can even see the Cheviot Hills.

Early in the walk, Allt-na-giubhsaich is passed, used by Queen Victoria as a 'cottage' where she and Prince Albert would come to escape the formalities of life at Balmoral. The long descent follows the Glas Allt, 'green burn', and passes the 70-foot (21.3-m) Falls of Glasallt, before returning on a shoreline path around Loch Muick.

Right: The clear waters of Loch Muick.

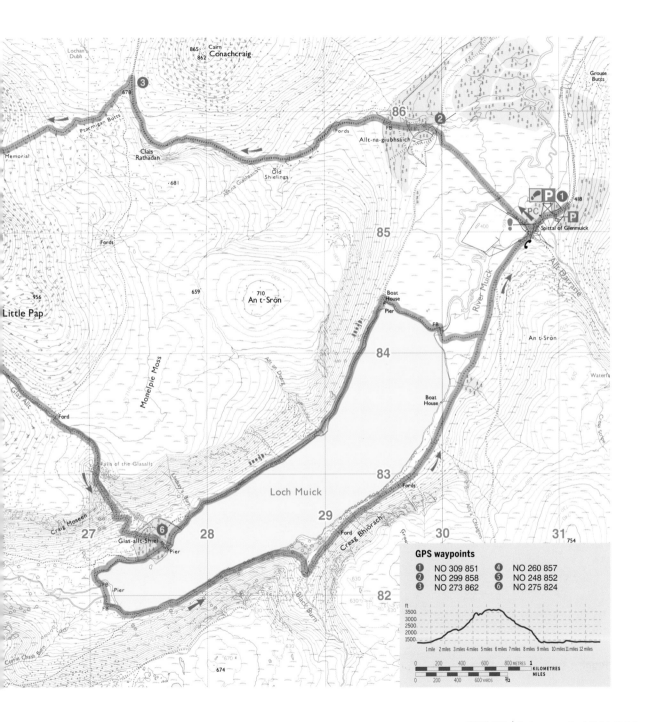

Conachcraig

Cairn
865
862

Lochan
Dubh

3

678

Memorial

Ptarmigan Butts

Clais
Rathadan

Allt na giubhsaich

Old
Shielings

Fords

681

Fords

86

FB

2

Allt-na-giubhsaich

Fords

85

P **1**
418

PC

!
400

P

Spittal of Glenmuick

956

Little Pap

659

710
An t-Sròn

Monelpie Moss

Glas Allt

Ford

Falls of the Glasallt

Allt an Dearg

Allt an Dubh Loch

Boat
House

Pier

River Muick

FB

Boat
House

An t-Sròn

Waterfa

Craig Moseen

27

6

Glas-allt-Shiel

Pier

FB
Pier

FB

28

Loch Muick

29

Fords

Ford

Creag Bhiorach

83

Grou

30

Allt a Chaorainn

Creag Sgiorr

754
31

Corrie Chash Burn

674

Black Burn

670.4

630

630

630

82

GPS waypoints

1	NO 309 851	**4**	NO 260 857
2	NO 299 858	**5**	NO 248 852
3	NO 273 862	**6**	NO 275 824

ft
3500
3000
2500
2000
1500

1 mile 2 miles 3 miles 4 miles 5 miles 6 miles 7 miles 8 miles 9 miles 10 miles 11 miles 12 miles

0   200   400   600   800 METRES
0   200   400   600 YARDS   1/2

1
KILOMETRES
MILES

Loch Lomond and the Trossachs National Park

One of the great joys of preparing my guide to the West Highland Way was that I could walk through the very heart of the Loch Lomond and the Trossachs National Park, plodding my laden way up the eastern shores of the world-famous loch. I also once managed the Ben Lomond Hill Race, although the winner was on his way home before I even reached the summit!

Because the National Park, established in 2002, lies not far north of Glasgow, close to the communities of Balloch, Aberfoyle and Callander, it is tempting to think of it as being heavily urbanised. But the hub of the park, north and south of Loch Katrine and Loch Arklet, is as wild as can be, with a menu of no fewer than 21 Munros and 20 Corbetts for those who enjoy the heights, plus myriad less demanding pathways, especially within the Queen Elizabeth Forest Park. The Great Trossachs Forest, which gathers around Loch Katrine and Glen Finglas, is the UK's largest National Nature Reserve – a park within a park.

Loch Lomond draws the crowds, but the autumnal colours of peaceful Loch Chon, to the west of Aberfoyle, also welcome walkers in search of nature's beauty. Nearby, Milton Narrows on the edge of Loch Ard, where the River Forth has its source, is a serene spot that will appeal to anyone.

The predominance of water in the landscape brings it to life, not least in the park's waterfalls. Inversnaid Falls were eulogised in a poem by the 19th-century poet Gerald Manley Hopkins, who asked: 'What would the world be, once bereft of wet and of wildness?'.

The spectacular Beinglas Falls above Inverarnan was the way I chose to access Beinn Chabhair, An Caisteal and Beinn a'Chroin on one of my Munro-bagging jaunts; the Ben Glas burn was in spate, and the falls made a thunderous roar that set my heart racing quite as much as the uphill effort. Another walk from Callander will bring you to Bracklinn Falls, where a stunning bridge, built in 2010 to replace the original, which had been washed away in flash floods in 2004, allows you to come face-to-face with the falls. Standing there, you will understand why the Victorians found this, and many other locations around the Trossachs, so mesmerising.

> **AMAZING BUT TRUE ...**
> Visitors longing to see the Northern Lights, or Aurora Borealis, often feel the need to head for Iceland or Norway, but this spectacular display is regularly visible from the shores of Loch Lomond.

Lochgoilhead and Donich Water

WALK 91

LOCH LOMOND AND THE TROSSACHS NATIONAL PARK AND LOCH LOMOND NSA

DIFFICULTY ●

START Lochgoilhead

DISTANCE 2½ miles (4km)

HEIGHT GAIN 625 feet (190m)

APPROXIMATE TIME 1½ hours

ROUTE TERRAIN Clear woodland paths with one short, steep climb

PARKING Forestry Commission car park at Lochgoilhead

OS EXPLORER OL37

OS PATHFINDER Loch Lomond, the Trossachs and Stirling

 **DETAILED ROUTE DOWNLOAD** os.uk/obw

Lochgoilhead is a magically tranquil spot, tucked at the head of a long, sinuous sea loch, seemingly remote in its stunning setting beneath the high mountains of the Arrochar Alps. This exceedingly agreeable short walk climbs to a sylvan spot in Gleann Donich Forest, where the confluence of Allt Coire Odhair and Allt Airigh na Creige to become Donich Water forms a pretty rock pool surrounded by lively waterfalls. Not only is this a delightful place to enjoy a picnic on a fine day, it is also well worth walking this route after heavy rain to see the falls at their gushingly spectacular best.

Once in the forest, the sound of the rushing stream drifts up from below, as the outward path contours above Donich Water. Nearing the midway point, breaks in the trees give glimpses to Loch Goil and the aptly named peak, An Stiobull – The Steeple. The return follows the Cowal Way around the base of An Stiobull, with splendid views across Loch Goil to the ring of mountains behind Lettermay.

Right: Lochgoilhead.
Opposite page top: Ancient bridge spanning the River Goil.
Opposite page bottom: Carrick Castle.

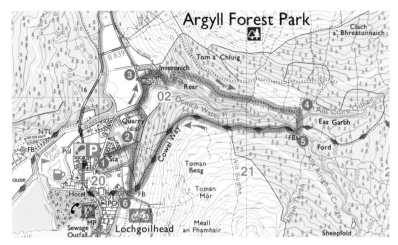

GPS waypoints

1. NN 200 016
2. NN 202 016
3. NN 202 021
4. NN 213 019
5. NN 213 017
6. NN 202 013

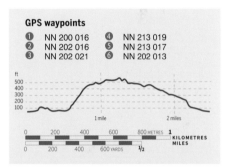

Loch Goil

Loch Goil is a small fjord-like sea loch, branching off the much lengthier Loch Long, in Argyll and Bute. It is entirely within the Loch Lomond and the Trossachs National Park and is surrounded by **Argyll Forest Park**, which was established in 1935 and is Britain's oldest forest park. The park, which covers 81 square miles (211km²) and is managed by Forestry Commission Scotland, is popular for walking, climbing, fishing, adventure sports and wildlife spotting.

Ben Lomond

WALK 92

LOCH LOMOND AND THE TROSSACHS NATIONAL PARK AND LOCH LOMOND NSA

DIFFICULTY ●●●

START Rowardennan

DISTANCE 7¼ miles (11.7km)

HEIGHT GAIN 3,135 feet (955m)

APPROXIMATE TIME 5 hours

ROUTE TERRAIN Clear woodland and mountain paths featuring a prolonged ascent

PARKING Car park at Rowardennan Pier

OS EXPLORER OL39

OS PATHFINDER Loch Lomond, the Trossachs and Stirling

DETAILED ROUTE DOWNLOAD os.uk/obw

Ben Lomond is perhaps the most climbed of all the Munros, thanks to its popularity with inquisitive travellers since the 18th century, its proximity to Glasgow and the inviting route along the southern ridge. Soaring above Loch Lomond, it is the first really big mountain you'll see when journeying up to the Highlands from the south. Much of the walk is through the National Trust for Scotland estate of Ben Lomond.

Although the path to the summit is clear, this mountain shouldn't be underestimated; a fine, settled day is recommended for the climb and to reap the rewards of the unfolding vistas. Bear in mind that conditions at the top are likely to be very different to those by the loch, with a marked drop in temperature and stronger winds making it feel much colder.

On the summit, the uphill toil is visually rewarded in abundance, with seemingly endless Highland mountains stretching away to the north and west, and contrasting views south and east beyond the Campsie Fells to the Central Lowlands and the Border country.

Right: View south from the summit of Ben Lomond.
Opposite page: Loch Lomond at Rowardennan.

GPS waypoints

1 NS 359 986
2 NS 371 991
3 NS 376 998
4 NN 372 024
5 NN 367 028

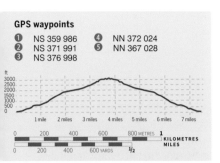

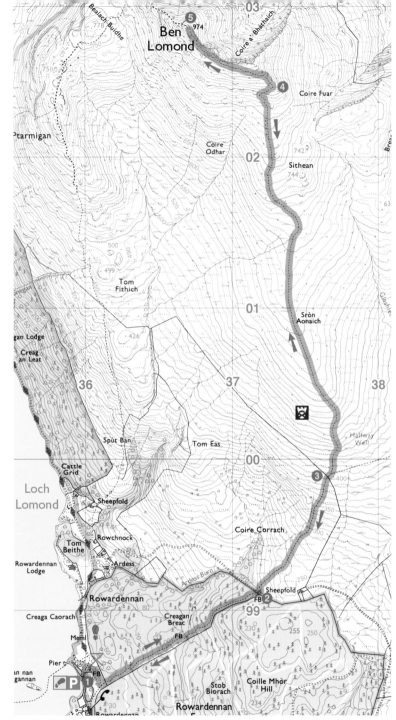

Ben Venue

THE TROSSACHS NSA

DIFFICULTY ●●●

START Car park beside the A821, ¼ mile north of Loch Achray Hotel

DISTANCE 8¼ miles (13.3km)

HEIGHT GAIN 2,670 feet (815m)

APPROXIMATE TIME 5½ hours

ROUTE TERRAIN Forest tracks and mountain paths; some boggy sections and a sustained climb

PARKING Ben Venue car park

OS EXPLORER OL46

OS PATHFINDER Loch Lomond, the Trossachs and Stirling

 DETAILED ROUTE DOWNLOAD os.uk/obw

Ben Venue is a rugged mountain. In terms of height classification, at 2,384 feet (727m), it qualifies as a Graham. Munros are mountains of 3,000 feet (914m) and over, such as Ben Lomond; Corbetts, such as Morrone, are between 2,500 and 2,999 feet (762–913m); while Grahams are between 2,000 and 2,499 feet (610–761m) and with a prominence of at least 492 feet (150m). They are named after Fiona Graham, who produced a list of such peaks. Ben Venue is a key viewpoint for all the Trossachs. Featured in Sir Walter Scott's *The Lady of the Lake* and *Rob Roy* as 'huge Benvenue', it offers picture-postcard views from the summit trig point, along Loch Katrine and, further round to the east, to Loch Achray and then Loch Venachar.

A low-level alternative walk is also possible across the mountainside above Loch Katrine towards the narrow, rocky pass of Bealach nam Bo, a route used by Highlanders droving stolen cattle back to their glens after sorties in the Lowlands.

Right: Ben Venue reflected in the waters of Loch Achray.
Opposite page: Ben Venue.

Loch Katrine

Loch Katrine is the setting for some of the writings of the much-loved bard Sir Walter Scott, most notably *The Lady of the Lake*, published in 1810. One of the best ways to experience the beauty of this ribbon of fresh water, which stretches for 8 miles (13km) across The Trossachs NSA, is via a trip on the steamship *SS Sir Walter Scott*.

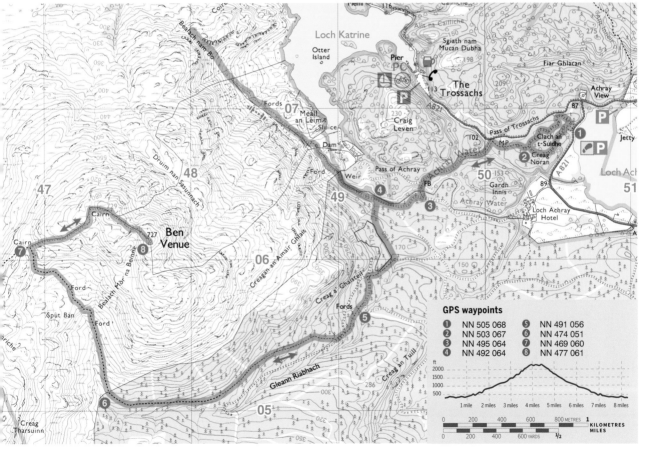

GPS waypoints

❶	NN 505 068	❺	NN 491 056
❷	NN 503 067	❻	NN 474 051
❸	NN 495 064	❼	NN 469 060
❹	NN 492 064	❽	NN 477 061

National Scenic Areas

The 40 National Scenic Areas of Scotland represent Scotland's finest landscapes. Considering the country's outstanding scenery and imposing mountain ranges, the wonder is that there are only 40.

Ben Nevis was the first Munro I ascended; I could have bagged many more Munros had I not been drawn back to the 'Ben' no fewer than 45 times, including one ascent for the annual Ben Nevis Race. When you stand on the summit of Ben Nevis, you are on top of the world; the sense of achievement this mountain bestows is immense. In 1979, I was in happy tears as I plodded up the Ben once more, this time after completing the 'Four Peaks', a challenge that had started 28 hours earlier on Carrauntoohil in County Kerry, Ireland.

At sea level, meanwhile, Loch na Keal on the west coast of Mull (*left*) is an engaging place of islands and geos, soaring cliffs, granite beaches and dashing waterfalls. Only a couple of years ago, while birdwatching here, I was held spellbound as a school of dolphin cruised up and down the loch. From here you can take a rising path up onto Ben More, the only island Munro, but there is also a fine and undefined amble along the long shoreline (where the evidence of glacial hydrology is a study in itself) that is perfect for a cloudy day.

Few places among Scotland's National Scenic Areas capture the imagination and inspire daring deeds in quite the same way as the Cuillin of Skye. This massive cirque of black jaggedness is not for the timid; even the simplest ascent, to Bruach na Frithe, must never be regarded as easy, and to complete the entire ridge end-to-end, is only for iron personalities with the stamina to match. Separating the Black Cuillin from the Red Cuillin, Glen Sligachan provides probably the best through-walk on the island; it needs good planning, but is an utter delight. The sense of elation you will experience anywhere among the Cuillin is unmatched; cope with the Cuillin, and you'll feel you're ready for anything. But, if you're planning to tackle all the Munros, be advised: make sure you deal with the Inaccessible Pinnacle on Sgurr Dearg as soon as you can; that's not a summit you want to have taunting you for years.

AMAZING BUT TRUE ...
Located 18 miles (29km) from Kinloch Rannoch, Rannoch Station is one of the most isolated railway stations in Britain. It lies on the West Highland Line between Glasgow and Fort William, which runs across the remote wilderness of Rannoch Moor.

WALK 94 Pap of Glencoe

BEN NEVIS AND GLEN COE NSA

DIFFICULTY ●●

START Glencoe village

DISTANCE 5 miles (8km)

HEIGHT GAIN 2,490 feet (760m)

APPROXIMATE TIME 3½ hours

ROUTE TERRAIN The old Glen Coe road, plus mountain track and path

PARKING Car park in Glencoe village

OS EXPLORER 384

OS PATHFINDER Fort William and Glen Coe

DETAILED ROUTE DOWNLOAD
os.uk/obw

The Pap of Glencoe is a fine summit, and as one of the great landmark peaks in Glen Coe, it makes a superlative viewpoint. From Glencoe village, the walk sets out along the old Glen Coe road for about a mile before the uphill work, initially relatively modest, begins. After the rough service track ends at a dam, the route continues up the gully formed by the Allt a' Mhuilinn burn over alternately rough, cloying and heathery ground, reaching a col, after which the final haul to the top of this quartzite cone is steep and rocky. There are magnificent views up Glen Coe, and a sweeping panorama eastwards over Loch Leven; to the west you can look across the Ballachulish narrows, over Loch Linnhe and onwards to the rugged landscape of Ardgour.

This summit is known as Sgorr na Ciche in Gaelic, *ciche* translating as 'breast', or 'pap' in the more straitlaced Victorian version.

Right: Pap of Glencoe from Glencoe Lochan.
Opposite page: Loch Leven as seen from Pap of Glencoe.

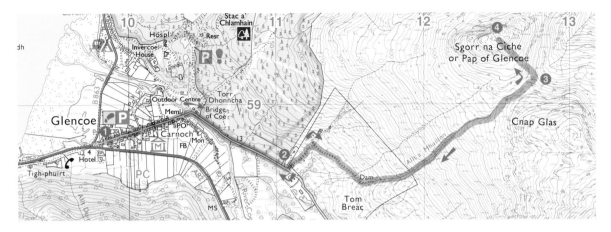

GPS waypoints

❶	NN 098 587	❸	NN 127 591
❷	NN 111 586	❹	NN 125 594

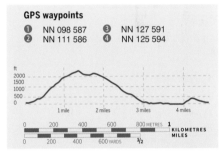

The Pap of Glencoe

The Pap of Glencoe's summit gives a feeling of great height, as peaks overlooking water tend to do (Ben Nevis itself is not any more impressive), and the far-reaching, all-round views are a special experience. The dominant peak in the scene up Glen Coe is Bidean nam Bian, at 3,766 feet (1,148m) the highest summit in Argyll. The local mountains rise steeply from near sea level and in the past made intimidating barriers to travel, as accounts from Wordsworth, Coleridge and Dickens testify.

WALK 95 Isle of Iona

LOCH NA KEAL, ISLE OF MULL NSA

DIFFICULTY ●●

START Iona, by the ferry terminal

DISTANCE 8½ miles (13.7km)

HEIGHT GAIN 690 feet (210m)

APPROXIMATE TIME 4½ hours

ROUTE TERRAIN Surfaced tracks, grassy paths and dunes

PARKING By the ferry terminal at Fionnphort, Isle of Mull

OS EXPLORER 373

OS PATHFINDER Oban, Mull and Kintyre

⬇ **DETAILED ROUTE DOWNLOAD** os.uk/obw

Easily divisible into two separate walks, the full route explores a large portion of Iona and touches upon all four compass points of the island's coastline. As Iona is fairly flat and many of the tracks are surfaced, the going is relatively easy, allowing time for the walker to appreciate fully the compelling scenery and beautiful beaches, and to get a sense of the island's isolation and peace, its rich historical significance and fascinating collection of religious buildings.

Iona's highest point, Dùn I, has far-reaching views over the whole of the isle, to some of the nearby islands, including Staffa and the west coast of Mull, with Ben More on the skyline. The walk visits the abbey, the 11th-century St Oran's Chapel, the ruins of the Benedictine nunnery, Maclean's Cross and Telford's 19th-century parish church. On the southern coast, the walk reaches Port na Curaich, also known as St Columba's Bay, where the saint is alleged to have made his landing in AD563 after crossing from Ireland on his evangelising mission to Scotland.

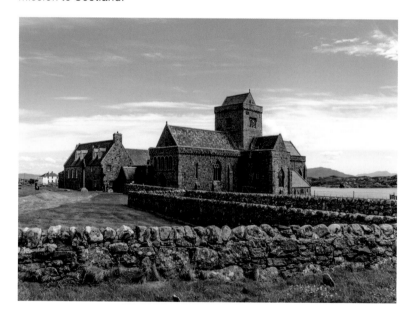

Right: The abbey on Iona.

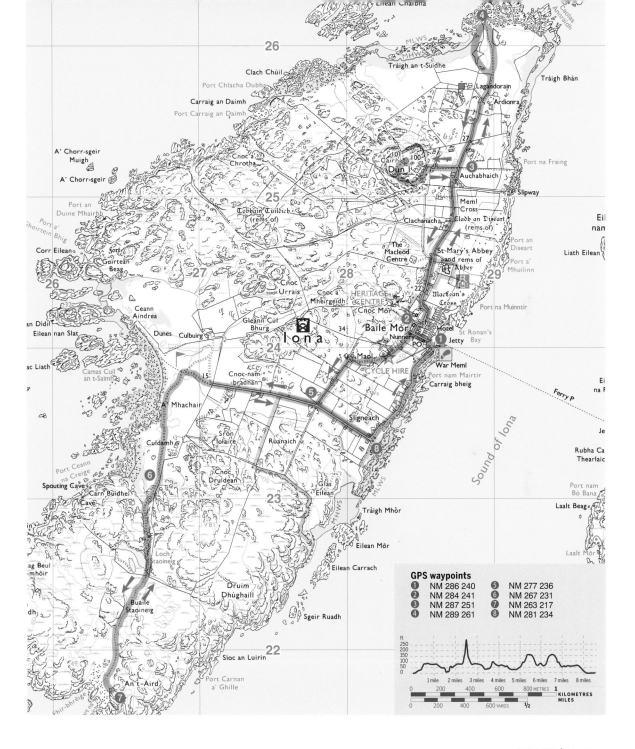

GPS waypoints

① NM 286 240		⑤ NM 277 236	
② NM 284 241		⑥ NM 267 231	
③ NM 287 251		⑦ NM 263 217	
④ NM 289 261		⑧ NM 281 234	

Dunkeld, the Hermitage and Birnam

RIVER TAY NSA

DIFFICULTY ●●

START Dunkeld

DISTANCE 7¾ miles (12.4km)

HEIGHT GAIN 655 feet (200m)

APPROXIMATE TIME 4 hours

ROUTE TERRAIN A short section of road walking, plus riverside and forest tracks and a moorland path

PARKING Pay and Display car parks in Dunkeld

OS EXPLORER 379

OS PATHFINDER Perthshire, Angus and Fife

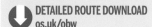 **DETAILED ROUTE DOWNLOAD** os.uk/obw

From the historic and compact cathedral town of Dunkeld, the route crosses the River Tay over Telford's fine seven-arched bridge, built in 1809, then threads its way beside the River Braan upstream, passing through the Hermitage Woodland, a pleasure woodland laid out in the 18th century by the Duke of Atholl. Here, the Braan is in an almost perpetual turmoil of rapids, falls and swirling pools. The famous folly of Ossian's Hall, originally built in 1758 and replaced in the 1940s, is a perfect vantage point from which to view the tumult of plunging water. Next comes Ossian's Cave, another 18th-century folly. Keep a lookout for red squirrels here. Later, the Braan is crossed by Rumbling Bridge, which provides another great viewing platform for the churning water. After walking over moorland and down through forest, the route reaches Birnam, the Beatrix Potter Garden and then the gigantic Birnam Oak. According to folklore, this is the last tree remaining from the ancient Birnam woods that featured in the witches' prophesy to Macbeth in Shakespeare's play.

Right: Ossian's Hall in the Hermitage.
Opposite page left: The cathedral at Dunkeld.
Opposite page right: River Braan.

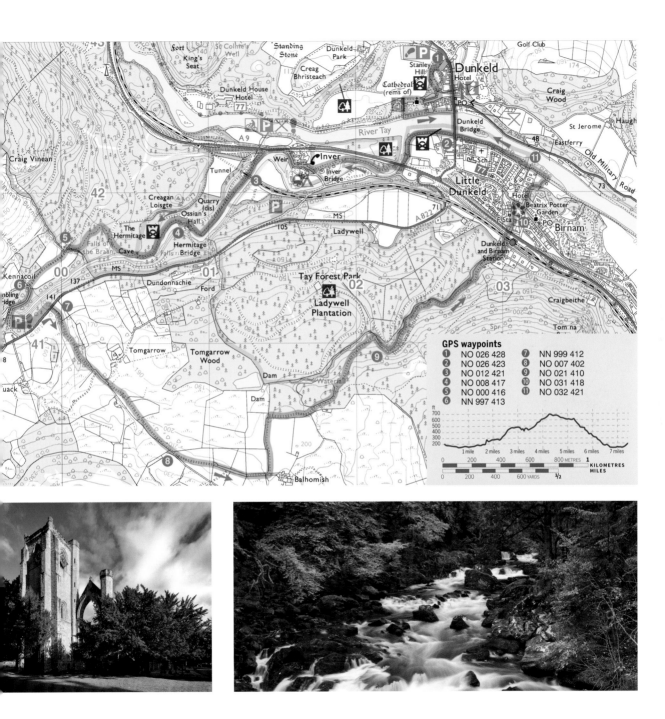

GPS waypoints

①	NO 026 428	⑦	NN 999 412
②	NO 026 423	⑧	NO 007 402
③	NO 012 421	⑨	NO 021 410
④	NO 008 417	⑩	NO 031 418
⑤	NO 000 416	⑪	NO 032 421
⑥	NN 997 413		

WALK 97 Camasunary-Elgol-Glasnakille

THE CUILLIN, SKYE NSA

DIFFICULTY ●●●

START Kilmarie, Strathaird

DISTANCE 11¼ miles (18km)

HEIGHT GAIN 2,280ft (695m)

APPROXIMATE TIME 6½ hours

ROUTE TERRAIN Stony tracks, rough hill slopes, minor road and coastal paths

PARKING Car park at the start (NG 545 172)

OS EXPLORER 411

OS PATHFINDER Isle of Skye

DETAILED ROUTE DOWNLOAD
os.uk/obw

There can be no more idyllic spot on Skye for peace and tranquillity than the lovely bay of Camasunary, or Camas Fhionnairigh to give it its Gaelic form. Lazy waves lap on a pebbly shore backed by the crags of Sgurr na Stri. This walk from Kilmarie is the most direct and easiest way of reaching Camasunary. From here, the walk strikes southwards along the coastline to Elgol, from where it crosses the main thrust of the peninsula to Glasnakille, there continuing northwards to return to Kilmarie.

For one of the most dramatic surprise views on the Isle of Skye, it is difficult to better the panorama from Am Màm, the broad bealach (hill pass) due east of the bay of Camasunary. For anyone wanting a brief walk, they need go no further than Am Màm (waypoint 2), but the curving bay is an irresistible draw and a splendid retreat from daily life. Kilmarie to Camasunary is a popular short walk, and deservedly so.

Right: Camasunary Bay.

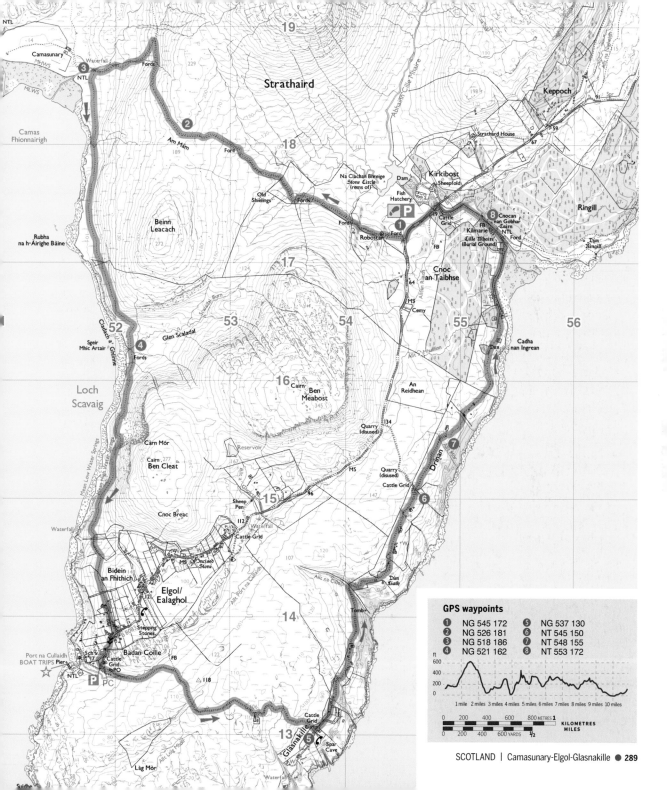

GPS waypoints

① NG 545 172	⑤ NG 537 130
② NG 526 181	⑥ NT 545 150
③ NG 518 186	⑦ NT 548 155
④ NG 521 162	⑧ NT 553 172

The Quiraing and Meall na Suiramach

TROTTERNISH, SKYE NSA

DIFFICULTY ●●●

START Bealach Ollasgairte, at the summit of the pass on the Staffin-Uig road, 3 miles (4.8km) west of Staffin

DISTANCE 4 miles (6.5km)

HEIGHT GAIN 1,360 feet (415m)

APPROXIMATE TIME 3 hours

ROUTE TERRAIN Rough mountain and moorland paths, and one steep grassy descent

PARKING Viewpoint lay-by parking

OS EXPLORER 408

OS PATHFINDER Isle of Skye

 DETAILED ROUTE DOWNLOAD
os.uk/obw

This is a splendid outing to one of Skye's most remarkable places: the crags and pinnacles of the Quiraing, natural rock sculptures with names such as the Prison, the Needle and the Table. The Prison is an enormous sheer-sided slab of rock, which merits its name. At the end of the last Ice Age, about 11,000 years ago, a bed of solidified lava about 1,000 feet (300m) thick broke away and began to slip towards the sea, creating the weird landscape of the Quiraing. Beyond this geological artistry, the walk leaves the landslip and follows a roundabout path up on to the vast summit plateau of Meall na Suiramach above, for an inspiring view of the Trotternish Ridge and the far-off islands of the Hebrides. The last part of the walk back to Bealach Ollasgairte is a steep grassy descent.

While the walk into the Quiraing is reasonably straightforward, the ongoing route up on to Meall na Suiramach should only be attempted in fine, settled conditions.

Right: The Quiraing.
Opposite page: The Needle.

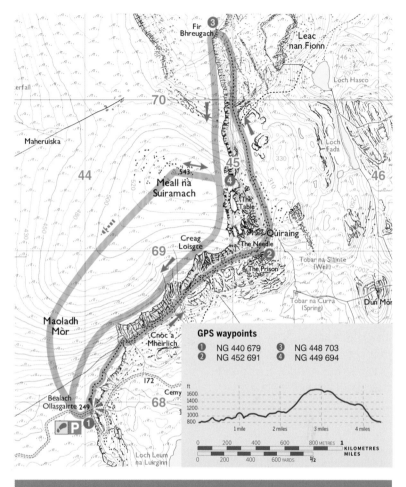

GPS waypoints

❶	NG 440 679	❸	NG 448 703
❷	NG 452 691	❹	NG 449 694

Trotternish

The northern-most peninsula on the Isle of Skye is Trotternish. Tròndairnis in Scottish Gaelic, this region contains the highest proportion of Gaelic speakers on Skye. Trotternish is remarkable for its geology and a feature known as 'the landslip', which runs the length of the peninsula's 20-mile (32-km) escarpment. It is the biggest landslide in Britain. A huge and much heavier layer of volcanic basalt lies over comparatively weaker Jurassic sedimentary rock, and over millennia the sedimentary strata have gradually given way. Resultant landslides have formed the curiously shaped blocks and pinnacles of the Quiraing and the Old Man of Storr.

Rascarrel Bay and Balcary Point

EAST STEWARTRY COAST NSA

DIFFICULTY ●●

START Balcary Bay, at the end of the minor road from Auchencairn

DISTANCE 5 miles (8km)

HEIGHT GAIN 310 feet (95m)

APPROXIMATE TIME 2½ hours

ROUTE TERRAIN Field and woodland paths, a short section of lane and coastal path, which is steep around Balcary Point and near the cliff edge in places

PARKING Balcary Bay car park

OS EXPLORER 313

OS PATHFINDER Dumfries and Galloway

DETAILED ROUTE DOWNLOAD
os.uk/obw

There is a succession of grand views over Auchencairn Bay and across the Solway Firth to the mountains of Cumbria on the coastal section of this walk, which joins the coast path at Rascarrel Bay along the edge of a stony beach, later climbing on to low cliffs and finally rounding the steep and dramatic headland of Balcary Point. Along this rising shoreline, look out for the sea-worn stacks with curious names such as Adam's Chair, Door of the Heugh and Lot's Wife. While the fine cliff scenery around Balcary Point is a highlight of the walk, the path is steep in places and sometimes exposed, so it may not be suitable for vertigo-sufferers.

The walk sets out from the attractive and sheltered bay at Balcary across field paths to Loch Mackie and then follows a woodland path through the peatland conifers of Rascarrel Moss, before taking in a short section of lane to rejoin the coast at Rascarrel Bay.

Right: Hestan Island in the Solway Firth can be seen from Balcary Point.
Opposite page: Rascarrel Bay.

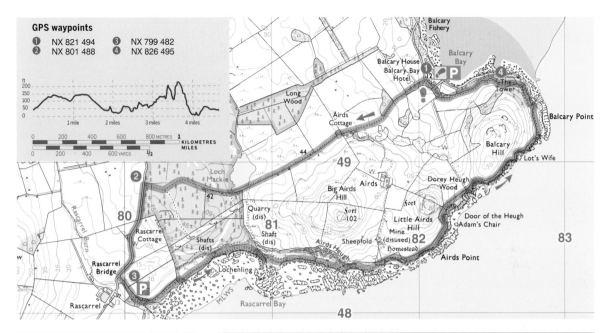

GPS waypoints
- **1** NX 821 494
- **2** NX 801 488
- **3** NX 799 482
- **4** NX 826 495

Solway Firth

The name 'Solway' is probably Nordic in origin, recorded as 'Sulewad' in the early 13th century. The firth separates Dumfries and Galloway from Cumbria and the mountains of the Lake District, and marks the boundary between Scotland and England as its waters open out into the Irish Sea. The tidal mudflats, estuarine salt marsh, beaches and low cliffs around the shores of Solway Firth are internationally important for wildlife, and there are in excess of 100 square miles (290km²) of Sites of Special Scientific Interest and nature reserves along the coast.

Edinburgh

The problem with Edinburgh is that often you can't see the wood for the trees; the city is bustling, animated, thronged with visitors, but a confusing place to visit if you want to see this exceptional urban landscape for what it is.

So, if you do nothing else in Edinburgh, take a walk up unmissable Arthur's Seat, a volcanic plug, located just east of the city centre. It is beloved of everyone and rightly so – just turn a blind eye to the ashes of the late departed that are frequently scattered up here. Arthur's Seat is a superb landmark, giving a demystifying overview of the city and its dominant castle. From here you can better observe the remarkable contrast between the medieval Old Town, which evolved organically to match its inhabitants' needs, and the planned Georgian New Town. Together, these two distinctive townscapes display exceptional architecture and plenty of historical and geographical interest. They also perhaps inspired Mendelssohn to compose his 'Scottish' Symphony (No. 3, Op. 56).

If you don't have time for Arthur's Seat, head for diminutive Calton Hill, regarded by Benjamin Franklin's business partner, David Hall, as offering the finest view anywhere.

The Old Town is characterised by a medieval herring-bone street pattern of courts, closes and wynds, while the New Town, built between 1767 and 1890, is a collection of planned residential developments on the glacial plain to the north of the Old Town. On the one hand, you have clear evidence of how things evolved naturally; on the other, an assemblage of ashlar-faced, neoclassical buildings designed by renowned architects, such as John and Robert Adam and William Playfair. It is this largely well-preserved juxtaposition of old and new that brought Edinburgh World Heritage Status in 1995.

Tying the heart of Edinburgh to the rest of southern Scotland is the John Muir Way, a 130-mile (215-km) long-distance route linking Helensburgh in Argyll and Bute in the west with Dunbar (birthplace of John Muir) in East Lothian. (John Muir went on to become a pioneer of the United States National Park Service.) This splendid trail keeps to the greener places as it crosses Edinburgh, before pressing on, past an area of low cliffs, skerries, dunes and saltmarsh beyond the city, towards Dunbar.

> **AMAZING BUT TRUE ...**
> It was in the Elephant House at 21 George IV Bridge that J.K. Rowling worked on her early *Harry Potter* novels; the view of Edinburgh Castle surely inspired Hogwarts School.

Grassmarket and Greyfriars

THE NEW AND OLD TOWNS OF EDINBURGH (UNESCO)

DIFFICULTY ●

START At the west end of Princes Street at its junction with Lothian Road

DISTANCE 1½ miles (2.3km)

HEIGHT GAIN Negligible

APPROXIMATE TIME 2 hours

ROUTE TERRAIN Pavement

PARKING Best to use public transport

OS EXPLORER 350

OS PATHFINDER Edinburgh City Walks

 DETAILED ROUTE DOWNLOAD os.uk/obw

This stroll through Edinburgh's Old Town uncovers the sordid world of the Resurrectionists, the charming tale of a faithful four-legged friend and the early years of a very well-known Hollywood screen legend. The walk offers good views up to Edinburgh Castle atop its craggy, volcanic perch, and passes through the West Port, one of the gates in the old Flodden Wall, built to defend the city between 1513 and 1560. It also visits the Grassmarket, where livestock and corn markets were held in times past; it was also an arena for public hangings. Maggie Dickson had a remarkable escape from the gallows and was afterwards nicknamed 'Half hangit Maggie'; her memory lives on in the name of the pub here. In Greyfriars, you can visit the Elephant House where J.K. Rowling started her writing career, but the real-life story of 'James' Barry, a distinguished medical school graduate is stranger than fiction and just as amazing.

Right: Edinburgh Castle, as seen from the Grassmarket.
Opposite page left: Ancient gargoyle in Greyfriars Kirkyard.
Opposite page right: Victoria Street.

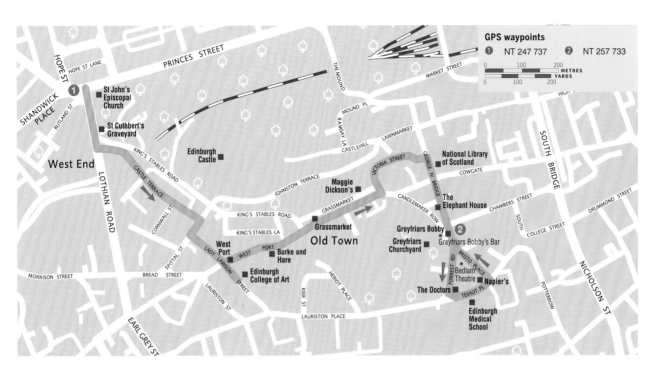

GPS waypoints

| 1 | NT 247 737 | 2 | NT 257 733 |

WALK 100B Georgian New Town

THE NEW AND OLD TOWNS OF EDINBURGH (UNESCO)

DIFFICULTY ●

START Princes Street, at The Mound junction

DISTANCE 2¾ miles (4.7km)

HEIGHT GAIN negligible

APPROXIMATE TIME 2 hours

ROUTE TERRAIN Pavement

PARKING Best to use public transport

OS EXPLORER 350

OS PATHFINDER Edinburgh City Walks

 DETAILED ROUTE DOWNLOAD os.uk/obw

By the 18th century the population of Edinburgh was growing fast, and the Old Town was very overcrowded. In 1767 a competition was held to design a new town. The winner was James Craig (1744-95), whose plan was to create three main parallel streets – Princes Street, George Street and Queen Street – with a grand square at each end. The new development was called the Georgian New Town after the reigning monarch, King George III.

Beginning at The Mound, created from earth dug from the foundations of the New Town, this stroll visits the home of Alexander Graham Bell, inventor of the telephone; the residence of Joseph Lister, a pioneer in antiseptic surgery, and the Oxford Bar, a favourite haunt of Ian Rankin, author and creator of the Rebus stories. Other famous literary associations are provided by Robert Louis Stevenson and Sir Arthur Conan Doyle. Near the end of the walk, there's a statue of William Pitt the Younger who introduced the Window Tax, a charge relating to the number of panes of glass in a property – a tax known as 'daylight robbery!'

Right: Charlotte Square.
Opposite page: Melville Monument.

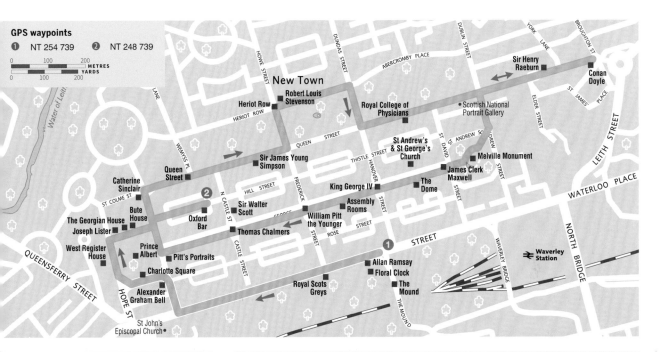

GPS waypoints
1 NT 254 739 **2** NT 248 739

METRES
YARDS

New Town

Heriot Row
Robert Louis Stevenson
Royal College of Physicians
Sir Henry Raeburn
Conan Doyle
Scottish National Portrait Gallery
Sir James Young Simpson
Catherine Sinclair
Queen Street
St Andrew's & St George's Church
Melville Monument
James Clerk Maxwell
The Georgian House
Joseph Lister
Bute House
Oxford Bar
Sir Walter Scott
King George IV
Assembly Rooms
William Pitt the Younger
Thomas Chalmers
The Dome
West Register House
Prince Albert
Pitt's Portraits
Charlotte Square
Alexander Graham Bell
St John's Episcopal Church
Allan Ramsay
Floral Clock
Royal Scots Greys
The Mound
Waverley Station

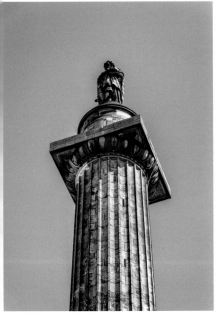

Famous authors

Robert Louis Stevenson (1850–94), author of *Kidnapped* and *Dr Jekyll and Mr Hyde*, lived at No.17 Heriot Row from 1856 to 1880. Stevenson was a sickly child and spent much of his time indoors. His bedroom window above the front door looked down on the street below and across to the gardens opposite, which were for the private use of the street's residents, and where as a young boy Robert sometimes played. In those days there was a pond with an island in the middle, which inspired him in later life to write his most famous book, *Treasure Island*. It is hard to imagine that Long John Silver and the 'pieces of eight' started life in this quiet Georgian Edinburgh Street.

Sir Arthur Conan Doyle (1859–1930) also lived in this part of Edinburgh. Conan Doyle studied medicine at the university, where one of his tutors was a Dr Joseph Bell. The young student hugely admired Bell for his enquiring mind, and based his famous detective Sherlock Holmes on him. You can see a statue of Mr Holmes, resplendent in his tweed cape and deerstalker hat, diagonally across from the Conan Doyle pub.

Walking Safety

UPLAND WALKS

The hills, mountains and moorlands of Britain, though of modest height compared with those in many other countries, need to be treated with respect. Friendly and inviting in good weather, they can quickly be transformed into wet, misty, windswept and potentially dangerous areas of wilderness in bad weather. Even on an outwardly fine and settled summer day, conditions can rapidly deteriorate at high altitudes and, in winter, even more so.

Therefore it is advisable always to take both warm and waterproof clothing, sufficient nourishing food, a hot drink, first-aid kit, torch and whistle. Wear suitable footwear, such as strong walking boots or shoes that give a good grip over rocky terrain and on slippery slopes. Try to obtain a local weather forecast and bear it in mind before you start.

Countryside Access Code (England and Wales)

Your rights of way are:
• Public footpaths – on foot only. Sometimes waymarked in yellow.
• Bridleways – on foot, horseback and pedal cycle. Sometimes waymarked in blue.
• Byways (usually old roads), most 'roads used as public paths' and, of course, public roads – all traffic has the right of way.

Use maps, signs and waymarks to check rights of way. Ordnance Survey Explorer and Landranger maps show most public rights of way.

On rights of way you can:
• take a pram, pushchair or wheelchair if practicable

• take a dog (on a lead or under close control)
• take a short route round an illegal obstruction or remove it sufficiently to get past.

You have a right to go for recreation to:
• public parks and open spaces – on foot
• most commons near older towns and cities – on foot and sometimes on horseback
• private land where the owner has a formal agreement with the local authority.

In addition you can use the following by local or established custom or consent, but ask for advice if you are unsure:
• many areas of open country, such as moorland, fell and coastal areas, especially those in the care

Do not be afraid to abandon your proposed route and return to your starting point in the event of a sudden and unexpected deterioration in the weather. Ideally, do not go alone, and allow enough time to finish the walk well before nightfall.

Most of the walks described in this book do not venture into remote wilderness areas and will be safe to do, given due care and respect, at any time of year and in all but the most unreasonable weather. Indeed, a crisp, fine winter day often provides perfect walking conditions, with firm ground underfoot and a clarity that is not possible to achieve in the other seasons of the year. A few walks, however, are suitable only – particularly during the winter months or in bad weather – for reasonably fit and experienced hill walkers able to use a compass. The level of difficulty of each walk is indicated in the information panel.

LOWLAND AND LOW-LEVEL WALKS

The reasonably gentle countryside of lowland Britain offers no real dangers to walkers at any time of the year, but it is still advisable to take sensible precautions and follow certain well-tried guidelines.

Always take with you both warm and waterproof clothing and sufficient food and drink. Wear suitable footwear, such as strong

of the National Trust, and some commons
• some woods and forests, especially those owned by the Forestry Commission
• country parks and picnic sites
• most beaches
• canal towpaths
• some private paths and tracks.
Consent sometimes extends to horseriding and cycling.

For your information:
• county councils and London boroughs maintain and record rights of way, and register commons
• obstructions, dangerous animals, harassment and misleading signs on rights of way are illegal and you should report them to the county council
• paths across fields can be ploughed, but must normally be reinstated within two weeks

• landowners can require you to leave land to which you have no right of access
• motor vehicles are normally permitted only on roads, byways and some 'roads used as public paths'.

Follow the Country Code
• Be safe – plan ahead and follow any signs
• Leave gates and property as you find them
• Protect plants and animals, and take your litter home
• Keep dogs under close control
• Consider other people

For more information please see www.gov.uk/government/publications/the-countryside-code

walking boots or shoes that give a good grip over stony ground, on slippery slopes and in muddy conditions. Try to obtain a local weather forecast and bear it in mind before you start. Do not be afraid to abandon your proposed route and return to your starting point in the event of a sudden and unexpected deterioration in the weather. Lowland and low-level walks, with due care and respect, should be safe to do all year round. The most difficult hazard likely to be encountered is mud, especially when walking along woodland and field paths, farm tracks and bridleways – the latter in particular can often get churned up by cyclists and horses. In summer, an additional difficulty may be narrow and overgrown paths, particularly along the edges of cultivated fields. Neither should constitute a major problem provided that the appropriate footwear is worn.

The Scottish Outdoor Access Code

1. Take responsibility for your own actions.
2. Respect people's privacy and peace of mind. When close to a house or garden, keep a sensible distance from the house, use a path or track if there is one, and take extra care at night.
3. Help land managers and others to work safely and effectively. Do not hinder land management operations and follow advice from land managers. Respect requests for reasonable limitations on when and where you can go.
4. Care for your environment. Do not disturb wildlife, leave the environment as you find it and follow a path or track if there is one.
5. Keep your dog under proper control. Do not take it through fields of calves and lambs, and dispose of dog dirt.
6. Take extra care if you are organising an event or running a business and ask the landowner's advice.
Further guidance is available at: www.outdooraccess-scotland.scot.

Glossary of Welsh Words

This list gives some of the more common elements in Welsh place names, permitting an understanding of these terms and an appreciation of the relationship between place names and landscape features. Place names often have variant spellings, and the more common of these are given here.

aber	estuary, confluence
afon	river
bach, fach	small
bont, pont	bridge
bryn	mound, hill
bwlch	pass
caer	fort
capel	chapel
carn, carnedd	cairn
castell	castle
ceunant	gorge, ravine
coed	wood
craig	crag
crib	narrow ridge
cwm	valley
drws	doors, gap (pass)
dyffryn	valley
eglwys, llan	church
fach, bach	small
fawr, mawr	big
ffordd	road
foel, moel	rounded hill
glyn	glen
hen	old
llan, eglwys	church
llyn	lake
maen	stone
mawr, fawr	big
moel, foel	rounded hill
morfa	sea marsh
mynydd	mountain
nant	brook
newydd	new
pair	cauldron
pen	head, top
pont, bont	bridge
pwll	pool
rhaedr	waterfall
sarn	causeway
traeth	beach, shore
twll	hole
ynys	island

Glossary of Gaelic Words

Many of the place names in Scotland are Gaelic in origin, and this list gives some of the more common elements, permitting understanding of these terms and an appreciation of the relationship between place names and landscape features. Place names often have variant spellings, and the more common of these are given here.

aber	mouth of loch, river
abhainn	river
allt	stream
auch, ach	field
bal, bail, baile	town, homestead
bàn	white, fair, pale
bealach	hill pass
beg, beag	small
ben, beinn	hill
bhuidhe	yellow
blar	plain
brae, braigh	upper slope, steepening
breac	speckled
cairn	pile of stones, often marking a summit
cam	crooked
càrn	cairn, cairn-shaped hill
caol, kyle	strait
ceann, ken, kin	head
cil, kil	church, cell
clach	stone
clachan	small village
cnoc	hill, knoll, knock
coille, killie	wood
corrie, coire, choire	mountain hollow
craig, creag	cliff, crag
crannog, crannag	man-made island
dàl, dail	field, flat
damh	stag
dearg	red
druim, drum	long ridge
dubh, dhu	black, dark
dùn	hill fort
eas	waterfall
eilean	island
eilidh	hind
eòin, eun	bird
fionn	white
fraoch	heather
gabhar, ghabhar, gobhar	goat
garbh	rough
geal	white
ghlas, glas	grey
gleann, glen	narrow, valley
gorm	blue, green
inbhir, inver	confluence
inch, inis, innis	island, meadow by river
lag, laggan	hollow
làrach	old site
làirig	pass
leac	slab
liath	grey
loch	lake
lochan	small loch
màm	pass, rise
maol	bald-shaped top
monadh	upland, moor
mór, mor(e)	big
odhar, odhair	dun-coloured
rhu, rubha	point
ruadh	red, brown
sgòr, sgòrr, sgùrr	pointed
sron	nose
stob	pointed
strath	valley (broader than glen)
tarsuinn	traverse, across
tom	hillock (rounded)
tòrr	hillock (more rugged)
tulloch, tulach	knoll
uisge	water, river

Publishing information

© Crown copyright/Ordnance Survey Limited, 2021

Published by Trotman Publishing Limited under licence from Ordnance Survey Limited. Pathfinder, Ordnance Survey, OS and the OS logos are registered trademarks of Ordnance Survey Limited and are used under licence from Ordnance Survey Limited. Text © Trotman Publishing Limited, 2021

This product includes mapping data licensed from Ordnance Survey © Crown copyright and database rights (2021) OS 150002047

ISBN 978-0-31909-086-2

This edition first published in Great Britain 2018 by Crimson Publishing.

Reprinted in 2018, 2019, 2020, 2021.

If you find an inaccuracy in the walks, please contact Trotman Publishing, 21d Charles Street, Bath, BA1 1HX
www.pathfinderwalks.co.uk

Printed in Spain by GrapyCems 1/21

Crimson credits

Editor Sophie Blacksell Jones

Layouts Emilie Crabb, Patrick Dawson

Cartography Cosmographics

Series Editor Kevin Freeborn

Production Manager Kate Michell

Design Jenny Semple

MIX
Paper from responsible sources
FSC® C007507

Contributors

Landscape and Heritage chapter openers written by Terry Marsh. Terry's zeal for country walking and mountain wandering began in the 1960s. He worked as a warden in the Lake District National Park, and began his career as a professional outdoor writer and photographer in the 1980s. He is the author of 17 Pathfinder Guides, including *Navigation Skills for Walkers.*

Walk introductions and the downloadable route directions based on the text in the respective walks published in the Pathfinder Guides and Short Walks Guides series contributed by the following authors:

South-West of England: Nick Channer, walks: 7, 17, 18, 19; Dennis and Jan Kelsall, walks: 8, 10, 16; Sue Viccars, walks: 1, 2, 3, 4, 5, 6, 9, 11, 12, 13, 14, 15

South-East of England: Nick Channer, walks: 22, 23, 24, 25, 26, 27; David Foster, walks: 20, 21, 29; David Hancock, walks: 28, 30; Deborah King, walk 31; Andy Rashleigh, walk 32

Heart of England: Nick Channer, walks: 34, 35, 36, 40; Neil Coates, walks: 33, 37, 38, 41; Dennis and Jan Kelsall, walks: 39, 42

East of England: Dennis and Jan Kelsall, walks: 43, 44, 45, 47, 48, 49, 50; Deborah King, walk 46

North of England: Neil Coates, walks: 67, 71; Dennis and Jan Kelsall, walks: 54, 55, 56, 57, 58, 59, 60, 61, 62, 66, 69, 70, 72; Terry Marsh, walks: 51, 52, 53, 63, 64, 65, 68

Wales: Tom Hutton, walks: 73, 74, 75, 76, 77, 84, 86; Dennis and Jan Kelsall, walk 82; Terry Marsh, walks: 78, 79, 80, 81, 83, 85

Scotland: Dennis and Jan Kelsall, walks: 91, 92, 93; Felicity Martin, walks: 87, 88, 89, 90, 96, 99; Terry Marsh, walks: 97, 98; Margot McMurdo, walk 100; Hugh Taylor, walks: 94, 95

Photography credits

Front cover: Daniel_Kay/iStock.com

Back cover: left Mike Russell/Shutterstock.com; centre left Phil Emmerson/Shutterstock.com; centre right Terry Yarrow/Shutterstock.com; right stocker1970/Shutterstock.com; flap Simon Bratt/Shutterstock.com

Interior: 39 (right) John Scott FRSA/Beer Quarry Caves; 45 (middle) Brian Conduit; 69 (right) Clive Perrin/Wikimedia Commons; 74 The Charleston Trust; 249 (left) Wolfgang Sauber/Wikimedia Commons; 252 Wikimedia Commons; 253 From the collections of the Imperial War Museum/Wikimedia Commons; 301 Patrick Dawson
The following images are from Shutterstock.com: 1, 2 (top), 5 (middle), 18, 29 (bottom), 82, 139 Helen Hotson; 2 (middle) Alexey Lobanov; 2 (bottom left), 54, 56, 91 (left), 228, 231 (right) ian woolcock; 2 (bottom right) socreative media; 3 (top & middle), 87, 119 (left & right), 137 (bottom), 162, 186, 187 (top & bottom) David Hughes; 3 (bottom) stocker1970; 4 (top) Keith Naylor; 4 (middle) ATGImages; 4 (bottom), 6, 206, 215 Michael Conrad; 5 (top), 183 (right), 216 Valdis Skudre; 5 (bottom) Petr Jelinek; 10, 193 (right) Mike S Appleton; 12 Paul Nash; 14 (top) Nick Stubbs; 14 (bottom), 21, 22, 29 (top), 44, 45 (bottom), 66, 163 (bottom), 233 (right), 257 (top) Mike Charles; 16 Simon-Hodgkiss; 19 (top), 32, 102, 113 (left), 169 (right) P J photography; 19 (bottom), 231 (left) FatManPhoto; 20, 237 DavidYoung; 24, 25 (bottom), 59 (bottom), 212, 250 travellight; 25 (top) Alexey Lobanov; 26 cparrphotos; 28, 29 (middle) Christian Mueller; 30, 256 Lukasz Pajor; 33 (left) Alexander Jung; 33 (right) ampersandphoto; 34 David Crosbie; 36, 84, 191 (top) Caron Badkin; 37 Philip Hector; 38 Peter Elvidge; 39 (left) marcin jucha; 40 Tom Meaker; 41 Lukasz Malusecki; 42 NORTH DEVON PHOTOGRAPHY; 45 (top) Georgios Kollidas; 46 nomadimagesuk; 47 George M Hiles; 48, 49 (top & bottom) Rolf E. Staerk; 50 Pecold; 52 Ian_Sherriffs; 53 Stephen Rees; 55 (left), 156 (bottom) antb; 55 (right) ieuan; 58 mubus7; 59 (top), 246, 247 (top & bottom) jax102189; 60 Justin Black; 62, 114 SuxxesPhoto; 64 (top) Louise Bottomley; 64 (bottom), 95 (left) Simon Greig; 68 Daniel Lange; 69 (left) Martin Fowler; 71 (top) Chris Button; 71 (bottom) Mark Christopher Cooper; 72, 75 Melanie Hobson; 76 Roserunn; 78 ian_stewart; 80 Philip Bird LRPS CPAGB; 83 M Rose; 86 ronald ian siles; 88 Gordon Bell; 90 Zoltan Tukacs; 91 (right) Stephen Clarke; 92 Dmitry Naumov; 94 Miikka Tuori; 95 (right) thatmacroguy; 96 asiastock; 98 godrick; 99 (top) Ints Vikmanis; 99 (left) MAVRITSINA IRINA; 99 (right) Jaroslaw Kilian; 100 I Wei Huang; 101 (left) Gagliardilmages; 101 (right) Renata Sedmakova; 104 (top) Matthew Dixon; 104 (bottom) A Shawyer; 106, 116, 233 (left) Andrew Roland; 108 Philip Smyth; 110, 111 (bottom) Sue Martin; 111 (top) sophiablu; 113 (right) Magdanatka; 115 (top) snapvision; 115 (bottom) chrisatpps; 117, 118 EddieCloud; 120 Nicholas Peter Gavin Davies; 122, 154 Paul Daniels; 124 Blenham Park; 125 (left) Paul Wishart; 125 (right) Foto-up; 126, 257 (bottom) Nicola Pulham; 128 Simon Annable; 129 (top & bottom), 185 (left) Oscar Johns; 130 William Kuhl Photographs; 132 (top) StevenDocwra; 132 (bottom), 144, 145 pxl.xtore; 134 Steve Lansdell; 136 Alan De Witt; 137 (top), 200 Steve Allen; 138 Damian Mooney; 140 Erni; 141, 148, 149 (right), 150, 152 Richard Bowden; 142, 146 ShaunWilkinson; 147, 149 (left) Electric Egg; 151 Capture Light; 153 capturelightuk; 156 (top) Paul Rookes; 158, 169 (left), 199 (right), 203 Kevin Eaves; 160 Derrick Dunbar; 161 Left) Steve Heap; 161 (right), 190 Neal Rylatt; 163 (top) Sue Burton PhotographyLtd; 163 (middle) chrisdorney; 164 JCEIv; 166, 168, 171 (right), 196, 214, 275 (top) Dave Head; 171 (left) coxy58; 172 Daniel J. Rao; 174, 175 (left), 204, 205 (bottom) Gavin J Dronfield; 175 (right) JaxxLawson; 176 Michael Stubbs; 177, 218 (bottom) BerndBrueggemann; 178 Philip Birtwistle; 180 Ian Law; 182 Glyn Swanson; 184 Andy Dines; 185 (right) Muessig; 188 PhilMacDPhoto; 191 (bottom) mattxfoto; 192 DMC Photogallery; 193 (left), 300 Lighttraveler; 195 Chris Frost; 198 Mark Caunt; 199 (left) Szczepan Klejbuk; 201 (left) Tom Curtis; 201 (right) dleeming69; 202 witchcraft; 205 (top) Nick Barber; 207 (left) carsthets; 207 (right) Gordon Bell; 208, 211 (top) Emily Marie Wilson; 210 Nicolo' Zangirolami; 211 (bottom) Phil Kieran; 213 (left) jekjob; 213 (right) Inspired By Maps; 218 (top) Sam Beckett; 220, 224 Billy Stock; 222 andreac77; 223 J R Patterson; 226 attilio pregnolato/Shutterstock.com; 230 Katarina Tauber/Shutterstock.com; 228 Gail Johnson; 236 Becker_D_Photgraphy; 238 Samot; 239 (left) Click Images; 239 (right), 255 meirion matthias; 240, 244, 245, 248 Henrykc; 242 Miroslav Orincak; 249 (right) JuliusKielaitis; 254 Harjit Samra; 259 David McElroy; 260 (top) Stockimo; 260 (bottom), 262 doliux; 264, 265 (left), 270 Jan Holm; 265 (right) Mark Medcalf; 266 Sander Groffen; 268, 297 (left) Heartland Arts; 269 JASPERIMAGE; 272 mountaintreks; 274 Hanna Grzesik; 275 (bottom) Samib123; 276, 298 Brendan Howard; 277 Julietphotography; 278 jwramsay; 279 Dale Kelly; 280 Neil Burton; 282, 287 (left) Targn Pleiades/Shutterstock.com; 283 DrimaFilm; 284 Alexey Seafarer; 286 Ross Pearce; 287 (right) Sara Winter; 288 Sue Wildey; 290 LouieLea; 291 christographerowens; 292, 293 Keith K; 294 David Ionut; 296 Gimas; 297 (right) Milosz Maslanka; 299 Atosan; 302 (left) bnl680; 302 (right) Euan Urquhart